On the Move

The opening of Chapter 1 of this book:

"Tourism without transport is – almost – impossible.

There are hardy souls who shoulder their backpacks, step from their front doors and stride out on great adventures on foot. Most plan to return home the same day. Others have more ambitious targets. They pitch tents or spend nights in hostels or bed and breakfast accommodation. Yet even those travellers are liable to tire of their home surroundings enough to hop on a bus, a train, a boat or a plane and start their hiking further afield."

From Chapter 3:

"Tourists carried knowledge to destinations. They gathered knowledge and brought it home. Guest and host interacted, questioned, explained details and shared new knowledge with others. Transport spread the effect more widely. ***Tourist information was a cargo"***.

Making Sense of Tourism

Book 1.1: On the Move

"Travel is more than the seeing of sights: it is a change that goes on, deep and permanent, in the ideas of living"

Mary Ritter Beard

Alan Machin

westwood start

Published in the United Kingdom by Westwood Start
33, Ripon Terrace, Akroydon, Halifax, HX3 6NA, UK

Web site: www.alan-machin.squarespace.com
Facebook: Westwood Start
Text, figures and graphics prepared for publication by the author. All
pictorial images based on photographs © Alan Machin, except where shown

ISBN: 978-0-9954924-1-7

British Library Cataloguing in Publication Data
A catalogue entry for this book is available from the British Library
The body text is set in Book Antiqua 10pt on 12pt
Printed and bound in the UK by Lightning Source UK Ltd

Dedicated to the memory of my parents,
George and Winifred Machin.
He was a textile millwright who cared for the
steam engine and machinery which so caught my attention,
leading to my later love of industrial archaeology.
She gave up so much in later years to get me to university,
enabling me to choose my own path in life.

Acknowledgments

Copyright permissions
London Transport Museum collection for permission to reproduce parts of the route map by F H Stingemore. **California State Railroad Museum** for permission to publish photographs taken by me in the museum, of the California Pacific Railroad locomotive and a celebratory track-laying notice. **The American Automobile Association**, for permission to reproduce part of a *Triptik* guide. **The UK Caravan and Motorhome Club** for the photograph of the *Wanderer* Caravan. **David R Machin** for the photographs of the Lincoln Highway marker and the Kitty Hawk workshops

People
Advancing years bring realisations about how many good teachers shaped my thinking. It is a pity most are longer with us, but it seems appropriate to record some names out of so many. From Westwood Primary School in Leek, Staffs, in the early 1950s, Mr Stephenson and Mrs Marianne Pickering; from the High School across the road, Mr Charles Pearce, Mr Jack Parrack, Mr Jack Chapman, Mr Tom Scott and Mr Keith Hughes; from teaching practice at Endon Secondary School Bernard Gilhooley, Ted Stubbs, Gordon Coates and Joan Hancock; from University College, Swansea, Professor John Oliver, Professor David Herbert, Dr Graham Humphrys, (now) Professor Michael Simpson, (now) Professor Peter Stead, Dr Tony Nelson-Smith; and Mrs Pamela Rees and the Reverend (later Bishop) Graham Chadwick, who both helped me, and so many other students, with endless patience; as well as in later employment, Mike Farringdon and Alan Gilmour. The mix of formal and informal naming above reflects the educational levels I had reached. Finally, my thanks to my wife, Pat, for putting up with me filling rooms with books and reference papers while I hid away muttering over my laptop. I thank them all.

A note about Currency Comparisons

At the time of writing, the online **UK National Archives Currency Converter** compares historic monetary amounts with 2017 values.   Values given in *The Beckoning Horizon* were based on a comparison date of 2005 used by the National Archives at the time. US comparisons are based on the excellent **Measuring Worth** website at www.measuringworth.com. The US site has a discussion on the difficulties of converting historic to modern values that is well worth reading. *Conversions in this book are only given to help visualise better the significance of the historic figures quoted.* Modern equivalents are shown in the present book in brackets preceded by the ≈ symbol.

Travel Authors on Travel and Transport

USA excursion and shipping company agent, 1889:

"It doesn't need an Exposition in Paris to induce travel. Europe is the lodestone! All we have to do is to show people that they can get to Europe at a moderate cost, and that fetches 'em"

Richard R John (2000) *Recasting the Information Infrastructure for the Industrial Age*

The coming of the railroad to the United States:

"reoriented the informational environment of the commercial republic from the seaboard to the hinterland. No longer would the primary information flows be transatlantic as they had been in the informational ancien régime that existed prior to 1787"

Emily Post (1916) *By Motor to the Golden Gate*

"I feel as though I had acquired from the great open West a more direct outlook, a simpler, less encumbered view of life. You can't come into contact with people anywhere, without unconsciously absorbing a few of their habits, a tinge of their point of view, and in even a short while you find you have sloughed off the skin of Eastern hidebound dependence upon ease and luxury, and that hitherto indispensable details dwindle – at least temporarily – to unimportance" (p240).

Laurent Eynac (1924) waxes lyrical about early flying: *Imperial Airways Guide*

"Life expands in an aeroplane. The traveller is a mere slave in a train, and, should he manage to escape from this particular yoke, the car and the ship present him with only limited horizons. Air travel, on the other hand, makes it possible for him to enjoy 'the solitary deserts of infinite space'. It allows him to look around him freely and at never-ending variety."

Contents

From the Introduction:

The Making Sense of Tourism *series, of which this book is a part, tries to update the popular perception of tourism. Marchand (1992) put it: "not so much by urging people to witness the difficulties and triumphs of tourism's processes of production, but rather, by offering them the chance to share its wider social and technological vision".*

Chapter opening images:

Photos and figures by the author unless shown otherwise below

Chapter

1 Enjoying a Countryside Panorama
2 Learning to Sail in the 21st century
3 Shipping Label
4 Oakworth station, West Yorkshire
5 Central Pacific Railroad Locomotive No 1, 'Governor Stanford' in the California Railroad Museum
6 London Underground Map of 1932, by F H Stingemore
7 Denis Bus, 1928
8 Bentley Tourer
9 Ordnance Survey Map Covers *(Ordnance Survey originals)*
10 The Wanderer Caravan *(Caravan & Motorhome Club)*
11 Barton Control Tower (Manchester City Airport)

Cologne Central Railway station

Figures and Images in the Text:

Barcelona tourists

Preface

On the Move is the second book of the *Making Sense of Tourism* series. I originally planned a single book to place the history of travel and tourism into a wider context.

It seems to me that most existing histories see tourism as a single, profit-making industry. After a working life split between public sector tourism, commercial tourism and degree-level teaching about tourism, I believe we underplay its importance. Tourism is fundamentally about how we discover our world. I wanted to place tourist activity into the context of the other three, main, world-revealing activities, namely the face-to-face contacts of family and community life, the mass media and formal education. I discuss this in detail in the Introduction. I had entered higher education to teach, hoping to share my experiences in public and private sector tourism with a new generation of would-be tourism managers. As ideas developed about new perspectives on tourism, I wrote and presented papers. Among them were

(1988) *The Social Helix: Visitor Interpretation as a Tool for Social Development* in Uzzell, David (ed) Heritage Interpretation Vol 2: The Visitor Experience pp149-155, London, Belhaven Press (from Second World Congress on Heritage Presentation and Interpretation, Sept 1988)
(1989) *Tourism and Historic Towns: The Cultural Key*, background paper Council of Europe 6th European Symposium of Historic Towns: Historic Towns and Tourism, Cambridge Sept 1989
(1997) *Tourism and the Information Society*, Leeds, Leeds Metropolitan University/School of Events, Hospitality and Tourism [*now Leeds Beckett University*]
(2000) *Datascapes: Tourism and the Historical Geography of Knowledge,* in The Surrey Quarterly Review 2 (4) pp 357-375
(2000) *Datascapes: Tourism and Education,* Sheffield Tourism and Culture Conference Sept 2000, Sheffield Hallam University, unpublished discussion paper
(2001) *Retracing the Steps: Tourism as Education*, Joensuu, Finland, ATLAS/FUNTS Proceedings of the Savonlinna Conference, Finland, June 2000
(2002) *Tourism and the Industrial Community: Aspects of Change,* Leeds Metropolitan University teaching presentation <u>and</u> *Tourism as an Information Stream System.* Lecture notes available
(2002) *Tourism as Education: Components for a Management System,* Huddersfield University Conference on Hospitality and Tourism presentation
(2010) *Back to Basics: Tourism, Entertainment and Education,* Havana, Cuba, Canadian EduTourism Conference paper, available from the author

It was soon obvious that one book could not encompass the ambition. The story had to start way back in prehistory. It should come up to the present time. To do that, one book became three. The first, *The Beckoning Horizon*, was completed and published in 2016. The second, *Bright Prospect,* was soon underway. Tracing the complex story of personal contacts, tourism, the mass media and formal education between 1851 and 1941 – *Bright Prospect's* period – began to get out of hand, mainly because of its need to cover transport developments. And so, this present book was born, dealing with transport and tourism alone. The numbering sequence was already established and now had to take account of an extra book between the main volumes numbered 1 and 2. Some decimalisation is the result, hence 1.1 *On the Move.*

At the present time, therefore, these are the planned books. But there will be another 'extra', on tourist photography. That is how travellers and tourists most usually record what they see. It is a personal medium that has been shaped by technology, commerce and fashion. The power of those *aide-mémoire* - still pictures and movies – becomes all-persuasive.

The books are to be divided between historical periods, as shown, but cannot be quite so clear-cut in content. For reasons of practicality, some major themes have to start or finish in either an earlier or a later work.

- 1 *The Beckoning Horizon*   *Prehistory to 1851*
- 1.1 *On the Move*   *1851 to 1941*
- 2 *Bright Prospect*   *1851 to 1941*
- 2.1 *Tourist Photography*   *1820 to the present*
- 3 *(Title to be announced)*   *1941 to the present*

While the aim is to compare and contrast developments in the United Kingdom with the United States, the author's experience gives a leaning towards British developments and examples. The influence of events in other countries must inevitably be noted, too.

I should note here some reasons for self-publishing, printing on demand and online marketing. Apart from what might be derided as do-it-yourself production, or mischievously claimed to be the craft of an artisan, it is a stimulating challenge in retirement. To research, write and control the style, content and appearance of each book is deeply satisfying. I am keen to avoid the stresses of full commercial schedules. I want to define the content and scope of each book. Self-publishing is presumptuous, probably over-confident and definitely risky. But our reach should exceed our grasp, in the words of Robert Browning, and the result is a little bit of heaven for the author, whether recorded on paper or in electronic form.

From the Introduction

"Earn, Inform, Educate, Entertain"

"Promote, Point Out, Portray"

"An epistemological model -
a basis for the study of
how we discover the world:
a theory of knowledge"

Chapter 1

Introduction

Tourism Without Transport is – Almost - Impossible.

There are hardy souls who shoulder their backpacks, step from their front doors and stride out on great adventures on foot. Most plan to return home the same day. Others have more ambitious targets. They pitch tents or spend nights in hostels or bed and breakfast accommodation. Yet even those travellers are liable to tire of their home surroundings enough to hop on a bus, a train, a boat or a plane and start their hiking further afield.

The 'classic' tourists – pilgrims, Grand Tourists, excursionists and package deal customers – used transport as the core of their journeying. They had the horse, the carriage and the boat. Later came the railway train, trams and trolleys, the coach, the car, the ocean-going ship and finally the aeroplane. As each new form of transport became popular, new forms of tourism developed, with more and more people going further and further to explore ever greater ranges of destinations. Bicycles, motor bikes, canal barges, pleasure boats and recreational vehicles of all kinds played their parts over time.

This book looks at the effects transport innovations had on British and United States' tourism, and much of the rest of the Western world, between 1851 and 1941. Railways turned coastal villages into resort towns. Steamships carried people across open water to islands and continents. Trams gave city folk the chance to explore the countryside, and rural folk the ability to discover cities. Cars and coaches offered the freedom to leave those fixed routes in favour of roads less travelled and far from the madding crowd.

Not until the peace and prosperity a decade after World War II did those internal combustion-engine crowds of tourists establish new problems, of traffic jams and overflowing car parks that demanded better roads, more signposting [see Willrich, 2013], traffic control systems and workers to clear litter and repair verges. The bright prospect of the late 19th and early 20th century was of years that offered carefree opportunities for travel. Only satirical cartoons in humorous magazines had thoughts of future chaos through overcrowding. They could be dismissed by travel-obsessed tourists as light-hearted humour.

A major change was slowly getting underway. The combination of road networks, independently minded customers and a greater choice of destinations, would begin to shift decision-making from the tourism establishments down to the grass roots. It would be a slow process. Mass transport would help begin it in the period between 1851 and 1941.

Then the electronic communications revolution a half-century later would confirm the shift of power. It would still be strongly influenced by governments and commerce, but the market would begin to wield power like never before. In the late 20th century, people would be able to buy comprehensive package holidays and travel if they wished, but they could also make direct bookings of every element – transport, accommodation, activities etc – with separate companies, by using online facilities. Details of offers could be studied. Users' opinions could be read, and questions asked of suppliers. Professional advice and guidance could be found.

Such future facilities were a long way ahead of our period, but on the other hand, 1851-1941 saw the consumer revolution beginning. Customers could book in the new travel agency offices or with the committee members of their social clubs. Already, postal services, typewriters, the telegraph and telephones were in use. Agency staff issued printed material. Even social secretaries had access to commercial letterpresses and simple office or even home-based duplicators. Teleprinters handled messages via keyboards and their remote printer stations were in common use. The principles would be one foundation of internet services decades later.

All the time, transport progress would be at the heart of tourism growth..

Detailed technological developments in transport have been extensively covered in other books. *On the Move* must note them and the social, economic and cultural context in which they came about. There are many good books and papers examining those contexts. I have endeavoured to refer to many of them, referring to their ideas where they have contributed to our knowledge. Our context of tourism requires *On the Move* to be partly a survey, partly a synthesis of historical strands relevant to tourism. I hope it helps to make sense of activities which are global and central to human progress.

Transport and the Travel Experience

The academic and author, Sean O'Connell, tells the following story:

> "A September 1905 edition of *The Times* offered readers a perspective on … the car … by recounting how the car enabled its occupants to travel to and through a number of culturally valued places whilst simultaneously ensuring that less esteemed sites were rapidly dismissed from view."
> (O'Connell, 1998:80)

The less esteemed included "rows of modern tenements" of parts of Oxford contrasted with, for example, the ancient streets of Burford, praised for its "complete freedom from any suspicion of modernity" (p80). O'Connell notes the irony of enjoying old places from a modern motor car. "Thus, the car facilitated what could be called a partial discovery of the nation". This was guided by maps such as Bartholomew's *Contour Motoring Map of the British Isles* of 1907, which carried an inset map marking industrial places to be avoided.

This, he sees as a kind of commodification, promoting some places over others according to the opinions of certain publishers and authors. "Car ownership provided the opportunity to continue another form of commodification, that of selected aspects of 'English' heritage and landscape begun by the late-nineteenth-century cycling boom." (O'Connell, 1998:79). It is an important topic in tourism. It relates tourist activities to a spectrum ranging from propaganda through marketing promotion to education, and it needs some examination (see Shepherd, 2002).

A commodity is primarily something that can be bought and sold. Tourist experiences often have goods and services for sale – entrance tickets, guidebooks, souvenirs, food and drink and so on. Not all tourist experiences do involve such transactions and when activities are examined, they often appear much more nuanced. A drive out in the country to admire the scenery, returning home without buying anything (and excursionists often take their refreshments with them) is difficult to see as commodification. Perhaps it was the result of some promotional work that might result in a purchase during a visit. That 'late nineteenth-century cycling boom' is often presented as including a meal in a public house, yet many excursions will have been made by cyclists who carried their lunch in a saddle bag. No purchase necessary!

What if the visit included having a picnic meal with food from a shop? Had they stayed at home the visitors would have eaten a meal using their normal shop-bought supplies. Buying food in a destination shop was hardly a major win for a tourism promoter. What if the shop was in neither the destination area nor the visitors' home area, but somewhere else along the way? A third-party benefits. Is a chance purchase, not related to the efforts of a promoter, 'commodification'? It was never commodified except by the person selling the food, for whom the goods in his or her store could have been sold to anyone.

It shows the limitations of the commodification argument and the need for some criteria to be set before it can be considered successful. "Car ownership provided the opportunity" was the point made, which has to be true. Except that it was "selected aspects of 'English' heritage and landscape" that were the suggested commodities, not consumer goods. Commodities are goods which can be bought and sold as parts of financial transactions..

A souvenir postcard, guidebook, food and drink are all commodities. But these are spin-offs from the tourist experience. They are not necessarily core activities of the visit. Many of them might well be products manufactured away from the destination, in which case there is only the retail profit margin accruing to the place visited. Is it really selling the *destination* as a commodity? Feeding hungry visitors to Wales with Black Forest gateau made in England under a German title would be hardly commodifying Wales.

So, what if the visitors were sold Welsh cakes, made and sold in the destination? Clearly a food commodity. Are they turning *Wales*, or *Welshness*, into a product? Would not the customer have to experience more than a delightful taste, such as some kind of instant perception of Welsh scenery or culture? It is a lot to expect from a bite into a dough product that might just be mistaken for a Cornish hevva cake, or a singing hinny from the North East of England.

It is possible to think of another kind of commodity – an opinion. Tourist promotions present destinations as historic, beautiful, exotic, fascinating, exciting, something for all the family to enjoy and so on. Visitor interpretation in one form or another (guidebooks, wayside panels, audio guides etc) present opinions about the meaning and significance of places, people and things. It aims to stimulate thought and understanding. Ideas are being 'sold' but not in a commercial way. A guidebook can be sold for money: are its opinions being commercialised? That is a tricky question. Take the example of an interpretive panel shown below. No money changes hands in reading it. An opinion is being 'sold', but without a cash transaction what is being 'commodified'?

Yet there are challenges ahead. The community must face up to, among others, climate change, rising energy costs and an ageing population. To conserve this lovely valley, we must create a more self-sufficient economy with jobs in new technologies, the care industry, tourism and agriculture.

Working together, and with forethought, the future can be bright.

Extracts from an interpretive panel on display in Church Stretton, Shropshire. Besides others describing the town's history, this raised questions about tourism management.

On the Move

It expresses an opinion. Few would argue with the first two sentences shown. Some might differ with the thoughts in the third. It did 'sell' an opinion, but again, did it commodify anything?

This digression into food may seem a by-road to the subject of transport, but it started with the relevant topic of cars and landscapes. The suggestion was that the driver and passengers experienced places by being *sold* them. A different view is that experiencing places depends on *suggestion*, *observation* and *interaction*. After responding to an idea (which might be the traveller's own thought) that a visit would be enjoyable and useful, it takes place. Observation arouses interest leading to close viewing, hearing, touching, smelling and possibly tasting. The last might be by eating food linked with the locality, adding to the experience, making it more memorable. Asking questions of local people, discussing the visitor's surroundings, or investigating by exploring places are forms of interaction. So too are activities like dipping rock pools, lifting fallen logs and clearing mosses off inscriptions. Whether an admission ticket is involved is incidental.

Car occupants can stop and explore as they wish. Other forms of transport might be different. Horses, bicycles, personal boats and a few others allow similar freedom. Most of the others, from trains to planes, do not. Yet even they can give limited viewing experiences through windows or from the decks of ships. The choice of which transport to use is both a matter of how to get to a place and how to experience that place. It is influenced partly by what help it offers towards enjoying the place and giving information about it. Examples of transport which have supplied some kind of guided information – visitors' place interpretation – will be noted in this book.

Visitor Interpretation and the Tourist Experience

Making Sense of Tourism: 1 The Beckoning Horizon divided the tourist visit experience into five phases. These were:

1 Preparation, at home
2 Travelling out
3 At the destination: activity
4 Travelling back
5 Reflection, at home

A tour, as opposed to a single destination visit, repeats phases 2 and 3 for each stage of the journey.

It is a fact of life in scholarly research that pioneering writers can be discovered late in the process of one's own efforts. It is only recently that I came across the writing of Clawson and Knetsch from over fifty years ago, even though their *Economics of Outdoor Recreation* was an important work [Clawson & Knetsch, 1966].

Marion Clawson and Jack Knetsch discussed their 'Major Phases of Outdoor Recreation Experience' under five headings. This predates my own, above, by several decades. Mine stemmed originally from thinking of the tourist experience in terms of environmental interpretation in the manner of Freeman Tilden's *Interpreting our Heritage* (1957) [see BH:50-51]. The weakness I saw in the Tilden book was of seeing environmental interpretation as being almost entirely an activity based at the destination. Thinking about the visit before making it and reflecting on it afterwards were important. This, the more so, because of knowledge built up before the visit and added to over many years afterwards. I envisaged a three-stage process at first [see weblist: Cuba] but analysing the full journey experience later it was obvious five stages were key to understanding what I termed the KATIE cycle [BH, 2016:58].

Clawson and Knetsch named the stages [p33-36] as follows:

1 Anticipation
2 Outward Journey
3 Experience
4 Return Journey
5 Memory

Their commentary was detailed and discursive. "The total recreation experience is almost always much broader than this; at least five rather distinctively different phases can be identified" [p33] though they did not look at others. They made the important point that individuals valued stages in different ways when comparing one with another. "A fisherman might get more enjoyment from tying his own dry flies through the winter than he will later get from the actual fishing itself" [p33]. Their subject is a discussion about the economics of outdoor recreation, its values, and how they are created, rather than education through travel, the subject of the *Making Sense of Tourism* series. Monetary and time costs underpin their experiences. Tourism as such is a minor topic. *Economics of Outdoor Recreation* is about leisure pursuits within culturally homogenous regions. Tourism is often – though by no means always – about crossing major cultural boundaries, into regions which may be marked out by differences of language, beliefs, politics and sociology, let alone by geomorphology and wildlife. In this, it was a book of the United States of America, a vast country with, broadly, a common culture.

The overlaps between recreation and tourism are many. The commonalities are clear to see in the book. What Clawson and Knetsch wrote is worth reading by all tourism managers. To pick just one other well-made point: "*travel back* is … unlikely to be a duplicate of the travel to the site. Even when the route is the same, the recreationists are different … they are now tired, while they were fresh travelling to the area" [(p34)] for example. It is a fact of excursions and tours that every leader and manager must know and be able to handle, whether it is leisure or learning that is the travel motive.

Transport and the Travel Experience

Phase 1 (my scheme, above) is the phase that might recall earlier visits to the same place. People thinking about possible visits can also draw on several sources of information that shape their expectations, for example, friends' opinions, travel books, catalogues, advertising, TV shows and others. It is where classroom teaching that inspired or dampened the individual's interest is remembered.

Commercial advertising material was used to promote the newly grouped railway companies. The London, Midlands and Scottish Railway [(Thomas & Whitehouse, 2002)] published *Walking Tours* based on stations in the Manchester area. Special tickets were sold to travel out from one station to another. Travellers using them walked distances from 4 up to 25 miles to a third station, then used the ticket again, to return home by train. The booklet detailed a few hundred walks, some with little details about places on the route, others slightly more, but the emphasis was on making sure directions for the walk were complete.

The company also produced *Residential Districts Served by the LMS from Manchester,* a detailed guide to towns and villages within commuting distance of the city. Information about housing, schools and leisure facilities was added to that about tourist attractions and nearby scenery. Local taxes were tabulated. Advertisements covered consumer goods, estate agents, business services and hotels. Readers could be tempted to visit towns other than their own, some of which were on the nearby coasts of North Wales and Lancashire.

Decisions are made in *Phase 1* about the travel and destination activity ahead and the return journey. Plans probably include taking a camera and perhaps keeping a travel journal or scrapbook. It may not appear that transport is involved in this 'domestic' phase. It may be needed, though, for a visit to the library or a travel agent. A town presents no problem that a bus service or car journey cannot solve. Being a distance away from these sources may take a little longer, that is all.

The real difficulty comes in situations where these mini excursions take too long or are too expensive. If personal media – telephone, letters, the internet - can stand in for the personal visit, then it becomes a matter of accessing commercial and non-commercial agencies and sites. Web pages designed to sell travel services will give free information along with what might be thought of as commodified travel offers, excursions, and locally themed restaurants, shops and entertainments. The costs and timing of transport becomes a push factor towards using personal media instead.

Phases 2 and 4, travelling out and back, are controlled by the transportation chosen. What is observed in these phases (seen, heard, felt, smelled, tasted) depends on the mode. The experience of cycling to a destination is different from that of flying there. The cyclist has to concentrate on riding the bike. Talking to other cyclists is possible. Sights, sounds and smells – and even some tactile sensations – are more marked than when travelling in enclosed vehicles. Social drinking and eating while riding a bike are not for any sensible rider, whereas on a train, boat or plane it is often part of the core experience.

On a plane journey these things are common – reading, listening to audio devices, watching seat-back entertainment, having a social drink and conversing with other people. On the other hand, the view through the window might be heavily limited by clouds and distance, although the take-off and approach to landing may have no equal. It is easy to compare the car, coach, train and ship experience with the bike and the aeroplane. Each may have its own variety according to the exact mode. A cruise liner is different from a canal boat in this respect. A railway coach is different from a tram and from a subway train.

Activity at the destination might consist of things done while walking through shops or exhibitions, lying on a beach or sitting in a theatre, etc. Even at the destination – *Phase 3* – there may be transport experiences such as taking a taxi, a coach trip or boat ride. So, transport could be influential in all of the away-from-home phases of tourism. The passing view of places may be all that they give the traveller. Exceptions to that include back-of-seat videos on aeroplanes showing the approaching destination, tour guide commentaries on buses and boats, audio guides plugged in to car entertainment systems and printed guides of the 'out of the window' kind that can be used on buses and trains.

One British example is a Great Western Railway book from 1924 onwards. It described the views along the London to Penzance line. Called *Through the Window*, (GWR, 1924) it stayed in print up to 1939 and has been reprinted in facsimile more recently. Another was *The Travelogue of Knowtoring* (sic) in the 1930s describing scenes along the routes of Western National Coach Tours (Harper, c1931). The coaches had a panel showing a number series that advanced as places were reached. A gong sounded to alert readers of the arrival at a new stage. The numbers apparently corresponded to descriptions in the guidebook. 'Knowtoring' was promoted as touring to learn about places. The books could be used by car passengers just as a normal route guide.

Tourism's Theatrical Transport

At the very end of the period covered here – 1851-1941 - an event took place that was a major milestone in the development of tourism. It was seen at the time as a spectacular innovation in automobile marketing. More than that, it combined industrial development strategy with the international power of tourism by introducing a remarkable multi-media attraction which had a very theatrical impact.

The New York World's Fair of 1939-40 introduced the public to an unusual form of transport. It was like a railway but one that did not take people from one place to another that was far away. It took them on a sightseeing trip within a building. It was like a fairground scenic ride that carried visitors past painted scenery, giving a sightseeing effect. But this one was much more interesting. The show was part of the General Motors pavilion. It foretold a world of road transport as part of a positive, optimistic future, one that would bring freedom of travel to everybody.

Instead of spotlighting General Motors' latest models, the *Futurama* display set out a vision of a landscape with safe and fast highways letting cars flow between and through the cities of America (General Motors, 1939). The year it predicted all this would be achieved was 1960. It was a pioneering combination of the theatricality of de Loutherbourg's *Eidophusikon* of 1786, described in *The Beckoning Horizon*, with the moving panoramas of the mid to late 19th century, detailed in the same book. It was a reminder of passengers' delight in scenic views from railway carriages (see BH chapters 13 and 14). The economist and writer, Stuart Chase, called it "a dream on a relief map" (Chase, 1940:173).

A long 'train of chairs' was publicised, linked and moving sideways, which gave an aeroplane-angle view of a huge model of road vehicles on highways. *Business Week* summed it up: "30,000 persons daily, the show's capacity, inch along the sizzling pavement in long queues until they reach the chairs which transport them to a tourist's paradise" (Marchand, 1992).

The New York World's Fair had a theme different from the earlier fairs. It looked to the future rather than celebrating what had been achieved in the past. In the words of the official guidebook, "A new and clearer view of today in preparation for tomorrow". It was an open invitation to commerce to display new products. There was an element of rivalry with the New Deal of President Roosevelt. It set out to show that commercial people and their work had an important part to play in future prosperity. General Motors was persuaded at a late stage to drop its original exhibit in favour of a proposal by the designer, Norman Bel Geddes. It had built a working production line at the 1934 Chicago show for its Chevrolet car and planned to repeat it in New York.

Bel Geddes used charm and inspiration to put forward a radical idea. In the insightful words of Roland Marchand, Bel Geddes

"discovered a way to involve visitors experientially with the corporation – not so much by urging them to witness the difficulties and triumphs of its processes of production, but rather, by offering them the chance to share its wider social and technological vision" (Marchand, 1992).

Norman Bel Geddes had a theatre-design background. His work had ranged from the Metropolitan Opera to a Cecil B DeMille Hollywood movie and an assistant role on the film version of H G Wells' *The Shape of Things to Come*. In the 1920s he had not only put a view of a medieval cathedral on the stage of a

11

theatre for a play, *The Miracle*, but made its whole auditorium look like one. Audiences had felt they had entered the scene of the action. Futurama aimed to make them feel they had entered the future. Bel Geddes wanted to reject the proscenium arch effect of the traditional theatre in favour of giving people "a sense of unity, intimacy, and audience participation" (Marchand, 1992 XX).

As *Business Week* had noted, long queues – often a mile (1.6km) long – had to be tolerated before admission could be gained through a narrow opening in a tall, blank wall. Some queues reached 15,000 in the number of patient visitors.

The visitors took their seats on a system of 600 chairs linked to run sideways along a sinuous track. They were in pairs divided from those ahead and behind by partitions. A small loudspeaker relayed a guiding commentary. The twists and turns in the track made sure the chairs were carefully facing what was being described. The first scene was of a map of the USA with the positions of cities and waterways shown. Highways were projected onto it as a tangle of red lines representing the 1939 distribution. Blue lines suggested super-highways of twenty-one years ahead, laid out in smoothly efficient sweeps connecting and running through cities. The United States Bureau of Public Roads had actually released a plan for six super-highways shortly before. Three would run East-West across the country and three North-South.

The chair system – called a 'carry-go-round' in the publicity – moved at 1.3 mph (2.19 km) a minute. 600 spectators were carried on each circuit. The track was 0.5 miles long (0.8 km). Visitors next viewed, through glass screens, an impressive model of much of the USA in 1960. Mountains and plains, cities and farms, with rivers and waterfalls, power plants and factories, were displayed at a regular scale, though as visitors progressed into new parts of the show the scale changed to represent closer views. It was a new world, of new buildings owing much to the architecture of skyscrapers, multi-level roads and walkways, with wide open spaces between city high-rise buildings with no old building styles, no slums.

Statistics again: half a million buildings were modelled, a million trees showing 13 different species and 50,000 miniature cars, 10,000 of which were moving along animated roads. It all occupied 0.40 of a hectare of exhibition space. Bel Geddes had arranged low- and high-level aeroplane flights for his model-makers to see what the real landscapes looked like from the air. Fairchild Aircraft Ltd took aerial photos of 48 varied sections of the United States' landscape to be used as references. Bel Geddes's idea was that viewers on the carry-go-round would have the impression they were flying across America.

The principle was of entrance and experience rather than one of external, detached viewing as in a traditional theatre show. The very end of the 18-minute journey provided an appropriate climax. The chairs came to a much-enlarged view of a city intersection with its buildings and vehicles, brightly lit and noisy. Then they turned a sharp corner to present their passengers with a view of the same intersection, full size, whereupon the commentary gave the signal for them to step off and walk through the street scene before leaving the show. It was unique and it was exciting.

As visitors left, they were given a little badge that proudly announced: "I have seen the future".

Roland Marchand quotes Stuart Chase, a usually sceptical critic of the day: "You know it is only a model … but the effect is very real". Could it be built in reality? The country was still recovering from the Depression and not yet entered the Second World War.

> "We have idle money and we have idle men" wrote Chase. "This world …
> can use them to the last dollar and the last man. Great sections of the
> American landscape must be torn down, redesigned, rebuilt; and this will
> demand intensive investment on a colossal scale" (Chase, 1940:194).

Marchand himself picked out the 'enter and experience' effect and makes a perceptive point when writing that Bel Geddes replaced the earlier car assembly line with what was a message assembly line. Visitors moved along the track to receive a sequence of information. It almost sounds like brainwashing on an industrial scale. Yet watching a movie or listening to a radio broadcast in the 1930s was similar, but without the element of being part of a moving audience of 600 people. Orson Welles's *War of the Worlds* broadcast in the USA in 1938 was a play presented like a live news broadcast that made many listeners believe that Martians had invaded Earth. Exhibitions could inspire, radio plays could frighten, movies could show vision and tourism – *real* travel – allowed people to go see for themselves.

In that same year, 1938, the Pare Lorentz film *The River* about the importance of the Mississippi had strong educational aims – or should we say it was propagandist? Both *War of the Worlds* and *The River* aimed to change opinions, one about the potential for countries to be invaded – world wars followed – and the other about culture and conservation in the New Deal. *Futurama* was about a world at peace and one that would become prosperous through commercial enterprise. World War II would intervene to delay further developments, but after it was over, many of these futuristic ideas would be put into practice. And there was new technology and innovative theatrical principles for tourist attractions, just waiting to be used.

Plans for a national grid system of interstate highways in the USA had begun in 1921. The first official topographical road map was produced to show which roads were of prime importance. Funds were used to construct new roads in Western states and the Appalachian Trail from Maine to Georgia was completed. The Eisenhower administration began the modern Interstate Highway System in 1956. It was officially completed in 1992. The 1939 World's Fair Futurama Exhibition was part of the movement to build major roads suitable for growing nation. It worked through tourism visits.

The *Making Sense of Tourism* series, of which this book is a part, tries to update the popular perception of tourism. To adapt Roland Marchand's comment on the Futurama exhibition quoted earlier, we need to do this

> "not so much by urging [people] to witness the difficulties and triumphs of [tourism's] processes of production, but rather, by offering them the chance to share its wider social and technological vision".

Promote, Point Out, Portray

Making connections between transport marketing and the informal education offered by tourism is crucial. Some thoughts about theory and practice are called for.

Marketing is a process by which a product is developed, promoted and sold to consumers who have themselves been targeted and readied for the transaction. *Education* is a process by which new knowledge is made available for, and acquired by, people. The people can be of any age and the education can be formal – through schools, colleges etc – or informal, through the efforts of individuals or groups who seek to learn more. We may think of education as *teaching* – something being imposed – and *learning* as something being gained, by those who seek after knowledge. It is better to regard the two as at the

14

opposite ends of a scale in which, however, the activities they inspire are almost always complimentary and intertwined.

The first in the present book series, *The Beckoning Horizon* (BH p52), describes a learning model based on four 'lifetime information streams', the *Circle of Contact, Mobility,* the *Mass Media* and *Formal Education.* The Circle of Contact is that of the individual who is surrounded by family, friends, informal acquaintances and co-workers who pass on and share their own knowledge and opinions first-hand. Mobility refers to travelling and tourism at whatever level. The Mass Media are many and varied, but generally well known. Formal Education is that supplied by schools, colleges, universities and adult education, as opposed to the informal learning of everyday life.

This offers an epistemological model: a basis for the study of how we discover the world - a theory of knowledge.

On the Move examines the history of tourism transport over a period when its technology advanced in leaps and bounds. Important benefits followed that helped travellers explore and make discoveries about their worlds. They could – the costs allowing – travel more, and there were interesting services introduced supplying information about where they travelled.

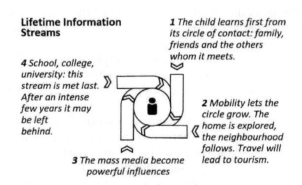

Lifetime Information Streams

1 The child learns first from its circle of contact: family, friends and the others whom it meets.

4 School, college, university: this stream is met last. After an intense few years it may be left behind.

2 Mobility lets the circle grow. The home is explored, the neighbourhood follows. Travel will lead to tourism.

3 The mass media become powerful influences

Process Model for Lifetime Learning: much more than just formal education

Earlier in the Introduction I described the main modes of transport and their potential for introducing travellers to the world through which they pass. The next chapters will examine closely how each transport mode developed its relationship with travel and tourism. It will be obvious that the relationships go back to the very start of humankind's use of transport and that they were crucial in contributing to knowledge. Understanding how they did so is what gives us the key to maximising these important processes in the future to everyone's benefit.

To make forms of transport useful as a means of understanding the world requires the landscape of each route to be promoted and appropriate information about it made available. The information might be low-key and incidental, or it might take centre stage and be direct. Older British travellers by train might remember the 'below the luggage rack' pictures framed within compartments (see Norden, 1997). They showed attractive images of places to brighten the carriage and promote rail travel. Passengers might well have picked up ideas of places to see on future trips. The paintings were nostalgic, reassuring and usually escapist. Chapter 4 will give examples of railway company promotions of their destinations. Chapter 8, on 'The Automobile Revolution', includes promotion of roads and their destinations by motoring clubs and pressure groups such as the Lincoln Highway Association in the United States.

These campaigns promoted out places of interest through posters and guidebooks. The age of motor coaches introduced the human tour guide, stood at the front of an open-topped coach, often with a megaphone, pointing out features and recalling events. Catherine Cocks (2001) describes urban tourism in the USA before World War I with guided coach tours like these. They had the advantage that the human guide could vary what was said according to the sort of tourists on board, or what was happening in the places being passed by.

Some attempts were made to do the same on aircraft, but engine noise and poor visibility made it a struggle. There was no all-round viewing as on open coaches. It was soon given up as a bad job. The American TAT airline handed out maps to passengers to help them identify landmarks. Daniel Rust (2009:54) writes that "Flying across the continent engendered a new appreciation in passengers for their nation's size and geographic diversity". High altitudes meant detailed examination through the window was too difficult.

Most on-location guiding was done for people on foot, indoors or out, by paid staff members or amateurs trying for tips or sometimes charging a stated fee.

Having a guide on board transport in Britain and America was usually limited to charabanc tours. The upmarket motor car tours such as those organised by the Atchison, Topeka and Santa Fé railroad in the South Western USA used human guides, but automobile tours were limited by expense..

A new service by the famous restaurateur Fred Harvey, called Harveycar Indian Detours [(1930)], started to take small numbers of tourists on excursions. They were making a side journey from their railroad travelling. Cars set off from the Castañeda Hotel in Las Vegas on a three-day tour of pueblos and cliff dwellings, finishing at Albuquerque's Old Town and the Harvey Indian Building. They were shown Native American crafts which were, of course, on sale. Each car had a driver and a courier-guide with four passengers [& Babcock, 1996]. An extensive booklet for the 1930 season (with a 25,000-print run) described the Detours available besides boasting of the hand-picked drivers and well-trained guides [Harveycar Couriers, 1930].

Whatever form tourist guides took – human beings or books – the job was to point out interesting features along the route of excursions [Cocks 2001, Dye 2007]. At each stage of the communication process, choices had to be made about what themes to promote, what features to pick out from the passing scene and what to say about each one. The tourist audience was being channelled towards specific information in a series of steps. Their journey and mode of transport was promoted so that they chose a particular activity over others that offered different routes and subjects. In the late 19th century, for example, they could have toured Chicago's great architectural features, the places where notable people had lived or still did live, or some of the industrial sites of the city [Cocks, 2001].

The Union Stockyards, abattoirs and packing houses made a popular coach and foot tour – if the punters were not squeamish. The advertised tour itinerary was followed. Visitors saw the details that the coach driver and guide had arranged with their coach company and the industrial owners. They heard history, descriptions, statistics and opinions that the guides and the owners wanted people to hear. It was largely a public relations exercise, modified perhaps by more personal comments by the guide and moderated by each visitor's own opinions on what they saw, heard, smelled and touched. And perhaps tasted in associated restaurants.

On the Move

Indeed, if those same people had later heeded a novel promoted by publisher Doubleday, Page & Co, and read what Upton Sinclair pointed out about the Chicago meat packing industry, they would have heard a very different account. *The Jungle* so portrayed the harsh conditions and insanitary surroundings of the factories in which thousands of immigrants worked that there was a public outcry that led to major new laws improving conditions.

The novel is a form of mass communication. A guided tour is another, created and delivered by people who decide, author and illustrate its messages just like those of the novel.

Not only guided tours but guidebooks, audio and video guides, visitor and exhibition centres, wayside interpretation panels, videos and a few other mass communication media are commonly used in tourism. By putting a selection together and presenting their work to an audience of tourists within a managed tourism operation, the communication medium that is tourism can be clearly seen. It has a history going back to the ancient world and forward to a future offering the bright prospect of better understanding between people and their planet. It is an important and challenging idea discussed at length in *The Beckoning Horizon*, Chapter 3.

Earn, Inform, Educate, Entertain

Forms of transport give access to places worth discovering. They take people to places beyond the range of walking. But there is more to their worth than just picking up would-be travellers and delivering them to somewhere else.

The *experience* of making a journey via a form of transport is two-fold. What is experienced inside the car, coach, ship or aeroplane is the first. The internal setting, the services and the other passengers contribute to this, besides the ways in which the individual traveller spends time reading, talking, eating and so on. The second is the nature of the scenery passing by. Human senses come in to play. Seeing is dominant. Hearing might have a part to play. Smelling might apply. Touching is virtually impossible while moving. A temporary stop might present a chance. Tasting is the same, although some coincidental activity might apply. For example, passengers on a train going through paddy fields in Asia might happen to enjoy a rice-based meal served on board. It would be a tenuous link to the scene outside but would relate. There are opportunities in travel management to arrange such meal experiences for appropriate tour groups.

Experiences of the world around form the foundations of tourism. The American radio pioneer and businessman, David Sarnoff, said in 1922 that "broadcasting represents a job of entertaining, informing and educating the nation" [Briggs 1961:59, Sarnoff, 1968)]. John (later, Lord) Reith of the BBC picked up on the idea. The phrase 'to inform, educate and entertain' would become the key part of the BBC's Mission Statement. It could equally well be applied to tourism in general so long as a fourth aim is added: 'to earn, inform, educate and entertain'. The *Making Sense of Tourism* series is about tourism as education. It integrates travel and tourism as mobility with the circle of contacts, the mass media and formal education. Yet tourism has to do with making money, though by no means always. Earning, and the other aims, are what makes it work. To enrich the visited financially and the visitors culturally and socially are laudable objectives. Good management of all the processes involved can only achieve a balanced range of outcomes by making sure the benefits are shared widely.

These experiences can be matters of chance or good management. A sight-seeing trip is planned. It takes in a chosen route offering a selection of vistas that a tourism manager wishes to show off and the passengers want to see. Cruises, railway excursions and coach tours rely for their market success on choosing routes and destinations well and matching the demands of the market. Families going for a day out do something similar without the commercial element. Some of its members enjoy the journey for what they see on the way. Others might fall asleep, play with a tablet computer, or do something else, with no interest in the outside view. Is it unfair to imagine that those are often the people who have not yet been led into the fascination of landscapes by their family, teachers and publishers?

Between the two World Wars printed guides to passing British landscapes began to appear, for example GWR's *Through the Window* and the Frederick Warne series of *Observer's Books* on outdoor subjects. Warne's first, in 1937, were on nature – birds, flowers, butterflies, trees and shrubs. In the post-1945 world *Observer's Books* on things like buildings and vehicles would appear.

It is worth glancing ahead to the 1950s, where we can find the first concerted efforts at blending entertainment and education about things seen through the vehicle windows. Charles Warrell was a teacher who devised *I-Spy* books in Britain in 1948. He sought to entertain children and make them more aware of the world around. They offered competitive points for spotting objects such as architectural features, animals, other vehicles, roadside items etc – on journeys from home. It was a sign of the times that *I-Spy on a Train Journey* was published in the first series and *I-Spy on a Car Journey* not until the second, cars not being so common in 1948. The *Train Journey* booklet was based on railway features rather than items in the landscape away from the tracks. Some would have been challenging to spot, such as the chairs and fishplates holding the rails in place.

The *Car Journey* covered a wide range of things which could be seen, even at some distance away. Children's *I-Spy* books are still published today under a deal with Michelin.

Travellers relate to places in different ways that can be understood better by considering them as being on different levels of activity. These are suggested in the graphic below. The least active is, of course, the passive level (1). Travellers use their five senses to absorb information about places passing by on journeys or surrounding them at destinations. Memories are the result.

Levels of Environmental Encounter

Passive ←				→ Active
1	2	3	4	5
Observation	Recording	Researching	Interaction	Integration
Senses:	**eg:**	**eg:**	**eg:**	**eg:**
Seeing	Souvenirs	Family	Internet	'Voluntourism':
Hearing	Diary	Friends	Residents	Conservation
Touching	Sketches	Guide Books	Other Visitors	Repair
Smelling	Photography	Brochures	Info' Centres	Regeneration
Tasting	Videos	Internet	Locations	Media Work

Forming, eg, home and museum collections, archives etc

Passive/Active Scale of Environmental Encounter

More active observers – here, meaning those supplementing any of the five senses – may want more than ephemeral memories (2). They might buy a souvenir postcard or other memento, or they may take photos or videos. Grand

Tourists and people inclined to art may have sketched what they saw or painted a picture. They often kept diaries with brief notes, or wrote more extensive journals, and some travellers still do.

A more active level is that of researching (3). It can take place before the journey, during it, at the destination or when back at home. This level depends on the use of media in its many forms. Questions are to be answered such as what is to be seen and heard, why the places to be visited are what they are, what happens in them – entertainments, cultural norms, events that are part of everyday life - and so on. These questions might only get answered after the visit is over and reference media are again on hand.

The visitor will find more by talking with other people (4), some at home, but usefully with many more at the destination. This information is best gained first-hand from tourist staff, local residents and other visitors who have collected their own travel knowledge. Perhaps the ultimate level of discovery involves learning by doing (5), integrating visitor and visited in shared, practical, activities of conservation and repair, regeneration, written reporting or the recording of interviews about residents' and visitors' views, memories, anecdotes and so on.

Travellers might enjoy observing the passing landscape on a journey for its own sake. They might note the way in which it forms a sequence starting at home and concluding at the destination. It is a kind of narrative to be read, a story of change that is often gradual, though it can also be abrupt. We are used to the idea of 'reading' a landscape. It underpins the published work of, for example, Tuan [1974, 1977], Cosgrove [1988, 2012] and Potteiger & Purinton [2008].

It was in 1961 that Gordon Cullen introduced the term 'serial vision' to describe the sequence of revelations produced when walking at an even pace through a location. He was relating this to a planner designing a townscape, striving to produce a sequence of stimulating, intriguing views. The urban experience should tell a story of some kind, whether abstract or meaningful. There should be contrasts to give impact. Norman Bel Geddes's *Futurama* had applied similar ideas to an exhibition narrative.

The illustration on the next page shows contrasts within a narrative read when a traveller leaves the land to cross the sea to a new land. It is a journey shown as one from an industrial region – perhaps from the North of England across the English Channel to the Costa Brava, or the Seattle region of the USA to Hawaii. Someone clued up about geography, history and biology will be able to read the landscape with understanding. Those touristic journeys would probably now be by air. But other, surface, journeys by road, rail and sea give similar results; indeed, probably better since they allow detailed, close, observation. Think of Hanover to Oslo entirely by car, Cape Town to Pretoria by train or New Orleans to St Paul along the Mississippi. Think, not only of the kind of views but of the sort of people using these different forms of transport. How would they interpret what they are observing, and how would they then think about the causes, the effects of geography, history etc?

Observing places from moving vehicles offers benefits just like those at tourist destinations: arousing interest, feeling escapist, being excited and so on. The traveller might come across them completely by chance. He or she will be happier when there are many observations to make and they are memorable. Tourism and transport managers will be happiest when their travellers and visitors take note of the surroundings along the chosen route. Landscape planners and managers who can bring about views that are positive and attractive have no easy job, but one that can be effective and memorable. Destination managers who can make places look attractive, filled with positive sounds and welcoming voices are especially valuable.

It is easier in the countryside or on rural-edge coasts. Managing urban sound is challenging, often limited to preventing excessive vehicle noise and late night rowdyism. It is possible to control smells and scents, adding suitable flowers and banishing industrial smells. Walking surfaces, walls, fences and hedges can be managed. Even tastes can be made to attract by encouraging good street food and restaurants. It may not be possible to succeed one hundred per cent, but every improvement made will increase visitor satisfaction levels.

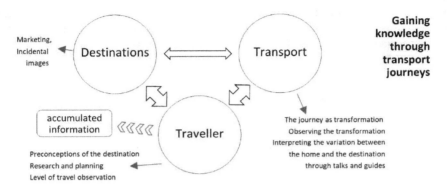

Partners in the Knowledge Process

The graphic above indicates the three main participants in the process. Travellers accumulate information about destinations and places along the route from previous activities (hearing opinions, scanning the media, remembering formal education teaching etc). Their own research and planning for the visit add much more, as will their observations on the journey and at the destination. How much those observations contribute depends on the level of attention they apply. Some will take little notice, while others will take a great deal. The journey from home to destination can be seen as a transformation in the landscape from the one to the other. Travellers will vary in their interest and understanding of what it signifies. Some might spend a journey reading or sleeping, others spend time watching the passing scene. Education, experience and interest affect the results. Astute geographers, historians and biologists, for example, will recognise changes in their surroundings and the reasons for them, making sense of the differences in the passing environments. Knowing something from subjects like geology, agriculture, industrial practice or regional culture adds more understanding and interest. They shine fresh light on the knowledge already gained from earlier sources.

Transport modes and managers exert the influences noted in the *Gaining Knowledge Through Transport Journeys (1)* above.

The third participant is the destination itself, centred on its official marketing staff but supported by the incidental images, sounds etc produced by others who promote their own products and activities. They might work with those

23

who supply relevant transport services and are at the same time influenced by their customers, the travellers, and of course the tour operators who are part of the wider set of agencies also including media workers, politicians and many others.

Enjoying the Views Across the Countryside

Chapter 2

Messing About in Boats

Exploration and Adventure on the Water

Pleasure boating may be said to have begun when human beings invented boats and rafts. Their simple craft had work to do, but their users probably managed to get some fun out of them as well. The same can be said for early sailing ships. Earning money was the priority. If that meant carrying passengers, who incidentally got some pleasure from boating, then fine. We have few accounts of anything approaching leisure touring before the 19th century. It would become big business in tourism, both in the UK (see above: Horning in the UK) and the USA. *The Beckoning Horizon*, Chapter 10, recounts one occasion, in 1774, when the Third Earl of Orford led friends and servants on a month-long barge tour on two stretches of open water near Peterborough. The noble lord wrote an account of the tour which was published much later and has been reprinted recently (Childers et al, 1868/1993).

On the Move

Any owners of small boats are likely to have used them for occasional leisure excursions. The simple craft, punts, were designed for carrying small cargoes or acting as platforms for fishermen on the River Thames. They were soon adopted by students in Oxford and Cambridge as pleasure boats, though with no keels, they were less practicable for any kind of distance travel.

> "Believe me, my young friend, there is nothing — absolutely nothing — half so much worth doing as simply messing about in boats. Simply messing about in boats — or with boats. In or out of 'em, it doesn't matter. Nothing seems really to matter, that's the charm of it". (Grahame, 1908:9)

Kenneth Grahame's famous praise of waterway leisure comes from his children's Edwardian classic, *The Wind in the Willows* (1908). Along with Arthur Ransome's telegram message "Better drowned than duffers, if not duffers, won't drown" from *Swallows and Amazons* (1930), it was the great exhortation to take to the water for entertainment and adventure. And people did in ever increasing numbers.

The Thames was the waterway that saw important leisure boats developed. Salter Bros of Oxford – now known as Salter's Steamers – was founded in 1858 when John and Stephen Salter moved from building and letting boats and operating a tavern in Wandsworth, to running a boat-building business in Oxford, formerly owned by Isaac King (Wenham, 2014). The business was immensely successful. Most of their craft were sold in Britain, but some others went abroad, to India, South Africa and South America. Their hire boats became part of their huge fleet, founding Thames pleasure boating (also see Leyland, 1897).

In 1877 this numbered almost six hundred of all kinds and sizes, including a steamboat, the *Isis*, "with cabin available for 10-20 persons" (Wenham, 2006:121). Their paired-oar skiffs were equipped with tent covers, mattresses and – as an optional extra – a cooking stove. The famous Jerome K Jerome story *Three Men in a Boat* (1889) refers to the men travelling to Oxford by train and hiring a boat, perhaps from Salter's, a common practice in those days.

A trip up and down the river was one thing. Expeditions abroad were another, but not quite unknown. For example, Robert Mansfield had enough money to spend his time exploring Scotland and Europe. He persuaded four friends to join him in making a rowing boat journey along rivers in Germany. Their

26

expedition, during the summer of 1851, was claimed by Mansfield to be the first where an English leisure boat was taken abroad (Vine, 1983). Their luggage was light since they sent travel bags on ahead to towns on the way and carried a carpet bag each on the boat. The rowboat, *Water Lily*, was also sent ahead from London to Rotterdam on board a steamer, transferred there to another, which took her up the Rhine to Mannheim, where the oarsmen launched it onto the river. Over the next weeks, they rowed to Cologne, Heidelberg, Wertheim and other cities. They finally retraced their journey back to London.

Another summer expedition followed with a new boat, also called *Water Lily*, and it proved more interesting than the first. The four oarsmen and their cox were skilled at their task, enabling them to travel much further and tackle difficult river conditions. The aim was to make their way to the Danube and on to Pesth (later linked with Buda as 'Budapest'). On occasion they put *Water Lily* on a steamer, travelled with it up a river and rowed it back down. They viewed many places and learnt a great deal on their waterway Grand Tour. In his short book of the journey, published after their return, *The Water Lily on the Danube* (1853), Mansfield implies that readers should be using a guidebook:

> "In this slight narrative of our personal proceedings, it is not intended to attempt any description of the well-known towns ... through which we travelled, or in which we stayed during our expedition; for such information, I beg to refer my readers to Mr Murray's excellent Guide-Book to Southern Germany" (Mansfield, 1853:3).

Mansfield makes several references to his 'Murray', showing clearly how useful for other tourists he thought it.

The five saw the railway being built at Schweinfurt, where the "Crowds of navvies, as many female as male, were busily at work ... till we hove in sight, then every mattock and spade was dropped, and they remained staring with eyes and mouths open till we were round the next corner" (Vine, 1983:7-8). Tourism could be a two-way learning process about the world and its peoples!

They followed King Ludwig's Canal that joined the North Sea to the Black Sea by linking the River Main to the River Danube. At one point they suffered a thunderstorm while rowing. The boat had to be bailed out desperately quickly: "I have reason to believe we passed the Castle of Hildegardsberg, according to Murray, one of the most picturesque on the Danube" (p81). Then,

27

in another downpour when making a road hike towards Salzburg, "We stumped steadily on. I have no doubt the scenery we passed through was very beautiful; if the reader will refer to Murray he will doubtless find out all about it" (p114).

Mansfield praises boats compared with the train:

> "Seeing sights go by wholesale is the most dreary of occupations; and I am convinced that the greater number of people who start for a month's trip, with the laudable intention of seeing as much as they can in that period by spinning from town to town by rail as hard as they can go, are, for one half of their time, supremely miserable" (p153).

He illustrates his view with a description of a (fictitious) noble Lord who has been trapped into making a two-week visit to Germany by his wife. Knowing it will be the last he ever makes, he determinedly visits churches, museums, castles, picture galleries and palaces. Lady C trots along on his arm, equally determined to consult her Murray at every step, "totally forgetting to look at the gorgeous carving over the old Gothic portal of the cathedral she is about to enter" (p154). The guidebook was replacing the reality!

The oarsmen opted out of passing through a stretch of more than thirty locks on the canal by sending the boat ahead on a barge while they explored more towns. After Kelheim, and again reunited with *Water Lily*, they rowed along the Danube. News of the group's adventure had spread ahead of them. Local people warned against their plan to shoot the rapids and whirlpools below Grein. The went ahead, and with great care went through without a problem. People turned out in numbers at Deggendorf to see them set off for the next rapids. Again, no problem.

The modern writer, P A L Vine, describes their journey, including a railway diversion to view a waterfall at Traun, and a 380-metre inclined plane used to carry salt barges past the cataract.

They were greeted by a choir singing a song composed in their honour at one place and the Union flag hoisted in another. More visits, more occasions to hear concerts and many encounters with local people. In Vienna, a policeman told one of the crew to return to his hotel to change his hat. It was a fashionable item known as a 'sporting wideawake', made of felt with a wide brim upturned at the sides: it was popular in Vienna with revolutionaries and therefore suspicious. *Water Lily* took them on to Budapest. They had spent 25 days on the water, rowing an average of 28 miles a day for that time. Having reached the city, the aim had been fulfilled. *Water Lily* was sold for £12 to a director of the Danube steamboat company.

The group returned home. Mansfield attempted another voyage in 1853, through France, but he had to return home to deal with a problem and his two companions abandoned the trip.

The Broads

That great boating district, the East Anglian Broads, continues its pre-eminence as a leisure destination today. In 1902, Nicholas Everett thought there must have been some sporting activity on its waterways back in the 18th century. Negligible tides and an almost complete lack of rapids and waterfalls meant easy boating for beginners and experienced sailors alike. He notes that regattas, known at first as 'water frolics', took place on Wroxham and Oulton Broads, at least by the beginning of the 19th century. Tourism was well established by the time he wrote his book, and it was based heavily on leisure boating.

"Pleasure boats of all kinds are as numerous as the rowing boats on the waters of the London parks, and one can, at the shortest notice, charter any craft from a sea-going yacht (sail or steam) to the tiniest rowing boat afloat. To all the hotels, fishing boats and punts with professional watermen, are attached. Besides these, there are many who get their living by letting small craft" (Everitt, 1902:3).

Carol Gingell (2009, weblist: Broadlands) sees that it was the coming of the railways that took away one water-borne activity and replaced it with another. Traditional sailing wherries had handled goods traffic and carried passengers on the Broads, but when the Norwich-Great Yarmouth railway line arrived in 1844, a revolution began. Within forty years, a network of lines connected the Broadland towns with each other and with London and the Midlands. She dates the first use of a wherry for a leisure trip as 1860, when a Reverend T A Wheeler adapted one for living on board during a three-week cruise on the tranquil Broads.

On the Move

Tom Williamson [1997] writes of the Broads taking part in the general increase in British tourism during the later 19th century. He acknowledges the view that a writer named G Christopher Davies was a prime mover inspiring tourism in the area, but writes that "he was, to some extent, catering for a market which was anyway expanding" [p154]. Davies's book was *The Handbook to the Rivers and Broads of Norfolk and Suffolk,* published in 1882. It is tempting to ask the chicken and egg question: which came first, the demand, or the books? But there is a third influence: destination services. Those water-frolic regattas were popular, using boats built, sold or hired out locally. Both Gingell and Williamson relate the importance of one John Loynes of Norwich, and later Wroxham, in pioneering a boat business similar to that of the Salter Brothers of Oxford.

Carol Gingell notes that Loynes began to hire boats in about 1878, effectively being the first in that trade on the Broads. Loynes had trained as a carpenter. He set up working in Norwich, built his own boat and sailed on the River Wensum. He built a larger boat that attracted enquiries from friends about hiring it. Loynes not only built more boats for hire, he made models of them to show on occasions like the Sportsmen's Exhibition of 1882 [Williamson, 1997]. He was charging between £1 and £2 5s (≈£66 to £149) a week for boats from 4 to 6 metres in length. It would have taken a skilled tradesman three days' wages to hire the smaller boat.

The business was moved to Wroxham in 1888. John Loynes then built cabin yachts with sleeping and cooking equipment. His new boats were fitted with raising and lowering roofs. Other builders joined in what was getting established as a boat hire industry for tourists on the Broads. Steam launches could be hired from about 1900, and Alfred Ward of Thorpe hired out the first motor launches in the early 1920s. Blake's hiring agency was set up in 1907: Hoseasons, just beyond the period of this book, in the late 1940s.

Christopher Davies's *Handbook* went through many editions. He gave buyers of his 1891 book an interesting idea. It was possible to hire the great working boat of the Broads, the wherry, for £8 8s to £15 15s (≈£689 to £1,292) a week. It would have been reasonable for prosperous customers, but not for the less well off. However, Davies suggested, "A good way of seeing the rivers is to give a wherryman a small sum to take you with him when he makes a passage" [p167].

Thirty-three new guides to the Broads were lodged with the British Museum Library between 1880 and 1900 (Williamson, 1997). Davies's 1891 *Handbook* showed thirty-seven companies advertising boats for hire, from wherries down to small yachts. Wherries could be converted to take private parties during the season, then turned back into trading vessels at the end of it. Hatches were raised to give better headroom and the hold was divided into several individual cabins.

Another well-known author was Ernest Suffling. He was a stained-glass artist and author of books on churches, the Broads, the Channel Islands and some adventure books. Besides titles such as *The Land of the Broads* (1887), he wrote *How to Organise a Cruise on the Broads*. The 1899 third edition includes chapters on the types of yachts and boats available, provisioning, comfort, cookery, first aid, routes to follow with distance tables and weather conditions etc. There is a chapter on fishing and shooting. The cookery pages deal in some detail with how to cook various fish. It makes sense as fishing was one of the major pastimes for people out boating. More surprising, then, is the lack of detailed information about places seen on any of the suggested cruises. But there were all those other guidebooks published, so Suffling was perhaps right in sticking to his organisational theme.

Arthur Ransome's *Swallows and Amazons* set his famous book in the Lake District. Ransome had absorbed his love of boating through his childhood holidays from Leeds spent in the Lakes, at Nibthwaite, on Coniston Water. Ransome's adult life became that of a writer of nature books, biographies, Russian folk tales and then newspaper reports on the Eastern Front of World War I and the Russian Revolution. He lived for a time in Moscow. Ransome approached a boat builder in Estonia and had a yacht built that he named *Racundra*. He sailed it to Helsinki and back, planning to return to England on *Racundra*, but never did, selling it to another enthusiast.

Out of the Helsinki voyage came *Racundra's First Cruise* (1923), not only a precursor to his children's story, but the source of his characterisation of both Peter Duck, who appears in several of the children's tales, and Simon, a wherry man in one of his East Anglian stories. When Ransome returned to Britain with his second wife, Evgenia, they moved to the Lake District, and it was there that his books about sailing helped to raise interest in new tourist activities – children's adventures on the water.

31

On the Move

American Adventures Afloat

The USA did not take to boating in quite the way that the British did, at least until after World War II. Leisure travelling by commercial riverboat or ferry along the Hudson River and the Erie Canal was an important way of reaching many popular destinations in the days before railroads served those routes and opened others. Packet boats looked after coastal traffic, including leisure travellers. Rowing boats and sail boats were things of necessity rather than fun. "When the 20th century dawned, spending time in a boat for any other purpose than wresting a living from the water was unheard of. Boating for the middle class only arrived, like so many other leisure pursuits, after World War II." (Lydecker & Podlich, 1999:81) It suffered from being thought a rich man's pastime, thanks, according to Lydecker and Podlich, mainly to the lifestyle associated with the multi-millionaire business man, J P Morgan. He owned several famously expensive yachts.

Upscale power boats did have a following from between the two World Wars. The splendidly named Christopher Columbus Smith built his first wooden boat, a skiff, in 1874 when he was aged 13. This was followed some years later by a duck hunting boat. In 1881 he joined his brother Hank, producing boats full time. The factory was in Algonac, Michigan, close to the motor city of Detroit and well placed to serve customers on the Great Lakes and many other waters. They made power boats for wealthy enthusiasts such as Henry Ford and William Randolph Hearst. The name of their business, Chris-Craft, appeared in 1924.

During the late 1920s, Chris-Craft changed from hand-building of boats to assembly line production, lowering the cost of the final products. They were able to buy power units from Chrysler and Ford in Detroit. Boat hulls were usually made from mahogany. To increase sales, instalment plan buying was arranged with advertising that promised "a piece of the good life" to potential customers among middle class Americans. During the Great Depression, the company sold basic power boats for just over $400 (≈$7,490 or £5,872)).

One area that bought speed boats in quantity was the Lake of the Ozarks, a hydro-electricity reservoir opened in 1931 in Missouri. It flooded the valleys of the Osage River and three tributaries to make a sinuous lake 92 miles long. The boats came from Chris-Craft, Garfield Woods and John L Hacker, power boat businesses near to Chris-Craft in Algonac. A 1934 published guide to the

Lake listed 57 resort properties already sprung up along its banks. Fishing and boating were the main attractions. Building the Bagnell Dam that impounded the lake supplied jobs and insulated the area from the worst of the Great Depression and helped to start the tourism industry around the lake.

The Great Lakes region, with those power boat builders at its heart, was equally busy with tourism. Steam ships were essential in the days before the railroads and automobiles (see Stone, 2015). Chicago folk could make visits to, for example, Harbor Springs in Michigan, a 300-mile journey taking 24 hours (weblist: Great Lakes). For $5.00 in 1898 they could make the trip and for a further payment could arrange meals and an overnight berth. Among the ships taking them was the SS Manitou. The SS Petoskey and the SS Charlevoix took 40 hours for $7.50 with berth and food included. There was even a demand for Michigan's Glen Haven residents to travel over Sunday night to Chicago to work, stay in the city during the week and go home over Friday night to their families. The SS Keewatin travelled between what is now called Thunder Bay on Lake Superior, and Port McNicoll on Lake Huron in Canada, working for the Canadian Pacific steamship service. It was, and still is, a long ship. Built in Scotland, it sailed up the St Lawrence to a point in Quebec where it was cut into two, moved up the Welland Canal where the locks were too short for the complete ship, and reassembled at Buffalo. The vessel is now preserved as an attraction in Port McNicoll.

It was all some way from the world of Huckleberry Finn. Britain had *Wind in the Willows* and *Swallows and Amazons.* It even had a boy on a raft adventuring in 1882: *Bevis* by Richard Jefferies, who made his craft from an old packing case and sailed it on a Wiltshire reservoir, Coate Water (see Arkell, 1933). The United States had *Adventures of Huckleberry Finn* by Mark Twain. Under his real name of Samuel L Clemens, the author had been a qualified riverboat pilot on the Mississippi. His hometown from the age of four was Hannibal, Missouri, an inland port on the great river. Huck's adventures with his friend Tom Sawyer were framed within the detailed knowledge of the author's experiences. They were also full of his knowledge of the antebellum life of slave ownership, crime, trade and poverty.

Twain described his protagonist as "hated and dreaded by all the mothers of the town, because he was idle, and lawless, and vulgar, and bad – and because all their children admired him so, and delighted in his forbidden society, and wished they dared to be like him" (Twain, 1884:70). This is a long way from the bucolic Edwardian summer of *The Wind in the Willows,* or the good, clean jollities of *Swallows and Amazons.* People might sympathise with the Southern State urchin, Huck, but it is much more difficult to empathise with him, let alone relive his life through fantasy play. And while Hannibal could enjoy tourism connected to its fictitious son, other communities would want icons more in line with the all-American ideals.

It is not to say there were no popular urchin heroes in American 19th century stories. There were. Horatio Alger Jnr wrote many, starting with his *Ragged Dick* series in 1868, before Mark Twain got started. Dick Hunter was a dirty, badly dressed boot-black in New York. In the stories, he shows what the writer John Rowe Townsend describes as his true character. "He was above doing anything mean or dishonourable. He would not steal, or cheat, or impose on younger boys, but was frank and straightforward, manly and self-reliant" (Townsend, 1983:73). He seizes an opportunity for betterment, washes, rents a room, learns to read and write, invests money in a savings bank and becomes a success. More of these poverty-to-riches characters follow from Alger's pen – Paul the Peddler, Tattered Tom (a girl) and Mark the Match Boy. Townsend points up the parallel with Andrew Carnegie, Henry Ford and others who went from humble origins to wealthy adulthood. Horatio Alger's heroes are largely forgotten today. Huck Finn is not. Twain's storytelling has more depth and light and shade. Yet American riverboat adventures did not lead to tourist activity in the style of Kenneth Graham's river bank animals, or Arthur Ransome's free-roaming children.

Cincinnati-born Daniel Carter Beard took up the subject of home-made boats in *What to Do and How to Do it: The American Boy's Handy Book* of 1882. He gave 37 detailed pages to the building of the 'Man Friday Catamaran', the 'Crusoe Raft', the 'Scow', the 'Boy's Own Flat Boat', (a kind of floating houseboat) and the 'Yankee Pine', followed by how to rig sails of different sorts. His much later work, *The Boy Pioneers: Sons of Daniel Boone* (1919) described making 'land yachts' with sails and wheels for road use, and with passing reference to canoes, but that was all. By the time that the Boy Scouts of America published its first *Handbook* in 1911, nothing was included about building rafts or boats, though there were about ten pages on rowing and sailing. Ernest Thompson Seton was by then Chief Scout of the American organisation, Daniel Beard a Council Member. The book paid homage to Lord Baden-Powell, the British army officer who had inspired the Boy Scouts' movement by his celebrated Brownsea Island camp in 1907 and his subsequent writings.

Ernest Thompson Seton gave no space to building a raft in his *Book of Woodcraft and Indian Lore* [1913] beyond making knowledge of it a possible step to gaining a Camper Degree among his Woodcraft Indians, founded in 1902. He had more about building a boat, using some tongue and grooved planks and other bits and pieces to produce a flat-bottomed craft. He did think it an important topic, however: "Most camp sites are selected with a view to boating; certainly, no camp is complete without it" [Seton, 1913:224]. It seems surprising that a country with a strong outdoor tradition of exploration and pioneering did not choose boating adventures for young people. Whitewater rafting and boating would only become popular from the late 1940s. Neither did the country adopt the kind of messing about in boats habits of Britain, born out of children's stories. But then the USA did not have that kind of story, either. There was no Arthur Ransome or Kenneth Grahame equivalent. Boating tourism was in the hands of the up-market and the adult.

Joshua Slocum (1844-1909) was one of those American writers who excited the interest of the well-off in ocean sailing. In the long term he inspired a wide audience to take up boating or sailing at all kinds of levels. The American Sailing Association judges that "Slocum ... introduced the world to the concept of sailing smaller boats strictly for the sake of adventure." [weblist: Slocum 2]. His exploits joined with those of others in creating an important tourist industry. By the end of the 1990s the USA would have an estimated 16.8m boats in leisure use, from canoes to yachts [Lydecker & Podlich, 1999].

Slocum was born in Nova Scotia where "the wonderful sea charmed me from the first. At the age of eight I had already been afloat with other boys on the bay" [Slocum, 1900:1]. He ran away to sea, became a (hopeless) sea cook at the age of fourteen, then a foremast hand on a merchant ship crossing the Atlantic. He gained experience and qualifications up to chief mate on British ships before moving to San Francisco, becoming an American citizen and from where he became first a part owner, then sole owner, of a succession of trading ships.

After more than fifty years maritime employment, Joshua Slocum, by now living in Massachusetts, rebuilt a former oyster boat and sailed it round the world, solo. His three-year voyage ended in 1898 at Newport, Rhode Island. The journey took so long because of stopovers for rest and exploration. One of these was for three months in Cape Town where Slocum took the opportunity of taking a railway trip to the Transvaal. In Tasmania, St Helena, Antigua and other places he gave talks to local people. One, at least, was apparently illustrated by lantern slides, though Slocum's modest style in his later memoire did not make clear where they came from. The modern style of making record-breaking journeys, often single-handed, leaves no time for seeing the world beyond the seascape surrounding the boat. Joshua Slocum was sailing for pleasure and discovery. Yet the feat of making his journey single-handed opened the way for the later racing challenges.

Two years after returning home, he published his book *Sailing Alone Around the World*. It was an instant success. Arthur Ransome later wrote "*The Spray* sailed on her last voyage, but she and her captain have joined the immortals and are sailing still, and will sail on so long as men can read his lovable and simple-hearted book" (weblist: Slocum 1). Ransome also made the much alluded-to comment "Boys who do not like this book ought to be drowned at once." Maybe it was a play on his phrase about duffers and drowning in *Swallows and Amazons*. "Joshua Slocum wrote the best sailing book in the world", he said to publisher Rupert Hart-Davis in 1947 (Hart-Davis, 1976:353).

Sternwheelers

Shallow draught river boats have been popular in many parts of the world, but nowhere have they symbolised river travel as strongly as in the USA. They carried goods and they moved passengers, and some were used as showboats moving from location to location to present dramas, music and even equestrian displays. A showboat was not usually a proper sternwheeler as it used a powered craft to push it to where it was needed. Having a steam engine to power it would have taken space needed for an auditorium. They followed the general design of sternwheelers. Publicity for Edna Ferber's 1926 novel *Show Boat* sometimes used images of both sternwheelers and sidewheelers, fixing the more romantic vessels in people's minds.

The first American sternwheeler to operate commercially was Robert Fulton's *New Orleans* in 1811. It ran between New Orleans, Natchez and St Louis (weblist: Sternwheelers). The first of a long line of sternwheelers named *Natchez* was launched in 1823 and served the route from Natchez to St Louis. As the *Idlewild* it operated as a passenger ferry from 1914 sailing between Memphis, Tennessee and West Memphis, Arkansas. In the 1920s it became an excursion boat offering short trips on various rivers such as the Mississippi, Ohio and Missouri systems. It is now moored at Louisville under the new name. The well-known *Delta Queen* started out in 1927 on the West Coast between San

Francisco and Sacramento. The ship ceased operations in 2008 and is now a hotel in Chattanooga, Tennessee.

Canal tourism in Britain

The *Leeds Intelligencer* reported, in 1774, on the opening of the magnificent five-rise staircase locks in Bingley, on the Leeds and Liverpool Canal. The canal and its locks are still in use - for tourism, lifting and lowering boats the 18 metres between the upper and lower sections of the canal, being a spectacle for boaters and passers-by alike. It was even more of a wonder for people in 1774. The canal symbolised industry and prosperity across the North of England; the working of double lock gates, barges, horses and bargees was a wonder of their world. The *Intelligencer* estimated that no fewer than 30,000 people turned out to see the great occasion. It would be almost two centuries before canals in the United Kingdom would be restored and equipped for leisure activities.

Within the period covered by this book, canals went from thriving industrial arteries to struggling waterways facing competition from railways. Yet there were signs of a new leisure interest, as shown by story books by Amos Reade, V Cecil Cotes, Anna Talwin Morris and Garry Hogg. At the very end of the period, an engineer named Tom Rolt bought a canal boat, *Cressy*, from his uncle. Rolt converted it into a barge that he and his wife could live in. They set out to make a journey on the Oxford Canal. In due course, Rolt would write a book, *Narrow Boat*, that would inspire generations of enthusiasts to take canal holidays on the waterway system. That, however, is a story to be recounted in the general tourism history book to follow this one - *Bright Prospect*.

Reliving a Maritime Tradition Today

Chapter 3

Life on the Ocean Wave

First - Life Over the Waves: Piers

A useful source of information on individual British piers is by Chris Foote Wood [2008]. Piers in the USA can be researched individually online.

Small boats could be launched from the beach. Passengers and cargo of any weight called for the boat to be loaded while floating, giving the extra advantage that it could be checked for trim as weight was added. A wharf required deep water alongside. A pier extending as far as deep water probably suited most conditions and could be used for mooring on both sides. Both piers and wharves offered the chance of fishing without using a boat. Add some social gathering and cultural activity and the transition from being purely aids for embarkation to places attracting more leisurely pursuits would be under way.

The idea of piers and docks as early places of leisure as well as transport must have been established long ago. Baiae and Puteoli, near Naples, became such places in the ancient Roman world. Nearby sulphur springs for bathing, plus restaurants, brothels and boats for hire on the Bay of Naples increased the leisure offer [(Feifer, 1985)]. Ports were obvious centres for entertaining travellers, where attractions could be opened in buildings both old and new. Piers came into their own where boats could not be unloaded and loaded again close to dry land. Where accessible by ordinary people they gave a chance of walking with quite different surroundings.

That was the case in Ryde on Britain's Isle of Wight. It was the natural arrival point for travellers from Portsmouth going to the island, but a muddy foreshore meant porters had to carry the visitors part way and leave them to walk across wet sand to the town. A pier was an obvious idea. It was financed by the landowning Lord of the Manor of Ashey, who claimed the right to charge tolls for landing. Ryde pier opened in 1814, with a walkway for people and farm animals to and from the pier head [(Foote Wood, 2008)].

A second pier was built alongside for trams in 1864 and a railway pier next to that in 1880. The tramway pier is now but a metal framework. The railway pier is still in use, running an ex-London Underground train from the pier head along the east coast of the island. After a public petition for appropriate entertainment facilities in 1864, a reading room, refreshment rooms, concert hall and an upper-level sundeck were gradually built. The pier became one of many Victorian pleasure piers round the coast of Britain as the idea spread..

By 1914 there were over a hundred pleasure piers. The basic attraction was that of being able to walk out above the sea at any state of the tide. Walking the pier, seeing and being seen, was an extension of the accurately named promenade, the seaside equivalent of the popular walking area in spa towns and public parks. It was a social activity and a health activity at the same time. Piers were better than walkways on the edges of towns in that they were more exposed to the fresh sea breezes, said to be "so bracing" [(see Cole & Durack, 1992)]. Pier owners built little shelters in case of rain, and restaurants, theatres and concert halls as additional entertainment were often added. Some had fairground stalls and rides. None of this was transport, just another extension to the resort facilities. But the transport attraction of piers came when excursion boats left the pier head for a short trip along the coast or a journey to another pier at another resort. Blackpool's North and Central piers would host trips to Llandudno in North Wales, Douglas in the Isle of Man, and Fleetwood, Morecambe and Southport, using many steamers over the years. In Blackpool, they took the place of harbours. Scarborough and Margate had harbours but did have – for some time – piers as well.

Ryde's pier had been built to serve the Portsmouth ferries. Others followed suit, with Clevedon (1869) acting as the English terminus of ferry trips across the Bristol Channel to South Wales. Paddle steamers set off on excursions from the pier. Bournemouth started with a wooden jetty in 1856, then built a longer pier five years later. It was itself replaced by a cast iron pier five years after that. Accidental damage and partial wartime deconstruction to prevent it being used by invaders in the 1940s gave it a chequered history, but it survives.

The well-known pier at Southend at the mouth of the Thames estuary dates from 1887 with an extension added in 1897. It was not the first Southend pier. A wooden pier was opened in 1830 stretching 180m (600ft) across the mudflats. These were covered by the high tide but exposed by the low, meaning excursion boats could only make limited use of it. The better docking arrangements across on the Kent coast captured much more of the London trip boats. Extensions followed so that by 1848 it reached out 2,100m (7,000ft) when it became the longest in Europe. The town relied on the river boat trade for most of its visitors, day tripping or overnighting. A railway from London arrived only in 1856, bringing large numbers of people more quickly out of the capital. That began to impose wear and tear on the pier. It was therefore replaced in 1887-89 by an iron structure, extended itself by 1897. A shore-end pavilion was added in 1923 and the electric railway along the length of the pier was completed in 1931. Post-war additions would include cafés and a theatre, but the pavilion would be lost in a fire in 1959. Many problems, restorations and replacements would follow over the next decades including a crisis period when it was almost closed for good. Today it thrives, known for its world-beating 2.14 km (1.33 miles) length and its use in films and TV shows. Trip boats occasionally make use of it, the paddle steamer *Waverley* sometimes making trips up the Thames to Tower Bridge, for example.

Blackpool's famous trio of piers date from 1863 (North Pier), 1868 (Central Pier) and 1893 (South Pier). All three were used for promenading and commercial entertainments, the North Pier being aimed at a more middle-class market arriving at the town's first railway station on Talbot Road. In Yorkshire, Saltburn's attractive 1869 pier is simple in form but is paired with a funicular railway from the town above. It had a landing stage for steamers at the end of its 1,500ft (457m) length but suffered storm damage and ship-collisions over decades which resulted in it being shortened more than once.

The USA

United States' piers had similar origins to those in Britain. Fewer of them seem to have been used as embarkation points for steamboat trips, having walking, fishing and entertainments as their primary functions. They may not have had transport links like many British piers, but they still transported visitors from the land to the world of water by acting as a bridge. Of those standing today, a number were only built in the last seventy years. Most of them are on the Pacific Coast with California's leisure resorts best endowed. The country's seaside resorts favoured the boardwalk tradition of wooden promenades and might later have added a pier. When they did, the choice was between a simple walking and fishing pier or a heavily built-on structure standing as a site for entertainments – fairgrounds, attractions, cafés, bars, gift shops and small theatres. Not so many were used as starting points for steamer trips. The famous wharves and piers edging Manhattan Island were built as ferry and liner terminals, constructed solidly as short oblongs jutting into the Hudson River rather than as elegant, narrow, promenading piers.

The Gulf of Mexico coast was excellent for tourism in good weather but terrible in bad, notably during hurricanes. Fairhope, Alabama, attracted tourists, being popular with writers like Upton Sinclair and Sherwood Anderson and artists including woodworker Wharton Esherick and the lawyer, Clarence Darrow. The Municipal Pier was built in 1894 and rebuilt after Hurricane Katrina destroyed it in 2005. It is mainly a walking and fishing pier, though it has a popular restaurant. In Florida, the St Petersburg pier of today is a successor to the first built in 'Saint Pete's', in 1894. That was a true railroad pier, up to 3,000ft (914m) long so that ships could dock in deep water. A bathing pavilion was soon added. Other piers were built nearby, with some being demolished after only a few years. The St Petersburg Municipal authorities built a recreation pier in 1913, but it fell victim to a powerful hurricane eight years later. It was repaired temporarily but replaced by 'The Million Dollar' Pier in 1926 funded by the city and by donations. It boasted a casino with ballroom and theatre, a beach, observation deck, solarium and tramway. The Railroad Pier and the Million Dollar Pier survived until 1952 and 1967, respectively. Other piers were built after them.

Across the Florida peninsula at Daytona Beach is the Main Street Pier. It was completed in 1925 with a restaurant and the attraction of fishing, stretching 1,000ft (305m) over the Atlantic.

On the Move

Navy Pier, in Chicago, was first known as the Municipal Pier, opened in 1916 as a docking facility for cargo ships and passenger steamers and a venue for exhibitions and pageants. The pier is unusual because of its size. Not only does it reach out 3,300ft (1,005m) but it encloses 50 acres (20.2 ha) giving space now used, among other things, by a park, a botanical garden, a theatre, a children's museum and a fairground.

There were changes of use over the years including for a time, post-World War II, as a university teaching centre. Today it is mainly a place of entertainment.

Manhattan Beach, Los Angeles County, California, has two wooden piers which were built by the new township in 1901. The first was on Centre St (later renamed as Manhattan Beach Boulevard) and the other on Marine Avenue. A storm destroyed it twelve years later. A replacement dating from 1922 suffered further storms, restoration, extension, more storm trouble and more restoration. It would gain a restaurant, aquarium and sea-life study centre after World War II but was until then was popular for walking and surfers. The first commercial surfboard maker and repairer was an enthusiast who started by using a space below the concrete pier.

Further north on the Pacific coast, Pismo Beach pier dates from 1924 and survived bad weather until the early 1980s, after which it had to be restored. It was financed privately but was open to the public from the start. Walking, fishing, watching the many surfers nearby and admiring the wide beach, the sea and beautiful sunsets added to its popularity in a busy tourist town. The pier is largely free of above-deck structures. The beach and coast behind are relatively low-lying and the views are panoramic. Walking to the end, seeing the surfers and the anglers along its length gives a strong intimation of being 'on the ocean wave'.

A busy, bustling tourist resort is that of Santa Cruz, close to the urban cities round San Francisco Bay. It has a famous boardwalk and the full infrastructure of tourism. There is a wooden rollercoaster claimed to be one of the world's most popular, having carried more than 60 million thrill seekers between its opening in 1924 and 2012. Known as the Giant Dipper, it was used in films like *The Lost Boys* and *Dangerous Minds*. Santa Cruz has had six piers on the site of the present one which was built in 1914. It is confusingly known as Santa Cruz Wharf. The structure is 2,745ft long (836.68m), making it the longest on the west coast. Its original use was for shipping potatoes to San Francisco, changing some years later to handle sardines for the North

Monterey Bay fishing industry. That industry declined and tourism began to take its place both in Monterey Bay and on the Wharf. From the 1950s tourism would be dominant with the Wharf having a typical mix of restaurants, gift shops and promenading. Viewing wildlife - sea lions on platforms below the pier - has always been popular.

San Francisco is to West Coast piers as New York is to East Coast piers. It has almost a hundred, many industrial but many others well known for their tourist attractions. Some are used by trip boats such as the ferry to Alcatraz Island. Others are good places to watch sea lions. Hyde St Pier leads to many old ships moored as museum pieces. Pier 45 harbours two World War II ships and a museum of coin-operated games. Pier 27 is the terminal used by cruise ships. Pier 15 has become the home of the hands-on science museum named the *Exploratorium* that used occupy a building on land that was once the Palace of Fine Arts of the 1915 Panama-Pacific Exposition .

Walking a few hundred metres out to sea, just a few metres above the waves on a solidly founded platform was cheap, decidedly cheerful and simple to do. But it was *terra firma* and not cresting the ocean wave. To do that in the 19th and early 20th centuries required boats, ferries and ocean liners.

And Then On the Waves: Crossing the Atlantic

The technical developments of the 19th century revolutionised transatlantic travel and tourism. At the same time, steam engines and iron rails revolutionised overland transport and tourism. The combination of land and sea travel powered by steam put a fast and relatively cheap circlet round the Earth. It is a story well known and not necessary to repeat here. But the linking of Britain, mainland Europe and the USA by passenger liners is central to the history, not only of general development, but of many forms of the tourism within those nations. Those links are important to trace.

Many examples of passenger ships have been preserved around the world. Wikipedia has a *List of Oldest Surviving Ships* giving summary details and links to longer articles. Below are details of a few passenger ships and a cargo clipper that are now tourist attractions in the UK and USA. They illustrate developments between 1812 and 1914. There are many others worth seeing and, of course, many more in other parts of the world: this list might at least whet the appetite to explore some of them.

On the Move

Comet 1812 – passenger boat – (replica) Port Glasgow, Scotland
Great Britain 1845 – ocean liner, Bristol, England
Cutty Sark 1869 – cargo clipper, Greenwich, London.
Lady of the Lake 1877 – steam yacht: diesel from 1936, Waterside, Ullswater
Columbia 1902 – excursion steamship, Buffalo, NY
Ticonderoga 1906 – paddle steamer, Shelburne VT
Keewatin 1907 – passenger ferry, Port McNicoll, ON
Nomadic 1911 – ocean liner tender, White Star line: Belfast, Northern Ireland
Sundowner 1912 – motor yacht, private touring, Ramsgate
Belle of Louisville 1914, sternwheeler, Louisville KY

The years 1837-1914 saw many steamship operations commence. The New York-based Black Ball Line operated sailing ships for many years, but it was the first to work to fixed dates and destinations – the definition of a 'liner'. There were many others. The table below picks out a selection of the most important foundations, including the New York Black Ball Line.

Black Ball Line (New York: sailing ships)	US	1816	
Peninsular S N Co/P&O	GB	1837*	
Pacific Steam Navigation Co	GB	1838	
Cunard	GB	1839	
White Star Line	GB	1845	
Hamburg-America Line (HAPAG)		Ger	1847
Collins Line	US	1848	
Black Ball Line (Liverpool)	GB	1851	
Compagnie Générale Transatlantique (CGT)	Fr	1855	
Norddeutscher Lloyd	Ger	1857	
Blue Funnel Line	GB	1866	
Holland-America Line	Neth	1873	
Compagnie Messageries Maritimes (CMM)	Fr	1881	
Scandinavian America Line	Den	1898	
Norwegian America Line	Nor	1910	
Swedish American Line	Swe	1914	

*Peninsula Steam Navigation Co 1837, Peninsula & Orient (P&O) from 1840

Transatlantic shipping benefitted from three passenger-market segments: business travellers, emigrants and leisure travellers. Shipping lines gradually brought in appropriate services. The emigrants wanted a low-cost, one-way passage in whatever comfort they could find for their money, and after that had no interest, unless they became prosperous in later life and could go back in style. People making a visit to the USA and then returning might be on tight budgets, but there were still plenty who were able to enjoy good service. Travellers in the 1890s and later were often seeking higher status cabins and state rooms, quality food, expensive drinks and the personal attention offered by stewards and other staff. Ships were bigger, faster, more efficient and safer. Coal-fired steamers really took over from sailing ships for the carriage of cargo and passengers during the 1860s ^(weblist: Trans-Atlantic fares). Industrialisation at home brought mass production with much improved prosperity, even though it was badly distributed across society. Passenger fares were becoming lower just as the numbers earning enough to make journeys like these were increasing. A paper, available online ^(weblist: Trans-Atlantic fares) by Dupont, Keeling and Weiss, analyses changes in fares during the 19th and 20th centuries. They point out the multiple classes of accommodation offered, varying by season, quality and on-board location, ie on which promenade decks cabins were located. Their analysis was based on advertised rates, which did not always cover the range available and at times were not advertised publicly at all.

The British sailing packets that made irregular crossings before scheduled liners appeared charged thirty guineas for a cabin in the 1820s and 30s ^(Chadwick et al, 1891). A rate of thirty guineas was part of a system of charging in which one guinea was worth £1 and 1 shilling (£1.05p), still used in some auctions today. Thirty guineas were therefore £31 10s, old style. Using the UK National Archives currency converter, that would have the same spending power as £1,903.14 in 2017. A skilled tradesman, according to the UKNA calculations would have had to work something like 157 days to earn that amount, and of course there was no such thing then as a credit card account. It does need to be remembered that it is difficult to be accurate as wage rates varied according to local conditions and the exact nature of the job, with a certain amount of wage bargaining going on. Given the costs, it was no wonder emigrants chose to travel by the basic steerage class when such accommodation was made available around 1850.

In the 1850s these steerage passengers paid £5-8, up to about a quarter of the price paid by first class passengers. Steerage space was arranged on the same deck level as the luggage, just above the cargo hold. It was named for the deck where steering cables connected the helm to the rudder. Passengers slept on straw mattresses with no bedding, perhaps several hundred occupying the open space with all ages, genders and married or unmarried mixed together. Early steerage passengers had to carry their own food and share simple cooking arrangements. After a while, food was supplied, but usually of poor quality, with stories of inedible bread and of grudgingly given water being commonly heard. Sanitary provision was poor.

The analysis by Dupont *et al* (2012) is based on drawing information from many sources and averaging ticket prices, as available, from different shipping companies. In broad terms, the first-class tickets that were likely to have been bought by American tourists to Britain cost around $115 in 1851 and fell to around $60 in 1900. The levels look low to our eyes until, using the American *Measuring Worth* calculator (website: $ currency) it is seen that these relate to 2017 purchasing powers of $3,800 (1851) and $1,810 (1900). It is well worth looking at the *Measuring Worth* website, however, for its detailed discussion of the difficulties of comparing historic costs one with another. At least, we can say that the average, advertised, tickets prices appeared to have halved between 1850 and 1900, the period in which trans-Atlantic liners established themselves and their services.

Dupont *et al* (2012:4) write that "Travel across the North Atlantic is one of the most significant and long-lasting phenomena in world history". The late 19th century witnessed the absorption of new territories into the empires of Britain, Germany, France and Italy on the one hand and, in a smaller way, on the other, the United States of America (Puerto Rico, Guam, American Samoa, the Philippines and almost, Cuba). World economic power was centred in Europe, with that of the USA growing fast. Developments in cultural, societal and technological life were rapid on the two continents and were being disseminated worldwide. The emigration of millions from Europe to North America moved important labour resources to the growing world power and fed new artistic ideas into the worlds of the theatre, music, art and new media such as cinema and broadcasting.

American tourists were making more Grand Tours to Europe by the 1890s, rather than the Grand Tours they had previously made through their own North Eastern States. They returned with ideas that also influenced their society and landscape; for example, the houses of the super-wealthy like Biltmore in North Carolina and Hearst Castle in California. Events such as the World Expositions on both sides of the Atlantic were enormously successful at drawing visitors across the ocean who returned home with ideas that invigorated every area of activity known to humankind.

The price of a ticket was not the only cost involved in an Atlantic voyage. Sea sickness had to be faced and endured. Stephen Fox recounts many 19th century shipboard experiences good and bad. An American woman named Adeline Trafton described her feelings while at sea in a book of 1872: as the ocean waves threw the ship about, she doubted "if any of [her] internal organs are firmly attached, after all; if you shall not lose them at the next lurch of the ship ... you feel dimly, but wretchedly, that this is but the beginnings of sorrows" (in Fox, 2004). "The clash of cultures aboard ship might confirm prejudices instead of softening them" Fox points out. Black passengers could be unacceptable to Americans, French passengers had strange lack of hygiene, the English were divided by class into those who felt superior and those who were seen as vulgar, and so on.

Cultural Cargo

A late 19th century book, *Ocean Steamships*, published by Charles Scribner's Sons in New York, gives much detail about the ships' physical nature and passenger life on board. The arrival of the British paddle steamer *Great Western* in New York in 1838 "had practically, at one stroke, reduced the breadth of the Atlantic by one half" (Chadwick et al, 1891:12) and the book clearly thought that human progress was then never going to stop. By 1891, F E Chadwick and colleagues wrote that nine passenger lines made seven-day journeys between Sandy Hook , New Jersey and destinations in Europe. "Their vessels are well fitted, the passengers find every convenience at hand, and, barring extremely bad weather, the traveller may imagine that he is confined but a few days to a first-rate hotel on land" (Chadwick et al, 1891:130-131).

American ideas of service were spreading to Britain:

> "The Midland Railway Company of England and the London and Northwestern [sic] Railway Company have both adopted the American system of checking baggage, and it is now possible to have your trunks checked at your house for delivery in London, although your steamship itself may terminate its journey in Liverpool." (Chadwick et al, 1891:131).

On the Move

The French Line (Compagnie Générale Transatlantique) had a variation on the luggage service. Baggage could be checked by it to any point in France. On arrival in Le Havre, passengers and baggage were put on a special train to Paris. From arrival there they were taken to the correct station for their journey in the country, along with their luggage
.

One of the great attractions for Americans thinking of going abroad was the Paris Exposition of 1889. *Ocean Steamships* is a little confusing, apparently reporting that a record number of 96,686 passengers landed in New York that year. It does not say they were all French, and the implication has to be that they were largely Americans returning from France. It does record that official records for 1890 showed at least 80% of arrivals in New York that year were US residents (USCB 1890). There were no surveys of travel intentions in those days about where passengers leaving New York were heading, though there were statistics on ticket sales to outgoing travellers. The record figure for 1889 was broken the following year, on reaching 99,189. "These figures mean that Americans are getting rich enough to travel, nothing more" (p134). We will see how "the balance of trade between Britain and America was shifting in America's favour" (Martin, 2012:127) when considering the flow of Americans with dollars and influence on the Underground railways of London, in Chapter 6. "The cultural and economic colonisation that has been continuing ever since was getting under way" (Martin 2012:127). Given that the USA population at the 1890 census was a shade under 63m, then 77,348 travelling was rather over-stating things.

One of *Ocean Steamship*'s authors, John H Gould, noted a comment by an agent of an excursion company in 1889 that

> "It doesn't need an Exposition in Paris to induce travel. Europe is the lodestone! All we have to do is to show people that they can get to Europe at a moderate cost, and that fetches 'em" (p134).

The influx of wealthy Americans to London helped build the transatlantic steamer services and it began to influence hotel quality. An imposing new hotel, the Langham, was opened in 1865 for a company whose president was the eighteenth Earl of Shrewsbury. It had 600 rooms, 300 water closets, the world's first hydraulic lifts and a form of air conditioning. The hotel was run on 'American lines' with suites of rooms including bathrooms with hot and cold running water. It had its own artesian well for drinking water and its in-house laundry. London still had a bad reputation for polluted water, leading to the popular phrase 'don't drink the water or eat a salad' (weblist: Langham).

An economic downturn brought an early change of ownership and the import of an ex-Union soldier from the USA, Colonel James Sanderson. His father was a hotelkeeper and James joined his trade. They ran the elite Merchant's Hotel in Philadelphia and added the Brandywine Springs resort hotel near Wilmington in 1839. James Sanderson served in the US Civil War of 1861-65. By 1867 he was managing the Langham Hotel, restoring its reputation and attracting many fellow Americans as tourists to stay there. Stephen Fox refers it at that time as 'A Yankee Island in the British Sea'. Besides the bathrooms, pure water and American management, "American men were drawn to the familiar smoking room and billiard hall. Their wives especially liked the hotel's location near the best London shops" writes Fox, quoting John Weiss Forney, journalist and editor, writing that "Gradually the Langham is becoming the headquarters of our countrymen" (Fox, 2004).

Fox describes the injection of American culture into upmarket inward travel and tourism to Britain. It flowed through the transatlantic steamers into the Langham and a few other grand hotels in London.

"Most of the cabin passengers, up to 80 per cent on a typical voyage, were American; so the steamship lines catered to Yankee tastes. 'The impetus of comfort in ocean travelling,' noted the *Nautical Magazine* in 1875, 'comes from America and … the wealthy Americans".

Tourists carried knowledge to destinations. They gathered knowledge and brought it home. Guests and hosts interacted, questioned, explained details and shared new knowledge with others. Transport spread the effect more widely. *Tourist information was a cargo.*

Cruising

A cruising industry was beginning to appear. "A first pleasure tourist visited the Arctic whaling ground in 1891,a New York yachtsman paying $25,000 for the three months' cruise in a Japanese steamer chartered at Yokohama" (Scidmore, 1893). This early voyage was recalled by Eliza Scidmore in an Appletons' *Guide to Alaska*. It was a book that began the important cruise ship business into the North West waters of the USA. Mansfield's *Water Lily on the Danube,*

On the Move

Scidmore's *Alaska* and Ransome's *Swallows and Amazons* had powerful effects on new forms of tourism.

Commercial marketing extended the operations of shipping lines into similar activities. The Orient Steam Navigation Company promoted a sixty-day pleasure cruise around the West Indies from London in January 1898 via Madeira, Tenerife and Bermuda. P&O advertised a Winter Tour to India, Ceylon and Egypt from London for £79..15s (≈£6,266.00) First Class, in 1908. They offered rail trips through India and world tours as well (Quartermaine & Peter, 2006).

All travellers have to start with small adventures, often guided by others and the advice of helpful notes. Edwin H Low of 949, Broadway, New York, operated a travel agency known as The Uptown Steamship Office. Edwin Low published a pocket notebook called *The Passenger* as a free guide for customers travelling to Britain late in the 19th century. It gave a wealth of general information about life on board ship – the captain, stewards, ship's surgeon etc – with cartoon sketches of typical passengers – the flirting couple (see the chapter-end image), the 'Kodak fiend', the seasick traveller – with advice about managing the voyage and the arrangements for arriving in Liverpool or Southampton. Concerts on board always included singing the US and British national anthems, so the words were included. Advertisements for hotels and family boarding houses were plentiful. In the 1895 edition there was an advert for a voice coach to help American would-be performers in London shows, some of which were listed in *The Passenger*.

Ships began to be fitted with radio equipment in the first decade of the 20th century. Those without radios had to rely on telegraph-cable messages, which were only available at coastal stations. Ships arriving off the coast of Ireland at the Fastnet Rock could signal their details to the mainland, from where they were sent by telegraph to warn Queenstown of their progress. The Marconi Wireless Telegraphic Company installed radio equipment on Fastnet and at Brow Head on the mainland in 1904. Edwin Low's passengers were able to have messages sent when their ships called at Queenstown in Southern Ireland, setting up arrangements for their arrival in Britain, buying railway tickets and hotel accommodation if necessary. Low's had its own cable code in which a single word or short phrase stood for a sentence, saving some of the cost of a telegram which was based on the number of words transmitted. The agency published a book of codes which, by 1900, included a claimed 10,000 code words. Low's could register a client's name and address against a further code word. This made it possible to send a telegram to, for example, relatives, without any of the confusion that could arise from surnames that were relatively common. For example, the 1900 code 'Humbug' meant 'get all the information and write to me'. 'Profusely' stood for 'remit immediately, by telegraph'. Other steamship lines provided their own coding lists for passenger use.

Crossing the Atlantic as a tourist required much more than a steamship, it required communication systems of many kinds, the invention and development of which allowed passenger lines to become reliable, safer and affordable. Shipping companies by the turn of the 20th century used both in-house and out-sourced printing facilities, producing posters and newspaper advertisements using artists' illustrations and photography; postal services, messengers, cable telegraphs, telephones, public presentations and lantern-slide shows. Promoting their liners meant everything from distinctive designs on ship's funnels right down to match books and menus to publicise their brand. Semaphores, flags and lights served for messaging other ships and shore stations, with some radio communications were beginning to be used for messages in Morse code.

Some ships carried printing equipment for announcements and shipboard news. When the *SS Great Britain* sailed from Melbourne to London in 1865, it produced on board a *The Great Britain Times* each week. The Cunard ship *RMS Ivernia* left Liverpool in June 1905 with a flatbed printing press and two printing staff on board. The purser had the responsibility of issuing a daily 24-page bulletin for the interest of passengers (weblist: *Ivernia*). The edition for 20 June was on high quality paper. It carried four articles, including one about the port of Palermo and another about the activities of children travelling on a Cunarder ship, and a list of the 72 First Class passengers on board (out of the 998 in total). Information from the ship's log gave passengers a note about the voyage, while there was a report about wireless contacts with other ships nearby. More than fifty adverts were included, most being for up-market products such as the latest fashions in clothing, smart hotels, choice foodstuffs, jewellery and Thomas Cook's tours. The paper was printed in the early hours of the day and made ready for passengers to read at their breakfast tables.

The *RMS Ivernia* printing press is a reminder that transport developments cannot take place on their own. They are part of a system of economic and

51

social activities, with the communication of ideas and services crucial to all of them. This book is about the changing modes of tourist transport. It is not about the media that helped to make those changes possible and successful. That, for the period 1851-1941, will be part of the book, *Bright Prospect*.

Setbacks to the Growth of Transport Services

The loss of the White Star liner *RMS Titanic*, on its maiden voyage in 1912, sent earthquake-like tremors throughout the Western world and beyond. The loss of over 1,500 lives from the supposedly unsinkable ship which had lifeboats for only half those on board was a tragedy and a scandal. It was a floating palace of luxury for the super-rich (ten-course dinners served) as well as a transport for third class passengers (rice soup, roast beef, brown gravy). Out of it all came stories of tragedy and heroism, mistakes and incompetence. British and American Boards of Inquiry resulted in recommendations that were incorporated into the Safety of Life at Sea convention of 1914. These covered the provision of proper and sufficient lifeboats, lifeboat drills, ship-to-ship communication, the comprehensive operation of shipboard radio (the US Radio Act of 1912) and the monitoring of icebergs affecting shipping. (Lord, 2012/1955; Ward, 2012)

The *RMS Titanic* was thought by many to be unsinkable, but so were other major liners of her day. It was big, but two sister ships were also big, and the German *Imperator* was even bigger and launched just over a month after the White Star liner went down (Ward, 2012). The sinking was a monumental disaster, but the sad fact is that all features of transport have their disasters, from roads and bridges to railways, ships and aircraft. The Tay Railway Bridge collapse in December 1879 took 75 lives and caused major changes in bridge construction. The Nashville train wreck in July 1918 took 101 lives and injured 171. Operating procedures had to be improved and the use of wooden carriages discontinued in favour of steel. A TWA DC-2 crashed in Missouri in 1935. Investigators identified communication failures, poor weather forecasts and many errors of judgement by ground handlers and flight crew. It led to the creation of the US Civil Aeronautics Authority. When the hydrogen-filled airship *Hindenburg* went down in flames, landing at Lakehurst, New Jersey in 1937, 36 died, with the result that the very idea of airships died too, at least for those using flammable gas. These tragedies, and many others, led ultimately to improved safety features and better operational management within their many industries.

The United States Government Would be Glad if You Would Go Away

World War I produced a shipping crisis for the United States, even before it entered the conflict itself. For many years, US shipping lines had been losing out to European companies. Edward N Hurley wrote in 1927 that "Little more than 10% of our water-borne foreign commerce (measured in dollars) was carried in American [ships]" (Hurley, 1927:Ch 3). Hurley had been the Chairman of the United States Shipping Board. The Board was created by Congress under President Woodrow Wilson in September 1916, just before the country entered the war itself in April 1917.

Germany, France, Austria and Great Britain had withdrawn their merchant shipping from normal international trade in order to serve their military needs. Germany's campaign of unrestricted submarine warfare saw 470 cargo ships sunk. The USA was quickly drawn into a fight it had tried to avoid, but the new situation forced its hand. It had been obvious by September 1916 that a radical shipping policy was needed just to preserve the lines of national shipping communication. Entering the European arena made it even more essential. An army, its weaponry and its continuing supplies of munitions and food would have to be carried by American ships. Ships were needed in a great hurry.

Congress passed the legislation required to seize 95 German ships in American waters and charter or purchase others that had been seized by other countries around the world. Some of Germany's biggest liners were included. Ships belonging to US allies were taken over, too. The British were pacified by a promise that its ships would only be used to supply British needs of cargo and personnel. A huge US shipbuilding programme was also added. By the end of 1918, the US had 1,386 vessels under its control (Hurley, 1927). The United States Shipping Board Emergency Fleet Corporation organised direct management of the fleet through government departments and commercial companies according to the type of ship and the jobs that were to be done.

The war came to an end with the Armistice of November 1918. One set of jobs was completed. Another – the building up of American cargo and passenger shipping – had still to be done. An unusual situation was now in place: the US Government was setting out to promote ship-borne tourism through the maritime industries it controlled. Cargo services were promoted by the Board at the same time. It had chosen six established steamship operators to oversee the activities of the key passenger vessels sailing on four main routes. These were from New York to ports in Europe (from Cherbourg to Danzig); from New York to Brazil, Uruguay and Argentina; Seattle to Japan, China, Hong Kong and the Philippines, and San Francisco to Hawaii and then those same South East Asia ports. A brochure issued in 1922 by the Board showed how close the system was to full nationalisation: "United States Government owned ships are now sailing the Seven Seas. Every man, woman and child in America owns a part of the American Merchant Marine" (USSB, 1922:2).

To build steamship services on US passenger liners, the Board arranged advertising for the available journeys by buying space in magazines and newspapers, as well as producing the usual brochures. It realised that there was a problem about the very idea of ocean travel. While some American citizens had made the trans-Atlantic crossing, by far the bulk of the population took vacations at home. Cost was one of the problems to be overcome. Another, for the Board, was that those who had travelled had done so mainly on European-owned ships. A third was the problem faced by many nations: that of would-be travellers being unsure about how an ocean voyage had to be organised and what ship-board life was like. The 1922 brochure, and others later, was aimed at solving these difficulties.

It was called *Going Abroad: A Booklet of Information for Travellers*, two dozen pages of clear and concise details on every aspect of buying a passage, living on board and a little about being a traveller in a foreign country. Edwin Low's *The Passenger*, already mentioned, was the kind of forerunner that earlier tourists found useful. Later travellers would use guidebooks such as those of Eugene Fodor from the 1930s, or Temple Fielding and Arthur Frommer after World War II about the best ways to plan travels, as well as details of what there was to see and do in other countries. They were lively and less encyclopaedic than the Murrays and Baedekers that had gone before.

Going Abroad was very detailed. 'Before Going Abroad' – one page – dealt with choosing a steamship company, booking directly or through an agent, applying for a passport and visas, labelling luggage, arranging travel funds through letters of credit, bankers' cheques or express cheques, arriving at the ship in time, boarding and having the stewards reserve a deck chair and a place at the dining table. Pages of detail followed on all these things and more. The system of the ship's bells to mark each half hour passing within each crew watch was explained. Terms such as 'crow's nest', 'port and starboard', 'knots'

54

and 'fathoms' etc were explained. Throughout the brochure no efforts were spared to show that United States' liners were at least as good, as safe and as enjoyable, as those of European shipping lines.

The US Shipping Board had little beneficial effect on its passenger liners. Many of the ships built during the war were not well suited to peacetime use. A Merchant Marine Act of 1920 gave preference to US-registered ships for carrying cargoes but did not result in stimulating new building. The Quota Acts of 1921 reduced immigration and steerage passengers from Europe, which meant, in Brian Lavery's words, "the USA took little interest in trans-Atlantic trade" (2005:301) and left it mainly to France and Britain, since Germany had lost her passenger fleet through confiscation during and at the end of the war. The damage to German national pride through defeat and confiscation would have not only a major effect towards the rise of the Hitler regime and a further war, but the growth of a new maritime tourism sector driven by a totalitarian ethos.

After a year or two of shipbuilding to replace wartime losses, the industry was in the doldrums. Those liners that had carried steerage passengers converted the space freed into a new, third class, style of accommodation. But economic depressions in the early 1920s and following the crash of 1929 meant little expansion of either fleets or market sectors. Maritime tourism offered luxury and leisure to those who could afford it, but most people could not. Their expectations were teased by newspaper and magazine reports, newsreels of celebrities arriving and departing, and the excitement raised by building new super-liners.

Cunard made a publicity film of the *RMS Franconia* in Hong Kong during its world tour and issued a smart passenger's souvenir book (1930). (RMS = Royal Mail Ship). Two Cunard ships built in the 1930s would become famous as liners and as wartime troop transports. British Movietone News reported to cinema audiences the launch by King George V of the *RMS Queen Mary* in 1937, with a claimed 250,000 spectators. The next year saw King George VI's wife launch the ship named after her – *RMS Queen Elizabeth*. British Pathé was on hand this time to record the event for a newsreel. Many London and regional railway stations were opening news theatres where travellers awaiting trains could watch cartoons and newsreels. They might not have been able to sail in real ocean liners: at least they could wonder at the magnificent forms of travel that were out there.

On the Move

There were movies set on board liners, such as the teasingly titled *Sin Takes a Holiday* (1930) by British Pathé, or Paramount's *Luxury Liner* (1933), a title that might tempt anyone suffering economic depression. It included shots of the *SS Germania* amongst its otherwise studio scenes. Sam Goldwyn's *Dodsworth* had shots of the newly-entered-into service *Queen Mary*. It was a drama about a failing marriage, scoring tourism content through ocean travel and Americans on a Grand Tour of Europe. Two Fred Astaire musicals, *Follow the Fleet* (1936) and *Shall We Dance* (1937) were widely popular, with a mix of maritime content. However, the travel mass market would never be served by liners until cruise ships became popular. It would be the aeroplane revolution of the 1950s that allowed the majority to consider, and to buy, long-haul travel.

Moving away from steerage provision for immigrants, towards more luxurious travel, was one reason for ship conversions and new builds in the 1920s and 1930s. A more narrowly defined market profile worked well with some European government strategies of national flagships. Brian Lavery notes the additional requirement of some governments for large passenger ships that could be converted quickly into troop carriers. The lessons of World War I and the threat of a rerun focused national policies. Financial policies were used to prepare for large scale tourist travel and the likelihood of military travel on a huge scale. Germany returned to large liners with *Bremen* and *Europa*, Italy unveiled the *Rex* and the *Conte de Savoia*, France the *Normandie*, Britain the *Queen Mary* and the *Queen Elizabeth*, Canada the *Empress of Britain* and the USA the *America*. They were all to be quickly drawn into wartime activities, some, like the Italian ships, never to return to carrying tourists. Germany was doing rather more than simple passenger liner development, however, using cruise ships as parts of a political, pro-Nazi, programme. Book 2 in this series, *Bright Prospect*, will examine that programme.

Back in Time for Tea

In the two or three decades before World War I there were plenty of good opportunities to take cruises along parts of the British coastline and, in the phrase of the time, be back in time for tea. Compared with ocean cruises these were mini, or even, micro-cruises. Small screw propeller or paddle steamers embarked passengers from piers or harbours for trips of an hour or several hours. Some went out to sea and returned home while others delivered their customers to some other destination. There were dozens. They plied down the Clyde, along the Lancashire and North Wales coasts, up and down the

Severn Estuary, round the coasts of Devon and Cornwall, in and out of Southern English resorts and as far as the Medway and River Thames.

John Megoran [(2016)] writes of the extensive paddle steamer excursions of the turn of the 20th century. "So prolific were excursion paddle steamers that you could have boarded one at Great Yarmouth and, with an assiduous study of the timetables and connections" made a journey round the South Coast into the Bristol Channel and across to Swansea and then Caldy Island. There could even have been side visits to France or the Channel Isles [(Megoran, 2016:Ch 1)].

The first paddle steamers in Britain to be of commercial use were in Scotland on the Forth and Clyde Canal and the River Clyde. 1812 saw the *Comet* carry passengers on the Clyde. The General Steam Navigation Company began operating on the Thames in 1824 where it tapped the growing passenger market represented by the city. Excursions to the exotic gardens at Rosherville and the resorts of Southend and Margate were popular. As railways spread towards coastal resorts, so were steamers able to offer trips to the day visitors who arrived. At the same time, they could react quickly to the new demands by adding destinations the railways had not yet reached. Flexibility of routes, timetables and on-board services gave them advantages.

Flexibility in some cases meant the chance to virtually take part in national events. August 1899 saw naval and army events take place on the Dorset and Hampshire coasts. Military manoeuvres were showcase events using tourism and media reporting, part of the growing imperial thinking running through the nation. The Second Boer War would break out in October in South Africa. Rivalries with Germany would grow in the years following up to 1914 and outright conflict. Megoran tells of five paddle steamers taking passengers from Bournemouth to sail through the Channel Fleet off Portland, a 'Grand Cruise' of Portsmouth Harbour to see Nelson's Victory and *HMS Terrible,* the largest and most powerful cruiser in the world, and a visit to Ryde to see a Review of the Hampshire and Isle of Wight Volunteers. There was also a trip to Cherbourg to see 'the French Port and Arsenal'.

The experience of travelling on open decks in beautiful weather, surrounded by the billowing sea or calmer rivers was more immediate than something only viewed through a window. As long as the weather and sea were calm the decks could be strolled, other passengers encountered, or the steamship observed at work. Bars dispensed refreshments and informality. Some steamers began to open dining rooms. Some steamer companies put on entertainment by singers or in running competitions. The comparison with Billy Butlin's holiday camp entertainments and the long-established concert party shows comes to mind.

Changes in the weather and the waves were potentially problematic. So were over-popular boats, loaded with crowds, making deck walking difficult. On the whole, though, this was travel with a great sense of adventure that railways could not offer, and it could be afforded by people for whom ocean cruising was impossible. These "happy little ships" as Andrew Gladwell has called them, "enabled holidaymakers of all classes to enjoy a day or a few hours experiencing the glories of the British coastline" (Gladwell, 2013:4). For steamers on the South East coasts there was the added attraction of possible cross-Channel visits to places like Ostend, Boulogne and Le Touquet. Some worked like ferries, allowing overnight stays, others as day trips, though for the latter, most of the time was spent at sea.

The happy hunting ground for lovers of pleasure steamers in the years before World War I was that around the Firth of Clyde. Forty vessels were being operated by eight companies in 1914 (Paterson, 1969). The extensive coasts of the Firth of Clyde, Lochs Fyne and Long, the Kyles of Bute, Kilbrannan Sound and other stretches of water offered varied scenery and were sheltered from much of the troublesome Atlantic weather. Mountains contrasted with lowlands, picturesque ports with industrial towns and notably, the city of Glasgow. It was the Glaswegians who made up much of the escapist crowds going 'doon the watter' for a few hours or days. Before coaches and cars became common features, the railways brought more crowds to the Eastern Firth of Clyde piers and harbours.

A line ran from Glasgow through Paisley and Kilmarnock to Ayr from the late 1830s. A line through Nithsdale connected with the Carlisle-Glasgow and Edinburgh line in 1848. Passengers could travel from England to reach the steamer and ferry ports between Ayr and Ardrossan. Edinburgh had already connected with Glasgow in 1842, bringing tourists from the East. When a line running along the Clyde coast from Greenock was completed in 1865 to Wemyss Bay, a steamer service across to Rothesay, Largs and Great Cumbrae Island began. The foundations of rail access to the Firth of Clyde ports were being put into place (see Robertson 1983, Ross 2014).

Way down the Clyde from Glasgow, the isle of Arran was already something of a destination, for health tourism. Andrew Boyle [(1994)] notes that in 1746 children from the town of Ayr made a trip in June to Brodick, on the island, to drink goat's milk for its health-giving properties. Visitors were more likely to travel from Glasgow or Saltcoats, the latter having a weekly crossing scheduled. The *SS Helensburgh* made twice-weekly journeys from Glasgow, returning one or two days later. Only prosperous tourists could afford the time and the tickets in those days.

The change towards affordable tourism came in the mid-19th century as Glaswegians "discovered in the Clyde coast a natural holiday area; fares were cheap, distances short ... the cult of the day trip 'doon the watter' ... from the grime, poverty and overcrowding" arrived [(Paterson, 1969:12-13)]. It was the beginnings of that love affair that took 7,000 passengers from Ardrossan to Brodick in 1836 [(Boyle, 1994)]. New piers on the island were gradually added, new rail links on the mainland opened and competition between steamer companies became fierce. A race to return people from Brodick to Ardrossan in 1890 left some passengers for the *Duchess of Hamilton* still climbing the gangplank as the ship moved away. At Ardrossan harbour it collided with the *Scotia* arriving from Arran. The captain of the *Hamilton* was fined, but racing continued [(Boyle, 1994)].

Day trips were not the only form of tourist activity. Small guest houses and self-catering accommodations were sprinkling the coastal resorts served by the railways and steamers. Advertisements in the Glasgow Herald in June 1898 for example, included these: Blackwaterfoot, Arran, a double-bedded room with cooking stove, £1 weekly; Ascog, Isle of Bute, charming bungalow with beautiful grounds, £20 monthly; Rothesay, attic flat, 5 apartments, splendid view, August £6 [(Paterson, 1969:265)]. Alan Paterson also quotes the July 1896 cruises on the *PS Neptune*. There were none on Sundays, a feature of many early railway schedules as well. 32 cruises are listed for the 25 days when there were sailings (1 July not shown, 17 July - no cruises). There were some days with two cruises. Destinations ranged from Arrochar in the north to Girvan in the south, Brodick on Arran, and Rothesay on Bute. Not only the resorts, mountains and islands attract the passengers, but seeing other steamers passing by and sailing yachts tacking to and fro. The Corinthian Yacht Club Regatta at Hunter's Quay, north of Dunoon, was to be followed on Saturday, 4 July after a sail up the Clyde.

On the Move

It seems right to round off this brief account of pleasure steamers in our period of 1851-1941 by remembering a radio broadcast by J B Priestley in 1940. The famous author had been given the task of making short reflections on the day's wartime events in short *Postscripts* after the important 9 o'clock news. On 5th June 1940 he spoke about the evacuation of British and Allied forces from the beaches at Dunkirk. German forces had driven the French, British and Canadian troops onto the beaches and were poised to annihilate them. A lull in the hostilities gave the chance to rescue 338,226 men using hundreds of naval and civilian ships. Many pleasure steamers and other small craft took part. Priestley's address took the form of a morale-boosting description of heroic actions after a disastrous defeat. He focused on the pleasure boats in a low-key, but highly influential judgement. After the war, a wave of nostalgia made trips out on pleasure steamers once more a popular activity. Holiday styles would soon change, but the memories lingered on:

"These *Brighton Belles* and *Brighton Queens* left that innocent, foolish world of theirs to sail into the inferno, to defy bombs, shells, magnetic mines, torpedoes, machine-gun fire – to rescue our soldiers ... but now - look – this little steamer, like all her brave and battered sisters – is immortal. She'll go sailing proudly down the years in the epic of Dunkirk. And our great grandchildren ... may also learn how the little holiday steamers made an excursion into hell and came back glorious" (Sevareid, 1967:6,).

Daydreams at Sea

Chapter 4

Railways and Tramways

Railways in Britain captured the imaginations of everyone who saw them in operation. Besides several early excursions, Gladstone's Railway Act of 1844, requiring low-cost passenger travel on at least one train a day from each operating company, had drawn more people to make journeys. Some who saw a train go by, or who had travelled in one, were excited and thrilled by the thoughts of what journeys they might achieve in the future. Others were alarmed. They worried that speeds of twenty or thirty miles an hour might damage the body or the mind. Mixing strangers together in closed carriages tempted risqué behaviour and worse. Unsupervised communication between different social classes, ages and genders would tempt untold immorality. Chapters 14 and 16 of *Book 1: The Beckoning Horizon* include many contrasting views on the issues. Doubtless, people would get ideas above their stations – or well beyond them, discovered on the highways and byways of the world. There were efforts made to keep the old social order. The Liverpool and Manchester Railway, for example, had timetabled no services to start running between 10am and 4pm. Journeys that matched the start and end of the working day seemed to be their idea. Some of its directors had wanted to run nothing at all on Sundays. Some Scottish and Welsh companies would do exactly that. When the Metropolitan Underground Railway opened in 1863, it incorporated a 'church interval' into its rail services so as not to clash with church services (Wolmar, 2007). It was like the BBC (and for a few months, ITV) policy that would prevail in television schedules during the 1950s. Between 6pm and 7pm there were no programmes shown, so that parents could get their young children to bed – the so-called 'toddlers' truce'. It was also intended to avoid clashes with church services on Sundays.

There were too many agents of change at work to leave lives undisturbed. Tramways, railways, the popular press, public speakers and classroom education ensured there would be change, no matter who tried to control and direct policies.

Simon Bradley has noted some of the landmark events in the growth of Britain's railways around the time of the Great Exhibition (Bradley, 2015). London's railways of 1851 had seen rises in passenger traffic of up to 38%. Railway companies were imposing standard times on their networks, based on London times. Before those, the turning of the Earth meant that exact midday, when the sun was at its highest in the sky, was often minutes later for places to the West, earlier for the East. Plymouth was twenty minutes behind London, for example. By 1851, railway lines ran from England through Southern and Central Scotland, and onwards via the East coast to Aberdeen. Of course, to the Scots, this meant that England was now being reached from Scotland to London and the South coast, making new opportunities for travel and trade. Wales had the important line along its North coast to Holyhead, from where ships could be taken to Dublin, or again, in the other direction, the cities of England. Ireland had no trains at the time.

Bradley quotes *The Times* newspaper in 1850: "Thirty years ago not one countryman in a hundred had seen the metropolis. There is now scarcely one in the same number who has not spent his day there" (Bradley, 2015:17). England was well served by 1851, notably from London into East Anglia, Kent, Sussex and Hampshire, though only one line crossed into the West Country via Bristol and as far as Plymouth. South Wales connections went via Cardiff and Swansea to Llanelli and into the coalfield valleys of the South. 1859 saw trains beginning to run into Cornwall, the last English county to be connected to the national network. 1864 was the year the trains first ran through mid-Wales to Aberystwyth.

Railways in late 19th century Britain had to do several things to attract passengers, especially tourists making longer journeys and any who needed to overcome a few concerns about trains. They needed comfort, safety and probably some way of getting meals. People were still only just getting used to how the railway systems worked. The correct tickets were needed for the most suitable route. Stations needed timetable information, signposting and helpful staff. Liverpool Street Station in the early 1920s had what was then called an evening 'crush' hour with intense working of trains in and out. The suburban railway lines feeding the station had handled over 107m passenger journeys during the year of 1919. Timetables and train movements were reorganised to cope. Part of the changes included number coding of the routes to the right platform and carriage compartments given coloured strips above doors, yellow for first class and blue for second class.

Bradshaw's railway timetables, produced from 1863 onwards, were ideal for the frequent traveller. Those who wanted to plan journeys by rail exploring towns and cities could use Bradshaw's *Railway Hand-Book*, and versions covering continental Europe were available for more upmarket tourists. Handbills and posters served those who did not need Mr Bradshaw's travel encyclopaedias.

George Bradshaw was a Lancashire-born mapmaker and printer, known at first for his canal maps. *Bradshaw's Railway Time Tables and Assistant to Railway Travelling* appeared in 1839 at a cost of sixpence (≈£1.51). Its name changed a few times, but its reputation became firmly established as the essential source of timetable information on home bookshelves. All railway timetable guides came to be called 'Bradshaws'. Numerous authors of crime and adventure stories from Conan Doyle and Erskine Childers to Philip Pullman have passing references to Bradshaws. The publication list of Bradshaw's more general guidebooks expanded rapidly to cover *Continental Europe* (from 1847), *Provinces of India* (from 1864) and then individual European countries, starting with *France* (1873). Many British TV viewers will be familiar with them from their use by Michael Portillo in his *Great Railway Journeys* series.

Passenger comfort was a class-conscious matter in the earliest days of rail travel in Britain. First class ticket holders got enclosed carriages of designs copied from road-coaches, well-padded and cushioned. Second class had open-sided wagons with wooden benches. They might have had a protective canopy, but the rain and wind could just blow through the open sides. Third class rode in open boxes with no sheltering cover and bench seating. As railways proved successful, finance was made available for investment in better carriages. Properly roofed and with side doors and windows, they were built with various combinations of compartments. Some had compartments for all three classes, others a mix of two classes and still others were dedicated to just one class. There might be a guard's compartment at one end with space for passengers' luggage.

The situation before lavatories were installed was that long-distance trains such as those on tourist routes had to make scheduled stops. Needful passengers could risk finding a platform lavatory or urinal in time or would have to wait for the slightly longer stops at stations providing meals. There were other possibilities: females might carry a chamber pot in a lidded basket, or a rubber bottle designed for discreet relief under a skirt. Males might make use of an open carriage window, being careful about the wind direction. Anything else had to wait.

Lavatories began to be built-in to carriages. They served one compartment each at first, some compartments not being provided with one at all. When corridors were added late in the 19th century, lavatories could be placed at each end of the carriage to serve all the passengers. At first, though, they were designated as they were in hotels, with one for men and the other for women. As it became obvious that was not very efficient, they lost their gender labels.

It is interesting to note how such a universal requirement was only introduced on a class basis over half a century – and then, not always on every carriage. Hamilton Ellis gave relevant dates in his book on railway carriages in 1965 (quoted in Bradley, 2015):

1848-50 Royal saloons
1850-60 Family and invalid saloons

1873   Sleeping cars
1874   Pullman cars
1881-82 East Coast 1st class coaches with side corridors
1886   Manchester, Sheffield & Lincolnshire 3rd class saloons
1887   Midland Railway 3rd class saloons
1889   East Coast route, 2nd and 3rd class coaches with side corridors
1891   Great Western Railway side corridor trains: all classes

It must have been a relief (pardon the pun) when potential long-distance travellers heard that lavatories were installed on trains on their chosen route. Efficient heating was another boon that took time to make its presence felt. There was little to be done about being cold in the early days with open carriages. First class passengers might have been able to rent metal hot water containers to use as foot warmers. But warmers cooled down after a while. Some stations were equipped to replace a cold foot warmer with newly filled hot containers as trains pulled up on long journeys. Station staff had to have them ready, collect the old ones and hand out the new, taking the money for the new hiring at the same time. Another version from 1881 contained sodium acetate, permanently sealed in, having been warmed in a simmering hot water tank for a while. It was claimed to stay hot for three times that of the water version [Bradley, 2015].

The Midland Railway, under James Allport, abolished second class accommodation, turning the carriages into third class, but with properly upholstered seats, more leg room and compartment partitions that reached the roof to give a better feeling of privacy. Christian Wolmar [2007] quotes C Hamilton Ellis, who said rival companies gave "squeals of dismay and disapproval" as it was "pampering the working classes". Allport bought US Pullman cars for his first-class passengers. They were attached to his Midland trains but staffed by Pullman attendants. Pullman cars had oil-fired systems with heated water pipes below the carriage floors. During the 1930s there were hairdressing salons, newspaper sellers, cinema cars, record players and radios in them [Palin, 2015].

Other companies began to use the luxury coaches in their own first class services. It was not long before radiators were installed in carriages, heated by steam supplied from the locomotive. Comfort from rugs, radiators, lavatories and better seating made the prospect of making long holiday trips to ancient towns, the coast and countryside much less of a challenge. Railway trains helped the growth of holidays for everyone, and not just the prosperous few, but they had to be more than just draughty, sooty people carriers. They also needed to provide food where possible.

Travellers took their own food as needed on the early journeys. Long distance trains began to make stops at key stations where refreshment rooms had been built. London to Scotland trains called at Preston, York or Normanton according to the line they were using. Twenty-minute stops for six-course meals at a fixed price were claimed to be usual, something that seems quite impossible to do properly looking back from the present day. They were, in fact, served in baskets to be taken onto the train, a harbinger perhaps of the miniature multi-course meals that would be served cabin-class on airliners. Bookings for the railway meals often had to be telegraphed ahead. On arrival, the rush to get to the food must have been horrendous, with another rush to regain the correct carriage – and presumably make a lavatory visit as well. It was worse on shorter journeys such as London to Birmingham. The stop at Wolverton was only five to ten minutes [Simmons, 1971].

The Railway Traveller's Handy Book (1862) worked carefully through the three-act drama of taking a long railway journey in the early days. Everything, from packing a portmanteau to finding hotel accommodation on arrival at the destination, was covered. Finding simple refreshments was a battle:

> "The counter is besieged by hungry and thirsty applicants, urging their various requests for sandwiches, buns, biscuits, wine, brandy, etc. But as there are usually some two or three hundred persons requiring refreshments, and only about a dozen hands to supply them, it stands to reason that the task of serving out the viands is no easy one … Walk to that part of the counter where one of the attendants is stationed … if you desire a basin of soup, never mind the words "a basin of" but simply utter the monosyllable "soup" … call out distinctly and in a loud voice, have the precise sum ready … On the whole, we should always advise the railway traveller to take his refreshment with him … " [Simmons, (ed) 1971 edition: 69-70]

Smaller stations might only serve individuals or families in their refreshment rooms. Brecon station in 1891 was leased to a David Williams. The lease gave details of what might be sold and at what price: examples below. When it was renewed in 1905, the list and prices remained unchanged.

Breakfast, plain, with marmalade	1s 6d
Ditto, with cold meat and marmalade	2s 0d
Teas, plain, with marmalade	1s 0d
Ditto, with cold meat and marmalade	2s 0d
Luncheon, cold meat and cheese	2s 0d
Large cup of tea	4d
Large cup of tea with bread and butter or with bun or biscuit	6d

A range of wines (Port, Sherry, Claret, Moselle, Hock etc) by the bottle, pint or glass; spirits (Brandy, Whiskey, Rum, Gin) beers, ales and soft drinks were on sale [weblist: Brecon]. Two shillings in 1891 would be the equivalent of £8.20 in 2017. The prices might mirror those of 2017, but incomes were lower and from the brief information given on the source document, the meals were more basic – and with no greens or salads, apparently. Railway catering on a large scale owed much to Felix William Spiers and Christopher Pond. They were both Britons who had emigrated to Australia in the mid-19th century, where they met and formed a business partnership operating top quality restaurants. Then, in 1863, they returned to England where they were soon in charge of the Holborn Viaduct Hotel in London. The partners found out how poor railway station refreshment rooms could be. It led to the change which made them famous. They took on a contract in 1863 to run the refreshment rooms at the new Farringdon Street station on the Metropolitan Railway. It was an opportunity to show what they could do.

They baked their own cakes, buns and biscuits, selling to busy city workers in a hurry. The journalist Henry Mayhew in 1865 thought them better than those at any other railway outlet. He noted that four hundred people ate at the rooms every day [Bradley, 2015]. At the time, food adulteration was common with alum added to bread flour, Venetian lead in sugar confectionery and the sweepings of workshop floors in loose tea [see Pittard, 2013]. Writers such as Isabel Beeton had been encouraging home cooking by middle class readers of her books. Refreshment room and restaurant owners like Spiers and Pond were showing everyday travellers what quality food was like. W H Smith's railway news-stands were feeding the minds of travellers and Spiers and Pond their stomachs. Spiers and Pond were by then operating the refreshment rooms on Victoria station and restaurants in the city. They picked up management agreements with two Midland Railway stations, Leicester and Trent. It was at the latter that they began to sell luncheon baskets containing half a chicken, ham, cheese and bread and butter with either a half-pint bottle of stout or claret. Trent, near Long Eaton, only served passengers changing trains or using its facilities. It was on the Midland Railway in 1884 that hot meals in baskets were first made available against passenger orders booked ahead by telegraph.

The first onboard train restaurant in Britain was a Pullman car containing a kitchen. It was attached to the London to Leeds services of the Great Northern Railway in 1879. The carriages of these trains had no means by which passengers could move between them, so anyone wanting a meal on board had to buy a ticket to sit in the restaurant car for the whole journey [Wolmar, 2019]. Inside the coach at one end was an open fire for cooking. The food might have been newly prepared, but passengers complained about smoke and even soot when the wind was blowing. The first corridor trains on the line only appeared in 1893. The United States had dining cars at least a decade earlier.

Simon Bradley [2015] gives a thorough examination of the improvements in British railway trains within our chosen period. Tourism depended on railways in the years before World War I and despite coach and car competition growing between the two World Wars train travel remained the essential holiday transport. Corridors and – somewhat later – inter-carriage links permitted the development of toilet facilities, and the provision of food and drink while travelling. Passengers could move around for exercise and socialising and go for help if the occasion arose. Communication cords were tested, rejected, replaced or redesigned. In some cases, they were installed, but for months were not connected to be ready to alert train staff.

Continuous braking along the train became common, using at first automatic vacuum systems. These held all the brakes off until a loss of vacuum anywhere along the train line, perhaps by carriages becoming uncoupled, caused the brakes to be applied without human intervention. Air brakes were brought into use that were more effective, using automatic valves and individual reservoirs of compressed air in each carriage. Management and safety systems like these reduced accidents and ultimately helped reassure potential passengers that travelling was safe and therefore more enjoyable.

Knowledge on Wheels

The traffic everywhere ranged from raw materials, especially coal, through manufactured goods, to farm produce and passengers. But Christian Wolmar points out in his *Great Railway Revolution* (2012), about United States railroads, something else that applied equally to Britain. The promoters of railroads there often said that education would be helped by the spread of knowledge. Information was an important 'cargo' on railways everywhere. Travellers came back home full of knowledge about what they had seen and heard (see BH Chapter 10). More than that, books, magazines and newspapers were distributed along the railway lines to networks of towns. Knowledge moved both ways.

It was becoming far easier for ordinary folk to go see for themselves what their country was about. Their mode of travel was most commonly the day excursion, followed by the transport, accommodation, food and activity package deals offered in tourism. Horse riding, stagecoaches and ships had spread information, but it was the railway train that made discovery a commonplace. Joseph Thomas had produced his *Railroad Guide from London to Birmingham* in 1839, describing the places that were seen along the route of the train. In the more media-conscious 20th century, the Great Western Railway published *Through the Window: The Great Western Railway from Paddington to Penzance*, based on a diagrammatic representation of the route to which notes of what could be seen were added. It was a guide to places like that of Joseph Thomas, but with less of a text book style. Just after our period, Stuart Pike compiled *Mile by Mile: An Illustrated Journey on Britain's Railways* in 1947/48. It was also based around three diagrammatic routes of LNER, LMS and Southern Railway main lines and aimed solidly at railway enthusiasts. It was heavily detailed about the physical track, signals, bridges, tunnels, level crossings and even water troughs and mail bag pick-up equipment. Places were marked and some industrial features shown such as collieries and factories. For those who used these guides there was much to be learnt about the railway heartland. A new edition of 2017 has added the GWR route to Cornwall in the same style as the original guide.

Thanks to the efforts of Thomas Cook and many other hard-working organisers, railway excursions were becoming common in the mid-19th century (see BH Chapter 14). They earned income for railway companies while supplying entertainment and education to their passengers, as discussed by Alan Delgado (1977) and Arthur and Elizabeth Jordan (1991). For example, the employees of the Portsmouth Dockyard ran an excursion to the Fisheries Exhibition in London in 1883. They had formed their own Excursion Committee to do so. It proved successful. 591 adults and 80 children took part (Jordan & Jordan, 1991). More trips followed. The Jordans point to the scale of activity by 1905, when two railway companies sent fourteen trains from Portsmouth to thirteen destinations with a total of 6,315 passengers.

A recent reprinted edition of the London & North Western Railway's *Programme of Excursion Bookings for the Summer Holidays* from London in 1914 lists hundreds of stations that could be reached on its network. They included places which needed a ferry crossing, such as Douglas on the Isle of Man, and places throughout Ireland using its own ferries and arrangements made with Irish rail companies. There were joint-working arrangements with other companies where it suited the L&NWR Co, so Penzance, Scarborough and Great Yarmouth did not figure whereas the Irish resorts did. As an example of a rail and sea excursion, on several days between early July and late September there were excursions that could reach Kenmare in the South West of Ireland. These started from Euston at either 6:30am or 7:30am. Arrival times were not shown, presumably because these depended on which Irish departure times were to be used by the passengers. Trains caught ferries from Holyhead to Dublin. There were two return excursion rates, Euston to Kenmare: third class travel cost £2..1s..6d (≈£122.41p) and third class with saloon on the ferry was £2..11s (≈£150.43p). Certain trains stopped for refreshments at Crewe or Chester for five minutes. Trains heading further north in England stopped at Preston for a more generous ten minutes (London & North Western Railway, 1914). More will be discussed about rail excursions in *Bright Prospect*, the next book in the present series.

Rack and Pinions

Three railway projects, in the USA, United Kingdom and Switzerland, are worth noting as being fully aimed at giving excursionists new experiences. The first is the Mount Washington Cog Railway in New Hampshire. At nearly 2,000 metres height, the mountain offers magnificent views across the Presidential Range of the White Mountains, long a favourite area for American tourists. By 1861 a road had been built to the summit. A railway was added by 1869 using a rack and pinion system devised by retired inventor and businessman Sylvester Marsh (Heald, 2011). The idea of a cog mechanism under a steam locomotive engaging in a toothed rail had been used from 1812 on the

Middleton Railway in Leeds, England. Marsh's version was the first used to climb up a mountain track. In 1871, the *Rigibahn* began to carry visitors up Mount Rigi in the important tourist district around Lake Lucerne, an area which would become a key development for British tourists (see Studd, 1950). Britain's only public rack and pinion mountain railway climbed Mount Snowdon, starting its journeys in 1896. The idea for such a service dated to 1869 when the London and North Western Railway connected Caernarfon with Llanberis. It was the year when the Mount Washington line was opened. A bill was put before Parliament to construct a line but was blocked by the opposition of the landowner concerned. It was two decades later that opposition ended. By then no Act of Parliament was required and the line was opened for the tourist season of 1896 (Johnson, 2010).

War and its Aftermath

As the railways of Britain entered the 20th century, their business was booming, but suffered from the effects of the 1914-18 war and the economic depressions of the '20s and '30s.

The war of 1914-1918 had left railways in Britain with many insurmountable problems. The 178 independent companies who made up the network were owed around £150m for a number of things, including handling military traffic during the war, according to the government's own auditor (Wolmar, 207). The physical system needed considerable maintenance. Fares and charges had been pegged by the government at levels below that of inflation. It had imposed an eight-hour day for the workforce, even during a time of heavy demand. The wages bill had more than tripled. Christian Wolmar continues the list of problems by recalling that Parliament had to agree to fares and freight charges being doubled in 1920 as a short-term solution. Post-war economic depression was at the same time reducing passenger numbers. After much debate, a major rationalisation took place which was completed in 1923. Known as the Grouping, it amalgamated most lines into a 'Big Four' of regional companies: London and North Eastern, London, Midland and Scottish, Southern and the Great Western. The government did not fully compensate the companies for their wartime efforts, and part of the legislation in the 1921 Act that led to the Grouping gave it powers to control fares. Building the new systems had to be done while suffering a cash shortage. The days of *laissez-faire* operation had been crippled by war. They would not return.

On the Move

Yet from a tourism point of view, the interwar period of 1919-1939 often presents an image of considerable investment in activity and successful growth. This was mainly thanks to national efforts to repair and rebuild the nation through publicity of increasing intensity. Wartime efforts were only part of the problem. The related economic crises of 1922-26 and 1931-33 had to be dealt with, in a context of frequent financial stresses and international upheavals. Social changes were coming more often. The position of women in society by gaining the vote and the changing relationships between social classes in a country which had had to rely on conscription were among them.

The kinds of holidays taken between the wars brought new opportunities for the railway companies. For example, countryside hiking was a growth phenomenon. It often began with a short train ride to a rural station well placed for the start of a ramble. Holiday camps, first of the informal tented variety and then of the Billy Butlin kind also relied on rail journey access. On the other hand, the Big Four companies were meeting competition from buses, long-distance coaches and even cars. They competed to win each year's holidaymakers. Londoners, well off or not, were on the doorsteps, railway concourses and motor car showrooms of all four. While trains and buses competed, they also helped each other as bus routes delivered new passengers to railway stations.

In many ways, the market-driven service improvements had begun well before the war. The London & North Western Railway (part of the London, Midland and Scottish from 1923) had enlarged its London base at Euston station. Its route to Rugby had been widened to four tracks. New locomotives, rolling stock and two ferries for its Holyhead to Dublin Service were added. The Great Western increased main line speeds, by 1914 running London to Bristol in two hours exactly, at 59 mph (94.9 kph). It required locomotives capable of sustained speeds, better track maintenance and reliable signalling. The London, Brighton & South Coast Railway promoted its *Brighton Belle* using seven Pullman cars mixing smoking/buffet and smoking/parlour designations (Wolmar, 2007). These were, however, prestige lines on systems which often had poor and untrustworthy services on the rest. Holidaymakers going to less popular resorts on branch lines had to put up with struggling conditions. Seasoned travellers may have decided to stay with the major resorts to a greater degree. *The Titfield Thunderbolt* (1953) type of whimsical comedy film might have entertained cinemagoers after the next war. It would have hit many a raw nerve in the 1920s.

After 1923, the Great Western (Roden, 2010) continued its policy of fast trains, thanks to the groundwork done by its locomotive designer, George Churchward. His had been the first loco to reach 100 mph (160.9 kph) – the *City of Truro,* in 1904. It was not promoted as an official record until 1922, however, so did not have the publicity impact of the 1934, officially recognised, run by the LNER 4472 *Flying Scotsman* would have. The London & South Western Railway opened its new London station at Waterloo in 1922, adding it in the following year to London Bridge and Victoria stations as part of the new Southern Railway.

Southern had a major electrification strategy that put a strain on maintenance of locomotive rolling stock. As part of its post-Grouping work, the company appointed the first railway public relations officer, J B Elliott (weblist: Elliott). Much improved commuter and holiday line services were achieved, with Mr Elliott placing articles in paid-for newspaper spaces, spreading the word about electrification's advantages supplying a fast and more frequent service. In 1930 he introduced 'Sunny South Sam', an avuncular character on posters who became popular – and effective. Sam was supposedly a member of the Southern Railway station staff. He was shown with Meteorological Office sunshine figures for the South coast, which were better than most others in the UK (Cole & Durack, 1992).

Picturing Perfection

Those were halcyon days for poster artists and for the holidays they promoted. Yet this is perhaps misleading, for posters were not always the dominant advertising medium that our heritage-collecting days make them appear. Roger Burdett Wilson quotes G E Orton of the GWR Publicity Department in 1925 – he was later in charge of it – as stating "quite categorically that 'newspaper advertising I place first in importance every time" (Burdett Wilson, 1970:41). "It is probably the pictorial poster which is most readily called to mind by the general public," quotes Burdett Wilson of G E Orton (1970:65), "this is not to say, however, that posters were the form of advertising which gave the best returns in terms of additional traffic". What they do give us today is a glimpse into the activities, growth and cultural focus of the railway companies' tourist aspirations. They promoted ideas of the perfect days out, of seaside scenes, heritage and family fun in a different age.

On the Move

Christian Wolmar has noted the perfection of train travel as shown in so many movies:

> "Homely and brightly polished engines ... pleasant, cosy compartments ... deferential porters in smart uniforms ... All the while, [the] train travels at a perfect pace, slow enough to enable [the passengers] to enjoy the countryside, but fast enough to enable them to get to their destination on time." (Wolmar, 2019).

He acknowledges the improvements that made rail journeys more comfortable in the years before 1914 but points out that less affluent passengers, or those travelling away from the main lines, enjoyed far less comfort. The poster collections published in books of nostalgia need to be treated with an element of scepticism, as romantic art rather than realism.

All kinds of subjects were shown in poster treatments that worked well in artistic and publicity terms. It was not always the case. Cole & Durack quote the writer on art, Walter Sparrow, in his *Advertising and British Art* (1924) on the subject of a certain well-designed poster for a resort. "Are the inhabitants of this town pleased? No. They look on decorative art as a window-pane, or series of window-panes, and wish to see on their hoardings a tinted photograph lithographed in all details into a very bad poster" (1992:21). Cole & Durack add "the need for designs to be approved by a local committee, often conservative in taste, led frequently to uninspired posters that made the resort appear worthy but dull".

Most famous and effective was John Hassall's 1908 'Jolly Fisherman' skipping along a beach with the slogan '*Skegness is So Bracing*' for the Great Northern Railway (see Cole & Durack, 1992). It earned Hassall £12 at the time. The slogan is said to have been the idea of the Chief Passenger Agent for the GNR, a Mr Hiley, who wanted to turn the town's North Sea breezes to his company's advantage. Hassall reworked it in 1925 for the LNER. It was used many times in the interwar years and indeed, since. Frank Newbould was another artist who continued Hassall's work with the Jolly Fisherman bounding along, led by a bright, flaxen-haired little girl. Billy Butlin chose the town as the location for his first holiday camp in 1936, as it was served well by the railway and had a strong marketing image. And the land Butlin chose "was a peach – the ideal situation. Bang on a main road, facing the sea and sitting on bad farming land that would not cost the world" (North, 1962:48). It was an example of how transport services follow early demand, but then create new opportunities and new demand in turn.

Hassall painted a poster for a *Daily Mail* holiday photo competition in association with Kodak. The 'Kodak Girl' in her usual striped dress, carrying a neat camera case, was seen on a beach with breaking waves behind. 'Kodak Girls' were a main part of the publicity efforts of the company. George Eastman's success with his Kodak company was based on selling the 'charm of photography' as much as his actual camera (West, 2000:20). In this, he was ably served by his advertising manager, Lewis Bunnell Jones, who knew exactly what excited public interest.

Walter Sparrow urged simplification and symbolism, qualities that many artists succeeded in using in posters.

> "Symbols ... convey by imagery what we should otherwise have to ponder over, and, unless the thing was of vital necessity, we should not bother about. But an idea conveyed by a symbol always has a quality of intrigue about it ... The symbol becomes, in my estimation, the most essential element in present-day poster design, by reason of its tradition and because it is the simplest form to understand" (Sparrow, 1924, 78).

The 'Kodak Girl' was such a symbol (see Jacob, 2012). She was presented in her blue and white striped dress, an elegant and lively outdoor figure in sunlit, fresh surroundings and often with her family around. George Eastman wanted to show how simple his photographic system was. Having a woman as the photographer rather than some alpha male was sexist and the forerunner of more than a century of domestic hi-tech advertising to come. Placing her firmly in tourist situations symbolised leisure, families and the memory of holiday exploration.

The interwar years began to embrace the symbol to its most powerful effect, from the political to the general commercial. See, for example, Robert Opie (2005) or the specifically tourist symbolism eg Keith Lovegrove (2000, 2004), Peter Quartermain & Bruce Peter (2006).

Edward McKnight Kauffer produced many distinctive symbolic posters for London Underground (and American Airlines and others) but was also a skilled landscape graphic artist bringing out the essence of locations in well-composed images. *Power: The Nerve Centre of London's Underground* (1930) and *Oxhey Woods* (1915) (Green,1990) were subjects that showed the contrasts.

Tom Purvis's *East Coast Joys: Travel by LNER* (Cole and Durack, 1992) from 1931 is an example and is still popular getting on for a century later. His posters are symbolic in a different way. He used flat colours and minimal shapes. The dominant colour is a deep blue, symbolic of Mediterranean seas, with bold streaks and swirls of pure white to represent clean, breaking waves. The beaches are likewise flat, with smooth sandy colour. Grassy banks and rocky slopes have pastel-effect green and browns. Holidaymakers match the simplicity and colour palette of the land and sea, bright, animated and above all eye-catchingly bold. Beverley Cole's LNER collection *It's Quicker by Rail* illustrates the company's wide range of posters.

A comparison of three well-known collections of railway travel posters and prints in book form suggests similarities and contrasts. *Travel by Train* (Zega & Gruber, 2002) surveys US railroad posters from 1870 to 1950. *All Aboard! Images from the Golden Age of Rail Travel* (Johnson & O'Leary, 1999) is a mix of US railroad material from the early 20th century. It includes a comparative section of British and European images. *Railway Posters: 1923-1947* (Cole & Durack, 1992) is of British material and has been referred to here already.

The Golden Age of Railway Posters (Palin, 2015) is another collection, spanning British posters from the 1930s to the 1950s. Michael Palin introduces this poster choice with wise words perhaps indicating a post-European Union age. Did these posters help shape the flag-waving beliefs of people who wanted none of the European future?:

> "Outrageously selective though their vision of our septic isles may have been, there is, nevertheless, something undeniably reassuring and comforting about the world of uncomplicated pleasure and unalloyed beauty which they defined … It's a Utopia, a Britain on which partly cloudy skies never set and in which the Industrial Revolution never happened: a jigsaw puzzle world from which strife and ill-health are absent, where everyone smiles and no one coughs or cheats" (Palin, 2015:6).

It is not quite true. Palin selected his posters to show seaside resorts, history-rich towns and attractive countryside. He comments that "one significant element seems to be missing from this poster paradise: the railway train" (p6).

That is true as far as his selection goes, but not as the railway output went in total. In the face of 1920s recovery from World War I, the 1930s great depression and the late 1930s threat of another conflict, the four rail companies commissioned work that was undeniably reassuring and comforting. On the other hand, they needed to promote locomotive progress, docks and ferries. The artist Norman Wilkinson was asked by the LMS for advice on improving its advertising. Among his suggestions was the use of industrial subjects as well as resorts and historic towns. "Beauty of another kind is to be seen in the great industries of the North" he said in a railway magazine (see Cole and Durack, 1992:14).

The LMS was happy to take his advice. Note the regional choice: London, Cornwall, South and North Wales had industry but were considered by the LMS as non-industrial destinations. Scotland had its cultural traditions and Highland scenery. The North of England, notably Lancashire, was therefore pigeon-holed as a place of industry, with Crewe locomotive works added from Cheshire, while Birmingham, the Black Country and Stoke-on-Trent were hardly mentioned. Perhaps the ticket revenue for the longer journeys from London to the North and Scotland was an important factor. In America, the New York Central Lines had a near equivalent with Herbert Stoops's *Ashtabula Harbour, Lake Erie,* distinctly not a tourist advert but a poster aimed at boosting the prestige of Ashtabula and the railroad in the eyes of armchair travellers. The Industrial Revolution never happened? Maybe it was played down in interwar posters, but by the mid- and later-20th century it would be a tourism growth area. Yet the sympathetic American travel writer, Rick Steves, presents his *Best of England* (2018) with nothing industrial, just the tourism 'milk run' circuit of old from London to Bath, the Cotswolds, Lake District and York. Then he tags Edinburgh which will upset the Scots.

During the interwar years, both Britain and the USA showed trains and locomotives. British posters of the period often showed railway works and other transport subjects such as ships. The Southern Railway promoted its electrification progress. The LMS had a short series that advertised industries such as cotton weaving, soap making, and its own locomotive works in Crewe. There were posters of ships as well as locomotives. Indeed, each of the post-Grouping companies owned docks and ships, and posters were used to promote them and the destination ports they served such as Zeebrugge and Flushing, Calais and Boulogne, Dublin and Belfast.

Both showed people: the Americans seen to be enjoying their rail experiences while travelling and the British their leisure time at their destinations. Seaside resorts figure highly in the British examples, not surprising for an island nation with a strong sea and sand tradition. The American posters have a few touches of cultural heritage – cowboys, Buffalo Bill, a tiny hint of Native Americans – but were overwhelmingly about views of their locomotives, with landscapes and townscapes as backgrounds to their railroad businesses. The *Travel by Train* (see above) selection incorporates Native American images. The Santa Fe Railroad was using ethnic elements to promote itself. This was a matter of some irony since railroad-based settlement of the West had resulted in the degradation of the Native American way of life The artist, Hernando Villa, was brought in to supply appropriate images. "They wanted a man in his prime – an Indian of dignity and poise" he said of the late 1920s campaign plan. Zega and Gruber describe the result as images "that inspired both dreams of adventure and a shudder of fear" [p76]. "The drums are calling you to Far West scenic regions this summer," read one of Villa's 1930 magazine advertisements [p79]. Images that promoted national pride presented native peoples as the 'others', the non-white from an earlier age that had had its day.

The British depicted heritage – castles, towns, cultural events and traditions in addition to the images of industry. The impression is that while there were overlaps, the Americans stressed geography and the British, history. Or, to use another phrasing, the Americans were selling their vast space and the British their ancient heritage.

This view is based on a limited examination of posters and other material in published books, but that is what the modern world also chooses to remember. Each collection today illustrates artistic styles chosen by commercial operators. Attractiveness and nostalgia play their parts, so the selections may not represent the original output. Yet it is a valid point to make that the nostalgia that attracts modern viewers was probably also effective with those inter-war travellers.

The contrast between the USA and the UK poster subjects may not be quite as marked. But if it is thought to have validity, it lines up with other conclusions that can be drawn. The first is that the United States has underplayed its own history by stressing modernity in its self-presentation and largely ignoring the rich culture of Native Americans. The second is that the United Kingdom has not just recently wallowed in heritage nostalgia during a period of economic decline [eg Hewison, 1987]. The device of countries using heritage subjects to present themselves to the world has had a long history, as travel posters and press articles have shown. Countries are today the result of their past, after all.

Railway services spread across most of Great Britain from Wick to Worthing, Cardigan to Cromer and throughout Ireland. The 1923 distribution of the Big Four lines grew out of the competing compromises and trade-offs between systems that had grown haphazardly. So LMS, for example, did not serve most of the English East, South, South West and Mid-to-South Wales lines. Its tourist regions included much of Scotland, the Lake District, North Wales and a corridor of historic towns from London to Carlisle. By using ferries, LMS could get people to the Isle of Man and Dublin.

The company advertised visits to the Lever Brothers' soap works at Port Sunlight to tour the factory, the model village and the Lady Lever Art Gallery. The passenger traffic to Blackpool was, of course, enormous. So were the FA Cup Final visits to Wembley and those to the Grand National at Aintree, requiring many special trains. When the Glasgow Empire Exhibition took place in 1938, 1,800 specials were needed. By then, a department dedicated to special traffic was running 22,000 such trains annually. Additional to this, the LMS owned a chain of 31 top-class hotels that employed 8,000 staff and took annual receipts of £3m (≈£118m) [Cole and Durack, 1992].

The Great Western Railway used posters showing landscapes and town views in traditional styles. They explored unusual artistry such as Ronald Lampitt's tessellated colour work for *Cornwall* and *Devon*, both of 1936 [see Cole & Durack, 1992]. Since industrial cities were well represented in their railway empire, the GWR people produced business travel posters, too, such as *Cardiff, the City of Conferences* in 1932 or Ernest Coffin's meticulous bird's eye view for *London* of 1936.

The company's promotional efforts have been covered in detail by Roger Burdett Wilson in his *Go Great Western: A History of GWR Publicity* [1970]. The company used press advertising, handbills, posters, guidebooks, children's painting books, postcards, jigsaw puzzles, lantern-slide lectures, movie films, window displays, a radio documentary with the BBC and visits to the Swindon locomotive works. All of them publicised the GWR while placing images and written descriptions of tourist destinations into the minds of the recipients.

More than just passing references, they were active propaganda via the colourful messages they carried.

The films made before World War I were, of course, silent shorts included in special film shows staged by the GWR company. In the late 1930s, it planned to have produced films for more general release, but only one, *Cornwall, the Western Land*, was completed before World War II intervened. Good publicity, however, was gained from cooperating with commercial studios wanting railway feature films. *The Hound of the Baskervilles* (1931), *The Ghost Train* (1931) and a thriller, *The Last Journey* (1936) used GWR locomotives, rolling stock and properties. The railway produced a folder *See the Ghost Train Country* for distribution to audiences at screenings of the film (see also Huntley, 1969).

Cinema and film society showings and the newly established radio service of the BBC made effective publicity tools between the wars. Newspapers and magazines had become livelier with better photographs and sometimes colour printing. Outstanding in Britain was *Picture Post*, launched in 1938 and therefore limited by threats of war from any immediate impact on tourism. Within a couple of months, it was selling 1.7 million copies. Its impact lay in strong journalism and superb photography, powerfully displayed (Hopkinson, 1970). Two years before, the American *Life* magazine, founded in 1883, was revamped as a photojournalism weekly, preceding the launch of *Picture Post*. Both magazines established themselves as popular visual reporters on the world around. When war ended it was the cinema and photo journalism that took up again the influences begun in the 1930s.

From the 1930s onwards, the impact of cinema and magazines made the awareness by the public of tourist destinations much greater. Their knowledge of what railways could do helped to fix holidays by train in the popular mind, though that meant competition from cars, coaches, and even aircraft for passengers, was being enhanced by the same media. The rail operators therefore chose speed, comfort and service as the means to attract tourists and business customers.

Railway races to the North by scheduled services in 1888 and 1895 had been unofficial – even denied by the companies involved – but were well reported events. After 1927, LNER trains raced from Kings Cross station in London to Edinburgh via the East Coast route through York and Newcastle-upon-Tyne, against LMS services from Euston station to Edinburgh via Crewe and Carlisle on the West Coast route. The LNER had introduced its new *Flying Scotsman* express in that year, using two crews who could change shifts by means of a narrow corridor through the locomotive tender, without halting the train. LMS joined the fray using one of its new *Royal Scot* locos and a Standard Compound 4-4-0.

Inter-war speed attempts did not usually involve direct route competition. Carefully managed speed measurement on 'testing days' was the tactic. The fastest train in those largely steam-driven days was 4468 *Mallard,* one of Sir Nigel Gresley's Class A4 Pacific locomotives. Four months after being delivered to the LNER in 1938, *Mallard* made its record-breaking run on the East Coast main line. It touched a speed of 126 mph (203 kph) south of Grantham. Earlier trains included *Silver Link* and *Silver Fox* of 1935, *Commonwealth of Australia, Dominion of Canada* and *Union of South Africa* of 1937. The latter three helped raise awareness of those countries at a time when the policy of Imperial Preference was busily campaigning for Britons to buy their produce and Imperial Airways was promoting tourism to them.

The LMS Railway started with a problem at its formation in 1923. It lacked powerful locomotives for the West Coast Main Line to Glasgow. It had inherited smaller engines from its Midland Railway predecessor. The LMS needed to get to work in a hurry. The outcome was a fleet of locomotives forming its Royal Scot Class that entered service from 1927 onwards. Route books that described the scenery between London and Glasgow were issued under the title *The Track of the Royal Scot.* Six years on, the organisers of the *Century of Progress* Exposition in Chicago invited the LMS to send a loco and carriages to take part. One of the Royal Scot Class was selected, overhauled and improved, renamed as no 6100 *The Royal Scot* and sent across the Atlantic. The publicity both abroad and at home supplied much prestige and awareness of the LMS services. That same year of 1933 the Company began to introduce its own Pacific-type fleet, its Princess Royal Class. One of the early designs was completed as a steam turbine locomotive in 1935, proving to give good service throughout the wartime years. However, it then failed and in 1952 was converted to use steam cylinders. It was given the name *Princess Anne.* After two months in service it was involved in the dreadful triple-locomotive crash at Harrow and Wealdstone. It was considered too expensive to repair and was scrapped.

On the Move

Tramways

New York got its first 'streetcar' (tramway) service soon after Shillibeer's buses opened in London - 1832. The scheme was led by Irish coachbuilder John Stephenson, backed by other Irish businessmen. They intended a railroad running up the Hudson Valley, so iron rails would be standard. New York streets at that time were poorly surfaced, so horse buses as in London and Paris were out of the question. A tramway, like the Swansea and Mumbles line of 1807, with horse-drawn carriages on rails, was the chosen method. Tramways had the advantage of a much smoother running surface.

We should note that in the USA these vehicles were known usually as streetcars or trolleys, in the United Kingdom as trams, and in other European countries by names in local languages if not 'trams'. For example, France uses 'tram', Germany 'Straßenbahn'; Russia, 'tramvay' (трамвай). This chapter will use 'streetcar' for US systems.

New York used a large, three-compartment carriage, with seating for thirty inside and thirty more on top. It was no one-horse affair but needed a team. The practice became to couple two more carriages behind, demanding more horsepower again. At first, the service only went as far as 14th Street, using double track. It would be six years before Harlem was reached and twenty-one before Chatham, on a route towards Albany. Steam locomotives began to serve the system, running into New York as far as 42nd Street, the city fathers being opposed to steam power in the city centre. Grand Central station was built in late 1871 at the limit of steam traction. By then, streetcars were using edge-rail tracks on the lines out of the city. Other US cities adopted streetcars, New Orleans from 1834, Boston, Philadelphia and others during the 1850s.

Alphonse Loubat had worked on streetcars in New York. He moved to Paris in 1852, where he applied for permission for a tramway from Vincennes in the east to Sèvres and the village of Boulogne (now Boulogne-Billancourt) in the west, a wealthy area with a famous pilgrimage church attracting many. Loubat was only given permission for the western arm from the Place de la Concorde. His response became the invention of a device to change flanged tramway wheels to flat-tyred ones. This enabled him to work his carriage as a horse bus to the Louvre. The tramway opened in 1853. He sold his business to the *Compagnie Générale des Omnibus de Paris* in 1855. Under its ownership the route was extended west to Versailles and the section to the Louvre was converted to tram track. It then became profitable and a core routeway along which urban development took place. The importance of tourism to transport development was clear. Loubat's work inspired William Curtis to run a service over a goods tramway line in Liverpool in 1859.

George Francis Train was an American who became the most famous early tramway pioneer in Europe. He was famous for several other things as well: making three round-the-world trips, one in 80 days; becoming a successful shipping magnate; standing as a candidate for the United States Presidency and somehow as a candidate to become Dictator of the United States. He claimed to have been the model for Jules Verne's Phileas Fogg in *Around the World in Eighty Days* [1873] and the begetter of Europe's first passenger tramway, despite the two earlier introductions in Paris and Liverpool. Business wealth, a habit of overlooking the truth and an effort to become either President or Dictator of the USA must have seemed an outlandish combination. Then.

Train visited Liverpool and Birkenhead in 1859. Charles Klapper [1974] suggests he might have been an emissary for Robert Morris of Philadelphia, a merchant banker. Morris had financed tramway schemes in the USA. Train approached the Mersey Docks and Harbour Board where Curtis had run a service. They turned down his offer of taking over that tramway. Then came the Commissioners of Birkenhead. The shipbuilder, John Laird, was their chairman and helped Train obtain permission for a new system. [Klapper, 1974:16]. A line was laid from the monumental gates into Birkenhead Park on Conway Street to the Woodside Ferry on the Mersey, a mile and a quarter away. It could serve people in the fine residential surroundings of the park wanting to cross into Liverpool. In the opposite direction, the trams could pick up passengers from the Liverpool ferry heading for the world's first publicly funded park, opened only thirteen years previously in 1847. Excursionists enjoyed two exciting forms of transport each way, with either shopping and culture at one end or parkland leisure at the other. Business travellers could have an equally interesting journey.

The Birkenhead scheme prospered. It was extended with a line around the park and new tracks serving residential areas nearby to the south. Some lines were electrified in 1901-02. As motor buses and cars became dominant between the two World Wars, the tramways were gradually closed. The story had not come to an end entirely. A museum with a short working tramline to the Woodside Ferry has recently been installed as part of a dockland regeneration project. Tourism is again helping revitalise this part of Birkenhead.

Tramways were added to the urban scene in many parts of Britain, Europe and the USA. Their relatively low cost compared with railways and the comparative ease with which they could be threaded through busy town and city centres gave them advantages. They could carry large passenger numbers. Operating them was easier than operating railway trains. British centres from Derry/Londonderry to Dover, Aberdeen to Swansea and Plymouth to Hull had tramway systems. European countries from Portugal to Russia and Norway to Greece, built systems. Although used mainly by people going to and from work or shopping in main towns, trams could be ways of making local leisure excursions. In some conurbation areas like East Lancashire, it was possible for a time to reach the resort of New Brighton for holidays by using a sequence of operators' routes. People in Littleborough could travel via Rochdale, Bury, Bolton, Atherton, Hindley, Ashton-in-Makerfield, St Helens and Prescot to Liverpool before crossing by the Mersey ferry to Wallasey and then on to New Brighton. They used one or more trams from eight systems.

Using trains was easier, especially with luggage, and it was much quicker. Trams were designed for district services with frequent stops.

The tram's peak use was in 1928 when 4,000m passenger journeys were made in Britain (weblist: Gould 2). After that they declined year by year as motor buses took over. World War II put a stop to many closures as financial efforts towards buses had to go elsewhere. After the war came more change, but that is a story to await Book 3 in this series. Two systems need to be highlighted, partly because they still exist and partly because their main source of passenger traffic came through tourism. The famous Blackpool trams were first run in 1885 as a seafront service, very quickly becoming one of the Borough's major attractions. Over several decades the fleet of trams was extended by buying from a variety of suppliers. Trams were kept running rather than being replaced. The result was a 'working museum' of trams of different designs, as well as an 18 km (11 miles) seaside line.

The second system was a tramway of a different kind. This was the Great Orme Tramway. It still runs from Llandudno's Victoria station up the headland known as the Great Orme, a notable promontory with spectacular views. The tramway is in two parts, one running through the streets of the town to a halfway point and the other from there to just below the summit of the Great Orme. The two are independent funiculars using two cars on each section of cable and track. As one goes up, the other goes down, the counterbalancing system helping what is now electrically powered instead of the original steam. Passengers change cars at the halfway point. It was opened in 1902 and 1903 as first the lower half and then the upper were completed.

The Great Orme Tramway was not the first of its kind in Britain. London's Highgate Hill launched the first cable system in Europe in 1884 and there was a second in Kennington in 1892. The complex Edinburgh Northern Tramways system began to carry passengers in 1888 (Klapper, 1974). As the cars established their routes it became clear how inexpensive they were to run compared with horse buses. As a result, the horse buses were replaced by cable cars in 1899. By 1903, Edinburgh had 36 miles of track and 205 8-wheel, double deck cars. The longest cable was a prodigious 10.5 km (6.5 miles) long (Klapper, 1974:49). It was the world's fourth largest system after San Francisco, Melbourne and Kansas City. The system never reached Edinburgh's port, Leith, since "traditional animosity between the City Corporation and neighbouring Leith Town Council made agreement about cross border operation impossible" (Green, 2016). It was an example of the reality of community life and politics, too often omitted from modern discussions of tourism development. Oliver Green points out that although the Edinburgh cable system was converted to use electric trams by 1922/23, there are two pieces of archaeology to remind people of it. One is a short section of track set into the road at the end of Waterloo Place, close to Princes Street. The other is a cable pulley unit in the former Henderson Row depot in Stockbridge, consisting of two large pulley wheels that carried cables, set in a stone opening. Tourism has an archaeology.

Cable cars had first been used in San Francisco over a decade before that of Highgate Hill.. A businessman named Andrew Smith Hallidie had witnessed an accident in 1869 in which a horse-drawn streetcar slipped backwards on a steep, wet hill, dragging its horses to their deaths. Hallidie's business was manufacturing wire rope. Arguing that the city's hills were too steep for horses or mules, he promoted a cable-based system with help from engineer William Eppelsheimer (weblist: SF Cablecars). Their Clay Street Hill Railroad opened in August 1873. The system used grip cars which locked onto a moving cable running in a duct, releasing it when a stop was needed. The cars towed passenger cars. Other, independent lines were slowly added, some using improved mechanics. By 1890 there were 23 lines, each either the sole route operated by a company, or part of multiple-line operations. One group of five lines converged on a terminus on Market Street where at peak times cars were leaving every fifteen seconds. As in Britain later, cable systems were opened in other cities, but as in Britain the introduction of electric vehicles or motor buses began to replace the American operations. San Francisco suffered badly from the violent earthquake in 1906. Much of the infrastructure and rolling stock was destroyed. Electric streetcars replaced cable cars on some lines. Five cable systems continued. Only two lines remain in use today, recognised as important tourist attractions (weblist: SF Cablecars).

Streetcar systems in the USA could cover immense distances. Klapper notes that "In the golden age before the internal combustion engine ruined them there were 18,000 miles of interurban in the States" (p251). Indianapolis in 1912 had a Traction Terminal serving twelve trunk routes and some five hundred cars arriving every day. Some services used trains of cars, electrically driven and running along the streets when in cities, or along reserved rights-of-way between them. They might have dining, observation, lavatory and even sleeping cars. Passengers and unpaved roads were their *raison d'être*, with their ability to serve many urban stops rather than the single stations of the railroad.

Trolleybuses

The idea of a 'trackless' electric bus was first tried out in Berlin in 1882. It was a demonstration vehicle, a converted landau with two electric motors driving the rear wheels. Werner von Siemens, its inventor, named it the *Elektromote*. Power came from a flexible cable connected to an overhead power line. An eight-wheeled 'contact car' pulled it along. After a few weeks, however, the test track was dismantled as impractical.

Although no further developments took place for several years, the advantages of lower installation costs (no need for tracklaying) and driving flexibility (rigid poles connected to pick-up shoes running on overhead wires would allow trolleybuses to move around other vehicles and pull over to the roadside when required), were tempting. The Italian, Cantono Frigerio, showed a system using six trolleybuses which was shown at the Milan International Exposition in 1906. It proved successful, leading to adoption by several Italian cities. 80 km (50 miles) of routeway were in use across various cities by 1916.

Britain's first trolleybus services opened on 20 June 1911 with routes in Leeds and then four days later, Bradford. As they proved themselves to be beneficial others were begun, ultimately reaching a total of fifty services across the country. In the USA, the first service was a seasonal provision at Nantasket Beach close to Boston, seven years ahead of the Yorkshire trolleybuses. Los Angeles operated the first all-year system from 1910. More than sixty places in the USA began to run trolleybuses, mostly starting them between the world wars, with many of those in the depression years of the 1930s. But they would be discontinued by and large in the 1950s and 1960s, notable exceptions being in Boston and San Francisco. Trolleybuses everywhere carried commuters and acted as feeders taking people to rail and coach stations. In this way they had some part to play in tourism.

A Long Way to Walk: Museum Tracks – No Trains!

Chapter 5

Opening Up a Continent

Railroads in the United States of America

There is some quality in the American term 'railroad' that sounds more pioneering that the British 'railway'. The British word connotes a guided route already set out for the convenience of travellers – which it is. The American conjures an image of an iron-hard trail to be followed and conquered to a destiny as much as a destination, as explorers, farmers and commercial men moved west.

The American story in the 19th century sees the railroad taking its part in building a continental empire, colonising from Appalachia to the Pacific. It was a communications empire based on the railroad, the mail service, the printed word and the telegraph, to which would be added the telephone and network radio within our chosen period. Railways in Britain were developing in the context of an already established country. They did so alongside postal, print and telegraph services, but did not have the role of what came to be seen in the United States as expanding the nation.

Railroads underpinned US tourism for a hundred years. In doing so, they were crucial to the communication of ideas, knowledge and culture. Richard R John (2000) has defined two important communications revolutions in the United States in a perceptive work. The first took place around the time of the American Revolution which

> "reoriented the informational environment of the commercial republic from the seaboard to the hinterland. No longer would the primary information flows be transatlantic as they had been in the informational *ancien régime* that existed prior to 1787 ... The second communications revolution recast the informational environment for the Industrial Age. This revolution began in the 1840s with the expansion of the railroad and the advent of the telegraph and accelerated in the 1870s with the elaboration of the Railway Mail Service and the coming of the telephone".

Railroads did not begin the opening of the hinterland (see Milward, 1999). New York used the Hudson River and the Erie Canal to drive deep into the North and West of New York State. The Lancaster Turnpike of 1795 stretched 100 km (62 miles) into Pennsylvania. By 1837 and at the start of the railroad age, the National Road linked the Potomac and Ohio Rivers, a 998 km (620 miles) strategic transport link for thousands of settlers. Four railroads pioneered the newest form of transport around 1830, not linking places along the Atlantic Coast but going inland from major cities. Baltimore pushed west towards Harpers Ferry and south to Washington DC. A line went from Charleston, South Carolina, to Hamburg on the Savannah River. It was longest at 219 km (136 miles). Boston was much slower. It built three lines by 1837 but all were relatively local, to the nearby cities of Lowell, Worcester and Providence. Albany, New York State, was not on the coast but enjoyed the River Hudson route from New York. It opened a short line to Schenectady, further to the North West. In 1843 a line opened between Albany and Buffalo, some 419 km (260 miles). It was at first a passenger route with three trains in each direction per day. The journey took 25 hours at a cost of "$10 in the best cars, $8 in accommodation cars" (Porter, 1888).

On the Move

> "There were no double tracks, and no telegraph to facilitate the safe despatching of trains. The springs of the car were hard, the jolting intolerable, the windows rattled like those of the modern omnibus and conversation was a luxury that could be indulged in only by those of recognised superiority in lung power"

continued Porter [(1888)], writing later of the early railroading days.

Being a tourist in this way required stoicism and stamina.

The spread of railroads became quicker as their advantages were seen. They did not grow 'organically' from those original lines, they appeared locally, where business interests demanded them. An effect of the philosophy that placed localism over federalism was that companies adopted at least six track gauges ranging from 4' 8½" to 6' (1.435m to 1.829m). The North-Eastern States had bought their first locomotives from Britain where 4' 8½" was the standard. With the use of different gauges, John Stover points out that passengers travelling from Charleston to Philadelphia in 1861 needed to change trains eight times. "Teamsters, porters and tavern keepers were happy that not a single rail line entering either Philadelphia or Richmond made a direct connection with any other railroad entering the city." [(Stover, 1999:26)]. At least, passengers could move between systems easily compared with cargo.

Similar states of affairs were to be found in other places. The 'break of gauge' situation meant cargoes and passenger luggage had to be unloaded and loaded at every change since freight cars and carriages belonged to their companies and could not be run onto other systems. There were a few 'compromise cars' able to run on either of two specific gauges. The Confederacy in the Civil War of 1861-65, in particular, struggled to move men and munitions quickly across the South.

It was becoming obvious that changes were needed. As a result, the Pacific Railway Act of 1863 stipulated that the transcontinental railroad started that year and funded by the federal government, must adopt a standard 4' 8½" measure. Commercial sense forced many companies to adopt the gauge in the 1870s. Southern States kept to their 5 ft gauge until 1886. When companies converted they did so over two days using tens of thousands of workers who pulled out the spikes holding one rail of each line, moved it three inches (76mm) towards its mate and re-spiked it into the wooden tie. On completion,

11,500 miles (18,500 km) of track were then set to the new standard, making train movements much more efficient.

With the Civil War over and the gauge problem being solved, railroads could expand westward with printed mass media and the telegraph supporting them. The Federal government continued its programme of land grants begun after the War of Independence to support military veterans, to do the same for those of later 19th century wars. Grants also funded canal building. It extended the system to help finance the railroads. Land close to the routes was given to companies from 1850 onwards, allowing them to sell parcels of it to settlers who might also become travelling customers. A rationale for taking land from Native Americans, who were moved to reservation areas, had to be found. One, with a so-called divine blessing, was invented. It was part of the political propaganda summed up by the phrase 'manifest destiny'.

The editor of the *Democratic Review,* John L O'Sullivan, used the words in 1845, first in an essay [O'Sullivan, 1845] and then in a column in the *New York Morning News* on 27 December. O'Sullivan wrote that Providence had given the continent to the USA for the use of its multiplying population. The expansionism that took a leap forward under President Jefferson with the Louisiana Purchase had been seen by some politicians as part of the role of the USA. This was declared to be one of setting a virtuous example to other countries, who ought to adopt similar republican systems. If force was required, it should be used.

Others opposed the idea, believing the nation should set an example, and not annexe territory by force. O'Sullivan thought the nation had a right to take on new territory, but by people of Anglo-Saxon origin settling in places like California, outnumbering the Spanish settlers and then applying to join the Union. The philosophy O'Sullivan advanced was racist, born out of a racist period. Native Americans and Hispanics would be the losers. The United States might have broken from the British decades before. It had not shed the mother country's imperial attitude and ability to colonise within its own growing territory.

The boom period for American railroads was on the way. "The West was seen as a land of plenty, a biblical vision" [Wolmar, 2012]. Anxious to open up the Western lands – the 'manifest destiny' argument – the Federal Government paid for its Army engineers to survey possible routes for the commercial companies to use. Then, land-grant acts gave Pacific-bound railroads over 130 million acres of land. These were then sold by the companies to new settlers on easy credit terms (see Stover, 2008). The economic effect was immense, with every subsequent development leading to many others. Mineral discoveries, ranching and agriculture prospered. Towns and cities populated lands previously the homes of Native American peoples. Manufacturing and services were added. 70,400 miles (more than 113,000 km) of new rail track were laid down between 1880 and 1889 (Stover, 2008). The potential for new tourism was clear and was rapidly turned into practical results. Much of the foundation work of American business success in the 19th and 20th centuries came from Federal spending.

Improved railroad technologies benefitting travellers included better braking systems, notably George Westinghouse's air brakes fitted to every passenger car, better heating and lighting and bigger, more powerful locomotives, though these were mainly for freight trains. Passenger trains did gain new locos, led by the Columbia (2-4-2) wheel arrangement in 1892, the Atlantic (4-4-2) in 1895 and the Pacific (4-6-2) by 1900 (Stover, 1997, Wolmar 2012). The middle figure in each classification of wheel arrangements indicates the number of driving wheels, gradually increasing the available power. The great influence on comfort was that of George Pullman's luxury carriages known as Pullman cars. Comfortable seating, sleeping arrangements and restaurant cars served long-distance passengers well. His 'Pioneer' car, first used in 1865, cost $20,000 when ordinary cars cost no more than $5,000 (Stover, 1997). Hand-carved woodwork, carpets and beautiful mirrors were installed along with well-upholstered seats, efficient heating and good lighting. Better passenger cars would form the basis of special trains as well as regular-schedule services.

Raymond and Whitcomb was a leading US tour operator, founded in 1879. The company used railroads for its extensive catalogue of tours, first from the Boston area and later picking up clients from other North Eastern cities. Their summer 1892 programme (weblist Raymond-Whitcomb) included 65 tours through popular New England destinations such as the White Mountains, Washington DC, and the Battlefield of Gettysburg. Niagara Falls featured prominently. There was a tour into Quebec and Montreal and another to Canada's Maritime Provinces. There were half a dozen long distance offers to Alaska, California, Colorado, Utah and Yellowstone. Many of their tours used 'Drawing Room Cars' as more comfortable means of travelling. Their advertising brochure highlighted the fact that these incorporated separate toilet conveniences for ladies and gentlemen. Sleeping cars featured as well. Pages of exciting descriptions of scenery on the routes were included, especially in relation to glaciers and icebergs in Alaska.

By the 1920s Raymond and Whitcomb were running their own nine-car trains, built exclusively to their specifications. A 1928 advertisement boasted of "Entertainment Cars with moving pictures, radio, gymnastics and library." A diagram in a hardback brochure issued to travel agents on a familiarisation tour in 1927 showed how they were arranged (Raymond-Whitcomb, 1927). They had double and triple bedrooms with many having private lavatories. Some rooms had connecting doors to join them into private suites. There were drawing rooms for families and sitting rooms for passengers who wanted to socialise while observing the passing scenery.

The company called these tours 'land cruises', suggesting to potential customers that they added just three days to regular trans-Continental journeys while including wide-ranging entertainment. The Aitchison, Topeka & Santa Fe Railroad operated in the same general area with popular 'Indian detours' as extensions to its through services. Raymond and Whitcomb started on the East coast with routes across the United States and developed major hotels on the West coast. They included Mexico, South America, and Europe in their later destinations.

From a Raymond-Whitcomb Travel Guide, 1913 (author's collection)

One effect emphasising the power of railroads was the adoption by them of railroad Standard Time Zones. These divided the contiguous States into four East to West Zones in 1883. British companies had adopted a nationwide Standard Time in the 1840s, though it was only in 1880 that it achieved legal status. The clock on the former Bristol Corn Exchange building in the UK still has two minute-hands, one for London time and one for Bristol time, ten minutes apart. Congress in the United States adopted the railroads' zoning principle in 1918.

The period of railroad boom became one of bust for many in 1893. A severe economic crisis resulted in what became called 'The Panic of 1893' which "pushed many railroads into default, and by mid-1894 a quarter of the nation's railroads representing over 40,000 miles and $2bn of capital, were in the hands of receivers" (Stover, 1997). There were other Panics – in 1819, 1837, 1857, 1873, 1907 (Wolmar, 2012) and perhaps the Great Depression begun in 1929 – labelled as such by the business, political and media communities. It may be thought that panicking was a feature of an irresponsible US commercial system. That would be unfair. Britain and other European countries had their own economic crises without having popular opinion label them that way. Crises led to reforms, revolutions or reversions to older ideas, initiated either by government or some other organisation. The 1893 Panic damaged railroads and the response from those which were left and were strongest was reorganisation through acquisitions.

Over the next decade and a half, seven major business groups evolved, bringing railroads under the leaderships of men like Cornelius Vanderbilt, George Gould, Edward H Harriman and J P Morgan. An Interstate Commerce Commission had been established in 1887 to regulate railroads and ensure fair setting of freight haulage rates. At first it was largely nominal. Two decades later it began to apply its powers to much greater effect, forcing companies to justify rate increases. On the other hand, the newly enlarged groupings were able to replace competition by mutually beneficial cooperation. Wolmar (2012) picks out the building of 'Union' stations used by several rail companies, as often happened in Europe, rather than competing facilities. The biggest is quoted by Wolmar as that at Kansas City, Missouri, used by a dozen railroads, which replaced an earlier building in 1914.

The big Union stations made changing lines much easier for commuters, excursionists and long-distance tourists. The number of passenger journeys increased threefold between 1896 and 1916. Over fourteen years from 1900, the number of Pullman services went up fivefold (Wolmar, 2012). Consolidated networks made it easier to enjoy long-distance journeys without changing trains. It helped Florida attract holiday makers from the North East in the 1920s, using such services. The national network reached its greatest extent in

1917 at around a quarter of a million miles. Companies turned their attention to improving their carrying capacity by four-tracking routes and improving the gradients and curves on their lines. They had much work to do as passenger numbers increased. New York's Grand Central Station had opened in 1870. Within ten years it was deep in operating problems [Martin, 1992]. The platforms were too short for the trains required by then, so trains had to be divided into two and accommodated on neighbouring platforms. The train shed was poorly ventilated. Locomotives therefore were kept with steam up just outside until being coupled at the last moment, after which the second half of the train cars could also be attached. Longer, heavier trains might need two or even three locos to haul them.

Travelling behind a coal-burning locomotive might have been increasing in popularity but it still had its challenges. One of these had a part to play in railroad history and the birth of advertising agencies. Passengers could get covered in soot from the locomotive's smokestack. The New Jersey/New York State Lackawanna Railroad brought in Earnest Elmo Calkins of the Calkins and Holden advertising agency. Calkins – who happened to be profoundly deaf as the result of childhood measles – was a $10 a week typesetter for a newspaper in Geneseo, Illinois. Before long he was experimenting with advertising designs. After a period working in New York with an agency, he joined a colleague there in setting up a new advertising agency.

When the Lackawanna asked him in 1900 to devise an advertising campaign for them, he invented a fictional character, Phoebe Snow. She was shown in print ads wearing a white dress while travelling on the railroad. The point was that the Lackawanna owned extensive anthracite mines. Anthracite is a form of coal that burns smokeless, allowing the Lackawanna to boast how clean its trains were run. Calkins wrote the words for the adverts, such as:

"Phoebe says
And Phoebe knows
That smoke and cinders
Spoil good Clothes
'Tis thus a pleasure
And Delight
To take the road
Of Anthracite"

On the Move

Both the railroad and Earnest Calkins drew on the campaign's success. The Lackawanna ran Phoebe Snow adverts until the 1914-18 war when they had to turn their anthracite over to government agencies for the war effort. Calkins and Ralph Holden wrote a 1905 book, *Modern Advertising*. His agency grew, counting among its later clients Edison Industries, H J Heinz and Pierce-Arrow Motor Cars.

The flood of passengers into railroad cities like Chicago altered the nature of those places. Besides the tracks, sidings and stations, hotels sprang up and the numbers of tourist attractions, theatres and night life centres increased. A large part of this activity was due to the fact that most rail journeys required Pullman Services passengers to change trains in the city. Train schedules often made it necessary to stay overnight. Hotels, restaurants and entertainments prospered. Albro Martin puts it this way:

> "Chicago was a popular town with tourists, for what other city in America was like it? The stores were famous: New York had Macy's and Fifth Avenue, but, then, Chicago had Marshall Fields, a far more widely recognised name in retailing, and its Gold Coast, and a not-bad night life, too ... There were "some of the most famous hotels in the nation ... the Palmer House ... the Grand Pacific ... the famous Auditorium Hotel ... the fabled Morrison ... and the mammoth Stevens" (Martin, 1992:118).

Support services grew in scope. The all-providing baggage handling and accommodation booking agency in the 1910s "not only attends to these details but also furnishes lecturers and literature descriptive of the places visited. It tells the traveller what he should see and what he should know about the places seen" (Stilgoe, 1983:254). The problem was that the glories of places such as the Grand Canyon and Yellowstone had to be visited by crossing vast spaces that were, in John Stilgoe's opinion at least, undistinguished. He recalls Robert Herrick's 1914 suggestion that the authors of novels should give "far more detailed attention to accurately seeing and describing the commonplace landscape" (p254). Speed and luxury in railroad travel meant that "vast stretches of the American landscape became increasingly less visible to the well-fed, drowsy passengers whizzing through them".

It has similarities to the modern phenomenon of passengers reading novels, using tablets and iPhones or listening intently to music fed through ear phones. Delight in the stimulation of landscapes, however superficially humdrum,

96

calls for a different kind of observing ability. Reading a landscape and what it tells calls for the senses of time, place, cultural form and function that were discussed in Chapter 4 of *The Beckoning Horizon*. There can be just as much romance, drama and inspiration to be found in landscape narratives as in any blockbuster novel, at least for those with the eyes to see and the skills to understand.

Competition and Decline

Valiant though the publicity efforts were, the interwar period continued the difficulties that railways had begun to suffer soon after 1918. Competition from the family car, the public coach and the establishment of air services was biting into the railroad passenger scene. It was severe in the USA, made more problematic by the growing popularity of automobiles, the use of buses and the speed advantage over long distances of aircraft. In 1925 there were 17.4 million automobiles in the USA, rising to 29.5 million in 1941. 17,808 buses were in use in 1925, 119,753 in 1941 (weblist: US transport). During approximately the same period, railroad passenger traffic went down from 42 billion in 1916 to 25 billion in 1940 (Stover, 1997).

The scale of tourist and excursion services was shown by a Chicago & North Western Railway Vacations booklet of July 1937. The 20 cms x 23 cms booklet had sixty pages packed with text and tables. There were many line-work images, including regional diagrams of routes. Profiles from these indicated some of the mountainous country crossed. Over the booklet's centre spread was a cat's cradle of a map with most US railways shown and hundreds of stations. As with many other rail maps of major systems, it was distorted to allow more space for the cramped layouts of the company's own system. The rolling-stock of C&NWR trains was listed in detail.

For example, the *Forty Niner* (named after the 1849 California gold rush) left Chicago at 09:10 on day one and arrived in San Francisco at 09:52 on day three, running five times per month. There were other named, less expensive, trains on the same route in between. The *Forty Niner* had a 'registered nurse-stewardess service', radios for passengers, barber and baths (the last listed for certain sleeping cars). A mix of single and double rooms were available. There were buffet/lounge cars and a diner/lounge car. Meals served on North Western diners were lauded: "The commissary department selects only the

97

finest foodstuffs our markets afford, the chefs are experts, the proportions generous and prices moderate" (C&NWR 1937:8).

Breakfasts ranged from what in the UK might be called a Continental breakfast for 50¢ up to a cooked meal, toast or muffins, fruit and coffee for 75¢. Dinner offered Entrees listed from Lake Superior Whitefish or Pork Tenderloin with candied sweet potatoes through Roast Beef or Lamb Chops to Ribs of Beef or Spanish Omelette, each with salad or potatoes and vegetables, with costs from 90¢ to $1.25. The one-way ticket cost was $44.50, meals extra. The US Measuring Worth website *Purchasing Power Calculator* makes the 1937 price equivalent to $510.00 today. At the time of writing today, the roomette-included, one-way Amtrak California Zephyr ticket price for Chicago to San Francisco Bay (Emeryville) is $900.00 with three meals per day included. Making comparisons must be done with care, especially as today's rates can vary and special deals might affect the price. Services like the *Forty Niner* were at the top end of the market. Its brochure listed short side-journeys and some 'All Expense Tours' such as a seven-day trip to the Black Hills of South Dakota for $47.50. The continent was crossed and now it was explored.

Transcontinental Encouragement

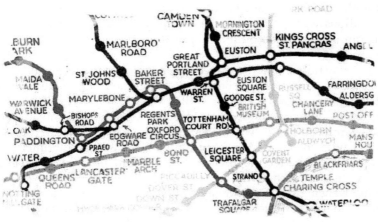

Chapter 6

The Underground and the Subway

Christian Wolmar summed up neatly the modern popularity of London's internal railway system: "The underground is the way to get around town, as demonstrated by the fact that it is used by both besuited City gents and their cleaning ladies" (Wolmar, 2004: Intro). It is now a general urban network along with the capital's bus system taking people from anywhere to anywhere. The origin was more focused: a means of linking mainline stations which had been prevented from building to the very centre of the city. Parliament had early concerns about railways affecting building conservation and urban character in London's central area. A Royal Commission on Metropolitan Railway Termini was set up by Sir Robert Peel in 1846 and reported within two months.

It had been prompted by the Railway Mania of 1845-47, when 19 new lines were proposed running into the centre of London. Many organisations were alarmed, either because they might lose business, for example, omnibus operators, or have their property values reduced. The Commission made recommendations that only one or two schemes be allowed to proceed. It could not impose these on developers. Parliamentary consent was needed for each proposal, but when they were debated in due course, the Commission's recommendations were generally accepted. Conservation of buildings, land values and omnibus routes would be among the criteria.

It had fewer worries about the effects on people or places away from its prestigious and wealthy heart. When the St Katherine Docks were built (1827-1830), 1,250 houses and a medieval hospital were demolished. 11,300 people lost their homes, with no alternatives provided. Mainline railway termini would have similar effects. The Midland Railway had been sharing King's Cross station with the Great Northern Railway. It was a new international tourist event that persuaded the directors of the MR to build their own London terminus. A second international exposition had been proposed to be held in 1862 in South Kensington. The railway company knew many excursion trains were likely to make the situation worse as there were estimates of 11 million visitors pouring into the capital. It quickly purchased land for its station, clearing a notorious slum known as Agar Town.

The site was outside the area the Royal Commission said should be free of railway development. It would also get rid of what some thought of as "the foulest North London development of all" (Swenson, 2006). The problem of slum clearance in those days was that old houses were demolished but no new ones appeared unless some local builder managed to divide old properties or throw up illegal shacks. Evicted people just added to overcrowding nearby. Steven Swensen (2006) puts figures for the clearance of slums to build St Pancras station at 4,000 buildings and 32,000 people, displaced with no compensation. As it happened, the Midland could not complete its new terminus until 1868, but it gained important goods facilities and new attractions were being opened regularly.

The new international exposition took place as planned in 1862, but it was a mixed success. It received only 6.1 million visitors, not 11 million. The event took place where the Natural History, Geological and Science Museums now stand, close to where the Great Exhibition took place. South Kensington was soon to become one of London's prime educational tourist complexes. As such, the ability to move people in, out and around that area and Central London in general was crucial to success. Besides residents working in the capital, the many tourist attractions, entertainment facilities and shopping developments would demand more than just horse omnibuses, trams and trolleybuses. Even so, the London General Omnibus Company would carry over 76 million passengers in 1885. Its horse drawn vehicles moved over 112 million in 1890 (Taylor, 2001).

Charles Pearson (1793-1862) was a solicitor who campaigned for many causes from reforms to the legal system to ending the monopolies held by gas companies. After being in private practice for several years, he became the official City of London Solicitor. He is probably best known for advocating underground transport systems in London (see Cudahy, 2003). Pearson published a pamphlet in 1845 proposing an underground atmospheric railway. It was to run in a glass tube with carriages propelled by compressed air, on a route along the Fleet River valley to Farringdon. It failed to gather any support. Another Pearson plan was backed by the City of London Corporation for a station shared by five railway companies at Holborn Hill. It was put forward in 1846 but was rejected by the Royal Commission on Metropolitan Termini because it would have been a major development inside the termini-free area that they had specified..

Then, in 1854, the Metropolitan Railway Company proposed a steam train line from Paddington to Euston, Kings Cross and on to Farringdon, close to the City of London. Pearson was not a significant shareholder or director but used his considerable influence to help raise the £1 million capital needed, including from the City Corporation. More important was his traffic survey of people entering London railway termini and the City itself in 1854 (Wolmar, 2004). Enumerators paid by him gathered the relevant information on all the principal City roads. 44,000 passengers arrived on horse omnibuses, 27,000 via Fenchurch St/London Bridge, though only 4,200 through Paddington, Euston and Kings Cross. 26,000 arrived by private carriages or hackney carriages. No less than 200,000 walked into the City. It was important information about passenger demand. We would call the in/out movement of workers commuting. Pearson called it *oscillation*. It occupied the lives of nearly a third of a million city workers. Today the figure is somewhere way over half a million.

Most people were coming from relatively local places. On the other hand, while the great termini showed relatively low figures, the evidence of the Great Exhibition and the 1862 event showed that excursionists and tourists put huge pressure on the stations and the London transport services. We have already seen in Chapter 3 how the flow of American tourists crossing the Atlantic with money to spend was boosting the ocean steamer businesses and influencing the quality of London hotels. 'The balance of trade' was tipping in America's

101

advantage. It would continue to do so and become an essential benefit to the United Kingdom. Gordon Selfridge arrived from the USA in the early 20th century. Noting London's lack of big department stores like Marshall Field's in Chicago where he had worked, or Le Bon Marché in Paris, he built his own on Oxford Street opposite the Bond Street Underground station. It opened in 1909, rapidly becoming a major shopping-tourism magnet. According to Andrew Martin, he wanted the station to be renamed Selfridges and a tunnel to be built for pedestrians to use visiting the store. All he got was a Central Line ticket office selling season tickets for the whole Underground system during Christmas sales [(Martin, 2012)]. Selfridge it was, apparently, who invented while in America the countdown slogan 'XX Shopping Days to Christmas'.

To return to the Metropolitan Railway's project. Work started on its line in 1860 and it opened in January 1863. Charles Pearson did not live to see it finished as he had died the previous September. On the first day it was opened to the public, the new underground line carried some 30,000 people.

The line was extended at each end within a few years of that opening day. A newcomer, the Metropolitan District Railway, began operating a line from South Kensington to Westminster. Further extensions and connections resulted in creating the Circle Line in 1884 and others pushed west towards Wimbledon and north west to Harrow and new suburbs beyond. Most of the outer area lines were brought up to run as surface railways, making them more attractive than the tunnels, prone to trapping dirt and smoke. They carried commuters into London. But as they necessarily made return journeys outward, it made sense to promote the trains as excursion transport into the countryside and towns on the city margins.

The Metropolitan Railway was extending its ambitions and its rails well outside London under the leadership of Sir Edward Watkin. He was involved in many railway schemes and had directorships in nine rail companies as well as interests in French, Belgian, Indian and Canadian projects. Watkin wanted to see a tunnel under the English Channel to France. One was begun in 1880-81, but after early excavations driven a short distance out from the English coast, the whole scheme was blocked by Parliament on grounds of national security. There were considerable fears at the time of an invasion by the French. In the opposite direction from London ran the Metropolitan Railway, out towards Wembley and beyond. The company "waxed lyrical" in Christian Wolmar's words: "Within 50 minutes from Baker Street and for the cost of less than a florin [two shillings, ≈£6.60], if the visitor be economically disposed, he can enjoy a feast of good things, fresh air, noble parks, stately houses, magnificent trees and sylvan streams." (Wolmar, 2004). Two shillings was still a sizable amount in the days when that amount might be needed to buy someone the main meal of their day. But what Watkins really wanted was a rail network from Manchester to Paris operated by the different companies that he was able to influence.

Watkin began work on an amusement park in Wembley that would attract customers to use the railway. It opened in May 1894. One of the attractions was a football pitch, something which would begin to dominate the village. Another was a tower in the style of the Eiffel and Blackpool Towers, which were opened in 1889 and 1904, respectively. There would also be a short-lived tower in New Brighton, near Liverpool, in 1900. Towers were popular attractions during those years. But the Watkins Tower never got beyond its first level. The public were invited to take lifts to the top of what had been built, though the paid admissions were never great. Even that first stage proved too much for the ground below. It began to tilt. In due course it was demolished. The site was used in the early 1920s for the Empire Stadium, part of the British Empire Exhibition of 1924-25. After that closed, it became most famous as the scene of Football Association Cup Finals.

A joint marketing initiative between the various London Underground railways had been launched in 1908. It began to standardise the stations' 'Underground' signs, to arrange for through ticketing and to issue posters and maps of the combined systems. Posters for the Underground were similar in scope to those of the surface railway companies (see Levey, 1976). But they had an advantage. They could be sited on the usual road-level locations *and* on the underground trains and stations. The latter had no distracting window views in the city's central areas, just the suburbs where lines surfaced. This meant that each poster on an escalator, platform or carriage became a substitute window on the world, controlled by the publicity department and carrying its promotion. Repetitive views of dominant images gave the posters much more power. Up until 1908, most poster spaces were sold to manufacturers to advertise their products. They were heavy with text.

The most important underground company by 1908 was Underground Electric Railways of London, or UERL. It was a holding company owning two tube lines as well as the main London bus operator and three tramway companies. Three new lines were launched in 1907, but they did not perform well in terms of passenger numbers. However, change was on the way. Sir George Gibb was appointed Deputy Chairman and Managing Director of the Underground Group, as UERL was commonly known. He made an English businessman, Albert Stanley, with considerable experience in several American transport companies, as the General Manager. Gibb also had brought with him Frank Pick, a solicitor and lawyer who had worked for Gibb in the North Eastern Railway. Pick was put in charge of publicity. He had no qualifications or experience in that field, but he proved an inspired choice (see Green, 1990).

Frank Pick may have been a beginner in terms of publicity skills, but he could see the goldmine offered by those underground spaces. Decades of bill posting had made a clutter that reduced the effectiveness of advertisements plastered across railway stations. Posters were often pasted up to obscure older posters. The effect was visually chaotic and distracted from the messages they carried. Even station information could be lost in the mêlée. This mass medium was not an effective aid for the travelling public.

Pick imposed order. Commercial posters were confined within delineated grids on platform walls and passages. Some spaces among them were kept for use by the UERL. There were illuminated spaces for use by the Underground at entrances to stations. Pick introduced eye-catching images. He knew that some railway companies commissioned colourful lithographs showing the destinations served by the trains. Oliver Green in *Underground Art* writes that Pick was soon "cultivating the notion that everything the great city had to offer was available through travel by bus, tram or Underground, which in turn were portrayed as the very lifeblood of the capital." (Green, 1990:8). The same subjects began to appear that were being paraded by the main railway companies. To some travellers they would have been familiar themes.

Within the first four decades of the 20th century came Fred Taylor's poster *For the Sunday Concerts* with an audience in formal dress (1912), and L B Black's *Summer Outings by Private Bus* with bright young things in sporting attire out for a picnic. Country life popped up in Mabel Lucy Attwell's *Hullo! Did You Come by Underground?* that two winsome children were asking of a rabbit. There were sporting scenes, theatres and cinemas, historic houses and country parks. Quite a few posters showed industry or transport scenes. Frank Brangwyn painted a docks scene of 1913 in *The Way of Business*. Esmé Roberts's *Steamer Cruises Visiting the Royal Docks* advertised trips from Tower Pier in 1934. Views during the 1914-18 war not only contrasted Belgian ruined cities with precious British countryside; the social changes at home were shown, for example in A S Hartrick's 1919 commemorative set portraying women and old men drawn in to help with war work.

Pick sharpened the way that text appeared across the whole network. He commissioned Edward Johnston to design a corporate typeface that had classic simplicity but was distinct and modern. Johnston's 'Underground' of 1916 was the result (London Underground, ?1920). It has been used, with slight amendments in the late 1970s, ever since. Station names, direction signs, notices and the Underground's own posters, employed Johnston's typeface, benefitting from its legibility in a way that was that of the friendly, dependable Underground, easy to locate, easy to use. Integration of purpose and design was the watchword. A comment in *The Moving Metropolis* claims that its "familiarity to Londoners earned it the soubriquet 'London's handwriting'" (Taylor, 2001:185).

The Underground symbol of a black (later, blue) bar imposed on a red circle was placed prominently to mark station buildings. As time went on, new buildings were added which were themselves distinctive. They were easy to locate. What mattered then was how easily travellers could find their way around the network. And that problem was at least partially solved by Harry Beck. Henry C Beck – known as Harry – was an engineering draughtsman in 1931 when he sketched out ideas for what was known as *The Diagram*. He was also out of work after several years with the Underground. Beck was taken on again to help with the Underground's growing workload, lost his job again as the company finances were under pressure, but then was taken back again for a third time (Garland, 1994).

Passengers on London's Underground trains were faced with eight companies and dozens of stations to be navigated. The first joint map of the system was issued in 1907. It was a geographic representation of each companies' lines, picked out in different colours. But in the top left-hand corner a key to the colours forced the artist to show part of the Metropolitan line more diagrammatically – as a straight east-west line. Not all stations on the edges of the system were shown as parts of the graphic. They had to be listed at the relevant margin because the map did not go as far as the outermost stations. It was made worse by the fact that, for example, the District Railway ran a service as far as Southend up to 1939, and the Metropolitan ran as far as Verney Junction, with the main-line Great Central Railway running inwards from the junction to Harrow. Should these extensions be included? If they were, the central London section became so compressed as to be no longer useful. Yet tourists especially might well have found these outer connections useful.

F H Stingemore was responsible for drafting several early maps. One of his, from 1926, introduced the device of compressing the outer areas and merely making marginal notes of which stations lines could reach beyond the edge of the area shown. Sometimes, other 'geographical style' maps showed some features such as parks and the River Thames to help show where the lines ran. These were generally large poster maps on show at stations, rather than free pocket maps, which were quite small. There were multi-fold pocket maps, eg by E G Perman in 1927, which showed places to visit and the times of the first and last trains of the day. They had to be much bigger.

Presenting a route as a diagrammatic element rather than a geographical account has had a long history. The medieval *Tabula Peutingeriana* map used the idea. It is drawn on parchment and might be a copy of a Roman original that was also carved in marble for public display. The Peutinger map rests in the Austrian National Library in Vienna. John Ogilby's *Britannia* of 1675 was a compilation of route maps through Britain [BH p143]. Each one showed a road as a strip or line marking off places along the route. Early British motoring guides often continued the practice. For example, the Dunlop Rubber Company sponsored a series of 'pictorial road plans' of seven main road routes from London to destinations including Edinburgh, Holyhead, Exeter and Dover. They described the routes and scenery and showed neat thumbnail sketches of towns along the way. Ed Burrow & Co produced them in both paper and hardbacked versions. Burrow's long- standing business was in making town plans with advertisements to pay for them. The road plans carried a nominal price tag of 6 old pence (≈£0.73) but since almost every left-hand page carried three or four paid-for adverts, they were probably distributed for free.

Ken Garland reproduces a map of LNER services out of North East London [Garland, 1994]. It used straight lines, vertical, horizontal or angled. The work of George Dow, it was a diagrammatic rather than a geographic representation. This map appeared in 1929 and may have been seen by Harry Beck. A 1930 Green Line country bus service out of London used similar principles, though with curves added to some straights. It combined a small part of the Underground near Tottenham Court Road, using lines with small circles for stations, then showed the bus route from Camden Town to Hertford using a double line and boxed place names.

Mark Ovenden [2003] has drawn attention to the Berlin S-Bahn diagram of 1931, the year Harry Beck worked on his London Underground diagram. "The first known network diagram to employ only 45-degree angles" (p13), that is, no lines at intermediate angles. It also used verticals, horizontals and a pure circle. The central area is enlarged. Stations are evenly spaced along route lines whatever the actual distances were between them. Route lines were only either red or orange, so not quite as easy to read as would be a diagram using more colours. This was a surface transit system diagram. It had a lot of complex information included.

Harry Beck sketched out ideas in an old exercise book. He kept Stingemore's route colours at first, with blobs for stations and rings for exchange stations. An important feature that helped customers visualise locations at least approximately was his pale blue, angular, River Thames. The Circle Line, so useful in the central area, was formed by a route using sections originally belonging to two companies and was not officially designated until 1949. His key rule was that the map used only vertical, horizontal and 45⁰ lines with small curves where changes of direction in the diagram had to be shown. It was the working style of an engineering draughtsman aged 29 – Harry Beck. At first, in 1931, the map was rejected by the Publicity Department. The following year, they changed their minds.

Beck had made some revisions. Stations were shown with 'ticks' pointing towards their names, and one line was shown in dark rather than light blue to avoid confusion with the District line. The order was placed in January 1933 for a printing of 750,000 pocket-sized, folded, copies. That was a large number – they were distributed free – but in the next month 100,000 more were ordered. Garland notes these statistics as well as the fact that Harry Beck, an employee, was given a ten guineas bonus, around £532 at today's values according to the National Archives Currency Converter. Over the years, other Beck maps appeared on posters and there were many amendments as the system changed. But there grew a whole range of tourist souvenirs as The Diagram appeared on postcards, mugs, small posters, tea towels and other souvenirs. The Beck approach to transit maps spread around the world, imitated and respected equally as one of tourism's favourite aids for travelling in big cities (see Ovenden, 2015).

1915: Metro-land

The ambition of Sir Edward Watkins to have a railway running from Manchester to Paris via a Channel tunnel came to an end after he suffered a serious stroke in 1894 and had to retire as the Metropolitan Railway's chairman. By then, the company's services reached fifty miles from the middle of London out into the Chilterns and Buckinghamshire. But in addition, it had been developing land, bought for railways, by creating new housing estates. The Metropolitan no longer needed the land, yet held on to it, unlike other companies. During the 1880s and 1890s it built houses on what it named the Willesden Green Estate close to Willesden Green station, with villas for rental by middle class families. Others followed. Railway extensions took the line from Harrow to Uxbridge. Two Pullman cars were added in 1910 for first class passengers, who could enjoy light meals for 3s (≈£12).

Wembley Park was another housing development. The amusement park and unsuccessful attempt at an Eiffel-style tower have already been mentioned. It was part of the company strategy to attract excursionists from London and Buckinghamshire to use the railway. Wembley Stadium replaced the tower idea and was far more successful, at a much larger scale. There were smaller additions to the marketing efforts of the railway. One began in the middle of the 1914-18 war, not on the face of it a particularly auspicious time, but it would prove a great success over the following almost two decades. The busy Metropolitan launched a new guidebook aimed at further development of the excursion traffic.

This was entitled *Metro-land*. It promoted leisure trips while advertising the halcyon days of living in any of the new housing park estates alongside the railway routes [Green, 2004]. Descriptions of picturesque villages, charabanc tours, golf courses, guest houses, hotels, cafés and theatres, besides houses on offer, made each edition as much a tourist booklet as an estate agent's catalogue. It is worth noting that William Gilpin's 18th century idea of 'picturesque' – rugged natural scenery – had by the 20th century become something that was more homely, domestic and shaped by the arts and crafts and *moderne* styles of architecture.

The *Metro-land* term caught on, being used officially through the years following up to 1933 when the government created London Transport, absorbing the Metropolitan along with the other companies operating in the capital. However, though *Metro-land* was then dropped as an official promotion, the name stayed in popular use in a 1920 song *My Little Metro-land Home*, a mention in Evelyn Waugh's novel *Decline and Fall*, a 1980 novel by Julian Barnes and a TV programme by John Betjeman [Green, 2004] and more. Railway fans today recall it nostalgically.

And Abroad

Other cities were adopting underground railways as obvious solutions to their transport problems. Paris had considered the need for a city transport network since the mid-19th century. A cable car system was first proposed, then a steam railway. There were debates about an elevated, or an underground, system. Agreement was reached in 1896 for nine below-ground lines to be built strictly within the city [Cudahy, 2003]. The suburbs were left to the surface railways. Tourism helped focus minds on construction, as with the London show of 1862, because the 1900 Paris Exposition loomed. Paris expanded its system quickly, much of it before World War I. The city stations and lines were largely in place by the 1920s and finally extended into the suburbs during the 1930s. They enjoyed a degree of uniformity from their Art Nouveau-inspired styling, the work of Hector Guimard. First and second-class tickets were in use and would be until the 1980s.

Opening day on 19 July 1900 saw twelve three-car trains in use consisting of a power unit followed by two unpowered units. The termini for each line were provided with a run-around loop so the trains could make the return journey with the driver's cab leading. Longer trains with motor units at each end were soon added to the rolling stock. Unlike London (and New York) each line was independent with no sharing of tracks and trains ran each way in the tunnels, as now. Like the earliest London examples, the Parisian tunnels were built using cut-and-cover methods that London had found disruptive. However, the man who became known as *le père du Métro*, Fulgence Bienvenue, devised an efficient system which reduced the disruption as tunnelling progressed in lines following the streets. In addition, the first line was connected by four side tunnels to the banks of the River Seine so debris could be taken to waiting barges without cluttering the roads [Cudahy, 2003].

New York in the late 19th century needed better transport. Manhattan might have been the powerhouse of its growth – and largely that of the nation, too – but the Bronx, Brooklyn, Queens, Staten Island, the rest of Long Island, the nearby cities of New Jersey and the Hudson Valley plus major urban centres from Washington to Boston and beyond fed it with traffic. Its ports handled ocean-going ships, its rivers and railways inland trade. Ferries carried flows of people in and out. At the focal point, Manhattan had the most important businesses, community services and entertainments used by New York's population. By 1860 this had just topped 1.1 million. 25 years later it reached 2m, and in 1900 3.4m. By1940 that had more than doubled to 7.4m.

Steam trains on four elevated railway lines were the first solution, all confined to Manhattan Island, from the 1870s. They were known collectively as the Manhattan El. Between 1881 and 1891 passenger numbers rose from 75.6m per year to 196.7m [Cudahy,2003]. Within twenty years of their opening it was obvious something much more was needed.

The result was the Rapid Transit Construction Company, which won the rights in 1900 to build a new subway line. Two years later, August Belmont, who as co-owner of the RTCC, set up the Interborough Rapid Transit Company to operate the line. Next came its leasing of the Manhattan El, enabling it to set up an integrated system when the Interborough's first line began running in 1904 [Homberger 1994]. Eight-car trains built entirely of steel were used, running in tunnels with four tracks. These allowed both local services and express trains to operate. They were the result of work by the important pioneer of electric traction, Frank Sprague, who worked out the energy savings of having trains that did not have to stop and start at every station but run through many *en route* to more distant places [Cudahy, 2003]. 600,000 people a day were soon using the pioneering New York subway. It, too, would grow into a giant system.

Finally, the Moscow Metro should be mentioned, though its full history deserves a glossy coffee-table book on its own. The fact that it does not get anything like that treatment here is partly due to the fact that it was only built in the 1930s with the first line opening in 1935. It would be way beyond the scope and resources of this book to show the immense splendour of its stations, which are unlike any others anywhere else.

The need for a system was acknowledged in the days of the Russian Empire but World War I, the Russian Revolution and the subsequent Civil War delayed it. The Communist Party of the Soviet Union then saw it as a state prestige project . After preliminary design work and scheduling against the country's other priorities, plans were approved in January 1932. Engineers were recruited from the London Underground. They recommended building by cut-and-cover work, the use of escalators instead of lifts, and the design of the trains themselves. Moscow specialists designed the stations and local workers carried out the construction. Unfortunately, the secret police, the NKVD, decided engineers from Metropolitan-Vickers Electrical Company had spied on the city's infrastructure. They were arrested, put on trial and then deported back to Britain in 1933.

The first stations on the line, opened in 1935, were smart but not splendid. Those of the second stage were magnificent, paid for, of course, by the state, not private enterprise. They established the architectural showcases that would characterise the Moscow Metro. Kievskaya station is shown below as it is today, part of what has become a world-beating system of 263 stations serving 408 km (253.6 miles) with around 7 million passengers a day.

It is also a unique tourist attraction for both Russians and many other international visitors.

Kiyevskaya station on the Moscow Metro. Opened in 1938.
Wikipedia Creative Commons, Antares 10. From the original, 2011.

Chapter 7

On the Road

Our early ancestors had to walk to get anywhere on land. They seem to have begun to use horses to travel around 4-2,000 BCE. Riding a horse, or having it pull a chariot, wagon or carriage, continued to be the dominant transport form until steam-powered vehicles and bicycles were invented centuries later. Steam buses, locomotives and steam cars are at the heart of the land transport history in this book. Bicycles had a key role to play in better road movements in Britain and the United States. On the other hand, in those countries they were mainly used to explore the great outdoors by individuals. They could not carry multiple passengers, nor could they be used by package tour operators. The importance of cycling in bringing about better roads is included in this chapter. They had a broader tourism significance, which will be discussed in 'The Outdoor Life' chapter in the forthcoming book 2: *Bright Prospect*. Readers wanting to find out more meanwhile might like to see Denis Pye's book about the Clarion Cycling Club, *Fellowship is Life*.

Horse Buses

The tourist could avoid using any sort of transport if he or she hiked the whole way. It would have had severe limitations. Perhaps, as a one-off experiment, it might be cheap and an experience. Hardy souls might relish the home to destination adventure, carrying a tent and their daily needs throughout. After that, the urge to explore would almost certainly demand that the hike began properly a distance away, beyond the too-familiar surroundings of ordinary life. A horse with a small cart would help. But what to do with the animal and vehicle when the hiking was to begin? A commercial transport service would be ideal, and an infrastructure would be built.

Horses have been domesticated in Eurasia since around 3,500 BCE. Some form of riding to explore would have followed, perhaps much later: brief excursions to satisfy curiosity. It would have been limited to those with a suitable animal, free time and a desire to go exploring. Travel on foot would have dominated most people's lives for millennia. Few would have gone far unless it was for some unavoidable reason. Such travel might have offered leisure time in a settlement, an inn or a trading place. It is hard to see it as tourism in our modern sense, yet such excursions are close to fitting our definitions.

The situation did not change for many centuries. When it did, in places like urban Europe, it might have been the result of someone organising a group outing for a community event. It might have been a festive occasion, an important celebration or, as industrial life grew, a brief escape to countryside. The start of stagecoach services in such a world was important, but few people would have afforded the time or cost of a stagecoach journey. 'Shanks's pony' in Britain – walking – was often still the only choice. The real opportunity came with the railways, bringing excursion trains and cheap fares. Buses, tramways and motor coaches came later.

There were some passenger services well before our period of interest of 1851 onwards. It is impossible to place a rigid time frame: complex historical themes overlap each other too much for that. So, the Swansea and Mumbles Railway featured in *The Beckoning Horizon* but must be noted here as it carried passengers from 25 March 1807, well ahead of any other railway system and long-lasting [Hibbs, 1989]. By 1813 when Richard Ayton rode on it as part of a journey round Britain, it was carrying tourists at a shilling (≈£2.33) a go [Green, 2016]. Was it a railway or a horse bus that ran on rails? At first, as a passenger service, it had one carriage, one horse and one route along a plateway begun four years before to carry coal, limestone and iron ore. It was operated like a turnpike road in those days. Anyone with a horse and wagon and who paid a toll could use it as a mineral line.

Paris had witnessed a short-lived attempt to run bus services in 1662. Blaise Pascal used seven carriages, each seating eight passengers. It was not a success since people apparently only tried it for amusement and after a few weeks they were unused. It was another operator, a man named Stanislas Baudry, who came up with the name 'omnibus' ('for all') in connection with his service begun in 1827 between Nantes and a spa he owned in Richebourg nearby (weblist: Gould 1). Within a short while, it was being used by residents rather than guests at the spa. Realising the potential, Baudry and associates managed to get permission to operate omnibuses in Paris. They had ten routes, all using the normal roads rather than rails.

London operators began to run their own services. Among these were Walter Hancock's steam carriages, the *Enterprise,* the *Autopsy* and later, the *Automaton* in the 1830s. The best-known was George Shillibeer, a London carriage builder who had worked in Paris with a commission to build horse-buses. Seeing a chance in London, he returned to England and by 1829 was able to start running coaches between Paddington Green and Bank (Hibbs, 1989). Shillibeer was successful. His vehicles had conductors "of great respectability" who "collected fares on the spot ... speed and punctuality were the ruling principles ... an immediate improvement over the short-stage coaches" (Hibbs, p26-27). By the next year there were 39 omnibuses operating in London for Shillibeer and others. But George Shillibeer had financial problems. By 1840 he had left the business. Even so, his service had made a positive impact, stimulating other operators, and persuading many to use his name as a general term for horse omnibuses.

Motor Buses

Petrol-engine buses were relative newcomers on the tourist scene, a long way behind trains, horse buses, trams and underground railways. At first, they were the servants of those systems, but in the long run they would exert a powerful influence. Early British operators used vehicles built by Benz and Daimler, soon adapting locally built units such as the popular Wolseley 24hp or the Leyland-Crossley 30hp, both of 1905 (Kaye, 1972). Motor buses might feed rail stations or run excursions to nearby destinations. The Lynton and Barnstaple Railway, a narrow-gauge line close to Exmoor, used motor buses as feeder services from its opening in 1898. The Great Western Railway ran motor buses in 1903 between Helston and the Lizard and from Penzance to Marazion. Their passengers were local people and tourists to the coastal resorts [Kaye, 1972]. Motor bus excursions were being developed during the same years. Stan Lockwood [1980] notes that the pioneering Thomas Henry Barton was running trips from Weston-super-Mare in 1901 to places like Cheddar, Wells and Glastonbury using a 6hp Daimler carrying around a dozen tourists. Small vehicles were not very profitable, however.

The charabanc or 'chara' made its motorised debut. It was based on the French-designed horse-drawn wagon in which bench seats filled the carrying space, each accessed directly from the road via an individual, open, entrance. Many had a distinctive appearance due to the bench seats being in tiers, higher towards the back. It was as though the cinema-type audience arrangement had been copied onto the new vehicle for viewing the world. Instead of gazing at a flat screen with limited dimensions, the excursionists entered a world they were actually visiting, with an almost 360^0, moving, panoramic view. Colour, sounds, smells, the warmth of the sun, the freshness of a breeze and the feeling of the charabanc moving, turning and bouncing along were sensations the movies could not reproduce. Granted, noisy engines and bad weather could be big distractions. But on a beautiful day, with a charabanc stopped to admire a view, the experience could be remarkable.

Then, travellers could get off and enjoy an even better encounter with their surroundings. They could pick flowers or pebbles as souvenirs, take photographs of the views and of themselves. They might have the chance to talk with local people, or to admire the wildlife, all occasions offering new subjects for photographs with memories to be recalled years later. Railway passengers might enjoy the 'moving panorama' that Wolfgang Schivelbusch [1980] identified, but the 'chara' trip was a direct, immersive, interactive audience experience for at least four of their five senses. Buy a cream tea? That would make a good experience for the fifth sense.

Charabancs became popular for works and church social club outings. Sharing trips with familiar companions was easier than with total strangers. Travel in new environments could be challenging, as 18th century tourists had found, for example, when entering mountainous country. In those days, women had been urged to view the peaks and ravines through the mirror of a Claude Glass with their backs to the view that supposedly could overwhelm them [BH p192]. It was a slightly concave, darkened mirror that reduced the impact of the view to a level which the gentler sex could endure. It also framed the view in a way that made it easier to sketch. It would soon become obvious how ridiculous the assumption about a gentler sex was when its members began to cross glaciers and scale Alpine heights with Thomas Cook's guides.

But there was always the chance of an uncomfortable encounter with local folk who looked different, spoke with a strange accent or even a foreign language. Safety in numbers! Charabancs lasted until the late 1930s when they gave way to buses and coaches with weather protection and seating no longer perilously open to the road. Even so, in 1937 there were approximately 20 million passenger journeys by charabanc, according to Michael John Law in his study of *Modern Britain* [2017], as well as an equal number partaken by motor bus.

David Kaye compared the effects of two great tourist events on public transport. The Great Exhibition created demand for more horse buses. The Coronation of King George V in June 1911 did the same for the motorbus. At the time of the crowning of King Edward VII in 1902 there had been only twenty motor buses in London. By 1911 there were 1,500. The London General Omnibus Company had to run its buses two minutes apart to deal with the crowds and they had tours at six pence a time to view the Coronation decorations round the capital [Kaye, 1972]. In the same year, a Bolton company ran a schedule of trips each week as follows: Sunday, to Ilkley; Monday, Morecambe; Tuesday, Blackpool; Thursday, Grasmere; Friday, Blackpool; Saturday, two trips to Southport. What happened on Wednesdays? The coaches were overhauled [Kaye, 1972:22].

By the end of the 1914-18 War the return of peace opened many opportunities. Buses had proved their worth during the conflict in Europe. The military travel into mainland Europe introduced a new confidence for many people in venturing abroad, despite battlefields. More women had taken on the factory and other work their menfolk had left behind to go to war. But the economic slowdown meant foreign travel was too expensive for many. The alternative was to continue the visits to British resorts popular pre-war while using mass transport to gain economies of scale. Stan Lockwood [1980, #28] shows a photo of a fleet of sixteen charabancs that were part of a larger number marshalled to meet a special train of tourists from Bolton arriving in Torbay. They ferried them to their hotels and took them on local excursions. Another photo [#35] shows 37 charabancs about to set off from Plymouth on a Dartmoor tour for members of the Ancient Order of Foresters.

Buses were showing major progress in the 1920s in the small vehicle sector. These had anything from twelve to perhaps thirty seats. Many were from overseas makers: in France, Italy, Germany and the USA. Coach companies would often buy a chassis from one manufacturer and complete it with bodywork from another. David Kaye [(1970:14)] shows how, in the 1920s, the finished vehicle was often cheaper using foreign chassis suppliers. Out of every five coaches completed by a Lincolnshire specialist, Morris' chassis came fourth against the others, who were all from abroad. The bodies that were fitted to these chassis were improving, with roofs and windows becoming standard and with double-decker buses making their appearance with roofs rather than open tops. Resort buses running along the seafronts from one end to another often stayed open to the sky, which is still a common sight today, in both city and seaside operations.

Railway companies in Britain struggled between the two World Wars, as we have seen. The Big Four left by the 1923 Grouping began to close some branch lines. The once-pioneering Canterbury to Whitstable line carried its last passengers at the end of 1930. July 1934 saw the end of passenger services on the Chichester to Midhurst line which was suffering competition from Southdown double-deck buses running every hour [(Kaye, 1981)]. Meanwhile, bus operators had been developing long distance coach services. As early as 1920, Royal Blue had been operating a twice a week route from Bournemouth to London, but by the following year this had increased to twice daily [(Anderson & Frankis, 1970)]. George Readings of Cheltenham had started cross-country routes in 1926 with two small, American-built, Reo buses under his Black and White Motorways banner. They operated services to and from London. Four years later, he had a fleet of 40 buses of different kinds travelling to Bristol, Gloucester, Hereford, Ludlow and Worcester. He sold it to a consortium in April 1930 formed by three other major operators. These brought five more long distance routes operating from Cheltenham, including those to Aberystwyth and Nottingham.

The new Road Traffic Act of 1930 aimed to bring some rationalisation of coach operations. In that year there were, for example, 18 companies running services between Oxford and London [(Flitton, 2004)]. The Cheltenham group played its part. July 1934 saw a new company called Associated Motorways at work. Black and White Motorways joined with five other major players in the new operation. Associated Motorways did not own or operate vehicles. The constituent companies agreed to provide set services for the new company using Cheltenham as a hub and spoke system, taking an agreed share of the profits. Coaches converged on Cheltenham during the morning, parking up while passengers changed onto their next coach around lunchtime. At 2pm a whistle was blown, and the rows of coaches departed one after the other on their return journey with their new passengers. On a personal note, I can attest to the impressive operation as I made my own way to and from university in South Wales and home in North Staffordshire in the mid-1960s. It was a procedure which lasted until 1974. By then, motorways were opening, making direct routes more sensible than the hub and spoke system. And I had bought a car.

Some coach operators went straight into the excursion business rather than stage services (plying set bus routes picking up and depositing passengers at bus stops). One such was Robert Barr, who founded a coach tours business that at the time of writing continues, though as part of a larger concern, to this day. According to Robert Davies and Stephen Barber's account [2007], Barr had an altruistic streak, a little in the Thomas Cook tradition. He grew up on the family farm in Woolley, near Barnsley in the West Riding of Yorkshire. The family were devout churchgoers and he attended Sunday Schools every week. His interest was engineering, practising by tinkering with what farm machines they had. Robert Barr made trips into Wakefield on market days. The contrast between the open countryside of his farm and the congested streets of the city struck him as disturbing:

> "I used to walk through the streets of Wakefield and was surprised and disturbed to find people living in such congested surroundings with little or no outlet from the streets and no outlook on nature and its beauties" [Barr, 1945:12]

Robert Barr overcame family resistance to his ideas and moved to a job with a garage in Leeds, earning a little more by running a bike-repair business on the side. By working overtime and saving from his meagre wages he managed to buy a small Karrier bus in 1912. In line with his more altruistic intensions, Robert used it to take city people on weekend excursions into the Yorkshire Dales, to the old abbeys of Rievaulx, Fountains and Bolton. And using the open-sided viewing advantage of the Karrier, he would stop in places to describe the countryside and scenery to his customers.

> "I was not, in the first instance, thinking in terms of the money that there might be in a new enterprise, but of performing a service of great educational value to people who, because of a lack of time, money and

118

transport facilities had not had much chance themselves to appease the hunger for Nature which we all feel" (Barr, 1945:14-15)

He also had a road haulage business using the convertible arrangement of the Karrier. The World War I interrupted proceedings as vehicles were requisitioned and he became regional commissioner for the Ministry of Transport. When war ended, he returned to build up the business again. 1920 saw him use a charabanc for a trip to London. It is worth remembering that it was a vehicle with solid tyres, a thirst for radiator water and running on roads of variable quality with a speed limit of 12 mph (19.3 kph) (Davies & Barber, 2007).

At the end of the decade there came an important step forward which was to create one of Britain's major coach tour operators. Robert Barr bought a busy company set up by Wallace Cunningham and Arnold Crowe. They ran five-day tours to London and Edinburgh at £8 (≈£328.47) a head, and nine-day tours to the Scottish Highlands at £16.16s (≈£689.79). Barr paid £800 (≈£36,628). The firm was named after the two men: Wallace Arnold. With the purchase, Barr became pre-eminently a tour operator. Book 2 in this series, *Bright Prospect*, will look again at his activities.

The United States by Bus and Coach

Albert Meier and John Hoschek's account of intercity bus transport in the United States, *Over the Road,* begins with the opening of the 20th century (Meier & Hoschek, 1975). They refer to a sight-seeing service operated by motor buses in New York in 1902. Internal combustion-engined double deckers ran along Fifth Avenue from 1905. But much of the earliest activity seems to have been in California, thanks to many small operators. East coast cities were often well served by horse-drawn rail cars, trolleys, steam trains and coastal boats. In Meier & Hoschek's discussion, The Midwest had electric interurban services, the South and Great Plains had railroads, even if they did have very infrequent services, sometimes only one or two a week. Bus and coach innovations took place in the mining areas of Minnesota, Texan oilfields, the timber country of the far North West and most notably, the new agricultural lands in California. The origins of coach building in the truck manufacturing industries were obvious in the long, front-mounted engine units.

"There was no such thing as a bus. Wagon makers turned into truck body builders by the advancing tide of gasoline power had to learn another set of new skills to satisfy early bus entrepreneurs. Parts were hard to get, if not impossible, and were often made in the neighbourhood, not infrequently by blacksmiths. Tyres, which never lasted long on the roads of the day, were seldom interchangeable between vehicles of different makes and models" (Meier & Hoschek, 1975:8-9).

Early operators included the California Transit Company using 'Pioneer Stages' as a brand name in the San Francisco area; Crown Stages Lines of Orange County, Southern California, and the Star Auto Stage Association with routes between Stockton and Fresno. The East would not be left far behind. The Curwensville Motor Transit Company in Pennsylvania of 1918 changed its name to Edwards Motor Transit Company in 1921, growing a network into Ohio, New Jersey and New York. Blue Club Coach Lines worked upscale journeys between New York and Bridgeport. Far inland came Purple Swan Safety Coach Lines serving Indianapolis, St Louis and Kansas City, and in Nebraska, the delightfully named Cornhusker Stage Lines. The Short Line had a White-built bus that was chartered by Clark University for a Trans-Continental Field Trip, out and back. Clark was in Worcester, Massachusetts. Its students were taken by the bus to Los Angeles, their transportation displaying its mission proudly in coach-painted lettering along each side. A few experiments of this sort took place in the 1920s, but they were largely ended by the economic restrictions of the following decade. The forthcoming *Bright Prospect* title in this series will consider one of these experiments, known as the Omnibus College of Wichita, Kansas.

Pickwick Stages

The big pioneer of the Pacific Coast bus industry was Pickwick Stages. For a bus company founded by people not called Pickwick, the San Diego pioneering outfit appears to have had an eccentric title. It had eccentric buses, too, though its business history was accurately centred on an ability to make money. The buses and coaches that looked so unusual – to our eyes, perhaps even ugly – were examples of the inventiveness that US citizens have long been celebrated for. They were experiments. That they failed to be widely adopted does not detract from the fact they were tried and achieved a certain success.

The Pickwick story began in 1912 when an ex-miner named A L Hayes bought a second-hand Ford auto in San Diego. He used it to run a stage line from the city to Escondido, thirty miles to the North. Hayes was successful, took on a partner, Herbert T Pattison and bought more touring cars. They were soon driving customers to Los Angeles on a stage-route basis. A merger with a San

Diego line owned by C W Grise and founded in 1911, took place in 1914. Grice would have a driver take customers on a 230-mile round trip to El Centro in the Californian Imperial Valley. The cost was \$25 (≈\$632). A detailed history online (weblist: Pickwick) refers to the cars carrying sticks of dynamite to remove any large boulders fallen onto the roadway. They also had firearms to ward off road bandits that were common during those early days. Both Hayes and Grise had used the Pickwick Theatre on Fourth Street, San Diego as a starting point. That was where the name of Pickwick Stages was born. The theatre was demolished in 1926, so the stage line, by then using buses, moved into offices at the Pickwick Terminal Hotel on West Broadway.

Another transport operator was Charles F Wren. He established a route in 1913 from central Los Angeles to Venice, 14 miles away. Wren attracted other operators to use the parking lot he had bought as a terminus. The Hayes Line from San Diego joined in. Wren developed routes to the North, reaching Santa Barbara and, in 1918, San Francisco. At that point, he and Hayes consolidated operations using the Pickwick name, Pickwick Northern Division and Pickwick Stage Line to the South. A Pickwick Corporation holding company controlled them and developed routes to Portland, El Paso, St Louis, Chicago and finally, New York. It reached fame as "the great Pickwick Stages system, largest in the nation" (Meier & Hoschek, 1975:2). Charles Wren became company president in 1922. He set up the Pickwick Motor Coach Works Ltd in 1923 (weblist: Pickwick) under Dwight D Austin, a skilled and innovative engineer and coach designer. Austin became responsible for several noteworthy designs. His 'parlour buffet' buses served meals on the Los Angeles-San Francisco service from 1925. The company built them on Pierce-Arrow chassis with sedan-style bodies and equipped with reclining seats. There was an 'observation buffet' coach in which a section of seating was placed on a raised platform. Passengers enjoyed a good view of the countryside by looking out through windows in the elevated roof space. A later version had the driver placed in a kind of cupola at equal height, and as it happened, partly obstructing the view forward of the people in the observation seats.

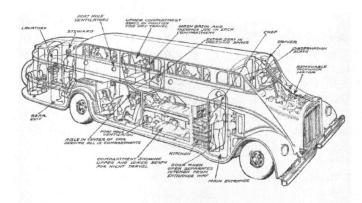

The Nite Coach

The most famous Pickwick Coach Works vehicle was the Nite Coach. It was a double-decked, all metal coach designed for 26 passengers, with an aisle set at a median height, from which single steps up and down led to the thirteen two-passenger compartments (see weblist: Pickwick). In each of these were upholstered bench seats for two, facing each other. At night-time they converted into upper and lower beds. A heavy curtain gave privacy for a dressing space equipped with a seat for dressing. There were two drawers for clothing and space for two suitcases. A wash basin had running water. There was a ventilation system for each compartment. At the rear of the coach was a lavatory with washbasin and mirror, built in what looked like an extension hooked onto the main coach body, but which was really just the lower deck extending further than the upper. Inside the entrance door at the front of the coach was a kitchen with cooking tables, percolator, toaster, ice box and utensils. Meals were served on tables in each compartment. The coach's engine could be disconnected quickly and replaced by another picked up from each coach terminal in the event of a problem. A driver, a steward and a porter formed the crew, with either the steward or the porter capable of acting as a relief driver.

During 1929, Pickwick inaugurated air services, firstly between Los Angeles and San Diego and then Los Angeles to San Francisco. They added a road-and-air route which was built to serve from the Pacific to the Atlantic. The Nite Coach took people to Phoenix, Arizona. The aircraft took them through the day in stages to St Louis, where a Nite Coach continued their journey to

Chicago. Those who wanted to go to New York were booked onto co-operating airlines' flights. Other routes were added into Mexico and Guatemala and the acquisition of two radio stations helped the business to gain publicity and an armchair audience. It was not quite the first bi-modal route from coast to coast. As we will see in Chapter 11, an outfit called Transcontinental Air Transport had started such a service the previous year, but it used rail and air and the train was faster than the coach.

It was still a time of pioneering for road traffic. The next chapter will tell how a US Army convoy struggled to cross the continent by road, in 1919. Long-distance coach companies had to choose their routes carefully because of the poor quality of many roads. Pickwick Stages used aircraft to pass over the worst stretches and to reduce the total travel time to a figure that could compete with the railroads. They had to deal with the need for sleeping facilities that could allow overnight travel, supply meals where appropriate when still on the move, and give their customers time to move around and exercise, at least at the transportation swap-over points. Their aircraft gave business travellers the speed they needed. Tourists were less time conscious, but perhaps enjoyed the new sensations of flight – if they could afford it.

The Great Depression triggered by the stock market crash of 1929 began a turbulent period for everyone. Bus companies were growing, merging or co-operating on route networks. Buying stock in each other's businesses for financial reasons made for complicated arrangements. The economic slump reduced demand for travel in many ways, putting pressure on operators. Pickwick Stages became owned by the Motor Transit Corporation early in 1929, ahead of the Crash. The MTC was strong in the Midwest. Charles Wren was persuaded to sell Pickwick Stages to MTC rather than compete with that company in further expansion to the East. The Motor Transit Corp was part of the Greyhound network, destined to become the USA's dominant inter-city carrier.

Before picking up the story of Greyhound, we can note that Britain had its own night sleepers for a limited period. A company called Land Liners Ltd started a service from Liverpool and Manchester to London in 1928. Its two vehicles were triple-axle, double decker coaches built on Guy chassis. At the same time Albatross Roadways Ltd ran a competing service over the same route with a coach on a Daimler chassis. It had two bunk beds on two levels of the floor – it was not a double decker – and like the Land Liner coach had a "lavatory and WC". Refreshments were available. The single fare was £1..5s (≈£51). The company then opened another service on 22 December 1928. It operated between London and Leeds and Bradford at a fare of £1..5s. single and £2..10s. return, as against the third-class railway fares of £1..3s..3d. to Leeds and £1..4s to Bradford, plus an extra charge for a sleeper berth in the ordinary compartments. The comfort on the road coach was claimed as almost equal to first-class on the railway. Three services a week in each direction were planned, starting out at 11pm and arriving at the destination about 8:30am (weblist: Albatross 02). Problems with the reliability of the vehicles, their weight damaging roads, and the economics of the depression seemed to have produced a rapid closure of all the services. (see weblist: Albatross 01)

Greyhound

Back in the USA, the bus brand that would outdo everyone was formed in Minnesota by Carl Eric Wickman in 1914. It was a name he adopted on arrival in the USA, his Swedish name having been Martis Jerk. Young Carl had emigrated from Sweden aged 17, worked for a while in Arizona and then moved to Hibbing, Minnesota where there was a Swedish-settler community. The work he found in the Mesaba iron ore mine was irregular. Carl Wickman tried taking on a dealership for Hupmobile cars and Goodyear tyres, but nobody bought from him. It was 1913. He paid for his demonstration car, a seven-seater, taking up another idea, using it to carry passengers between Hibbing and Alice, Minnesota (Schisgall, 1985). After setting up a partnership with another Swedish immigrant named Andy Anderson, business boomed. They earned $8,000 in 1915 and twice that the following year. By then the partnership had five members and five cars with Wickman in charge. It was called the Mesaba Transportation Company. Buses quickly replaced cars.

Carl Wickman made another change of direction – out of Hibbing and the business he ran. It was 1922, he was married and had two children. He sold his share of the company to his associates and moved to Duluth. Oscar Schisgall, the author of *The Greyhound Story*, believes Wickman wanted a town with more to offer his family and his business skills. It was a logical choice as the nearest major city was ninety miles by road to the South East, on Lake Superior. He had $60,000 from selling his share of the Hibbing operation. He might have shaken off the ties to Hibbing but not bus lines. Wickman invested in shares in some lines that looked promising. The first was the Superior White Company owned by Orville Swan Caesar. They were a well-matched pair and set about buying other bus lines, putting them into a holding company, the Motor Transit Corporation. It was formed in 1922. Three years later, with a new partner involved, it was turned into the Northland Transportation Company.

Schisgall notes their ambition to make bus travel simpler by overcoming the customer's problem of transferring themselves and their luggage from bus line to bus line when making a long journey. What could be more obvious than a strategy of buying up lines to create an ever-expanding network? A deal with the Great Northern Railroad helped. Train companies were also buying bus lines, so that they could be used to act as feeders to their rail stations. The GNR bought 80% of the Northland stock but left it free to expand in other areas, away from the rail/bus network. With the Federal government investing huge amounts in road improvements and the war over, people were much more willing to travel, whether by train or by coach. More lines were added to the network.

Oscar Schisgall tells one version of the story about the word greyhound being applied to coaches. It came from a Wickman driver named Clifford Graves. He said that an early bus operator was having lunch in Duluth with a friend. A Fageol bus swept past. One of them said to the other, "Look at that thing! Fast as a greyhound!" (Schisgall, 1985:9). However the description came about, it was soon being applied to buses and used in company names. Wickman's business was soon buying other companies that were using the word – Southland Greyhound Lines and Richmond Greyhound Lines amongst them. Pickwick Stages had done so. It became part of the Wickman operation in 1928, letting Carl tell his stockholders, "We now serve practically every city of importance in the territory between Chicago and St Louis and New York" (Schisgall, 1985:23). At the time, Pickwick was running its Nite Coach and Pickwick Airways service between Los Angeles and Chicago, so Wickman could not claim coverage of "every city of importance" between LA and St Louis: they were dominated by Pickwick.

As the 1920s came to an end there were over a hundred bus lines in Wickman's network. So, in 1930 the whole consolidated business became known officially as the Greyhound Corporation. It operated 1,800 buses every day. The parent company by 1933 contained three wholly owned companies and ten affiliated companies, with smaller lines, using their own names, also within the Corporation. The financing arrangements were complex and there were struggles through the Great Depression of the 1930s. 1933 brought the chance of a spectacular marketing ploy. The Corporation won the right to provide internal transport for the Chicago Century of Progress Exposition. Sixty buses were organised under a new company name – World's Fair Greyhound Lines. The buses were long, with a coach trailer hitched onto a standard lorry tractor unit. The buses gave tours of the fairgrounds, earning the Corporation around half a million dollars. But the business also reserved 2,000 hotel rooms for the duration of the Exposition. It transported people to the event, carried them around its exhibits and offered guaranteed hotel rooms for longer visits.

There was a worldwide piece of media publicity, too. A short story, published in 1933, was turned into a Columbia Pictures film directed by Frank Capra. It screened in the next year under the title *It Happened One Night*. A romantic comedy starring Clark Gable and Claudette Colbert, it had Colbert playing a spoilt heiress travelling from Miami to New York after having had a row with her rich father. Gable played an out of work newspaper journalist. They both took the overnight bus, and it was a Greyhound. The film was actually made in California using a bus loaned by the Greyhound Corporation. Today, the vehicle looks uncomfortable and sounds grimly noisy. The driver wears military style uniform complete with Sam Browne belt, a Greyhound idea to reassure passengers about reliability. In this driver's case, he matches with some of his male passengers' boorish behaviour.

It was a movie of its time. The five key Oscars came its way in the 1935 Academy Awards, the first time it happened (and it has only happened twice since). The public loved it, and they must have found the bus sequences tempting because the Corporation's business increased fast. Escapist, romantic comedy using low-cost travel to reach a prosperous conclusion was just the job in the years of the Great Depression. The movie audiences would relate to the mom-and-pop motel scenes with their air of cheerful economy contrasting with the overbearing, wealthy father hunting his daughter in a private aeroplane. Travel by bus would look to be a community singsong and party atmosphere affair to be enjoyed with conviviality.

1934 saw another bus film, *Cross Country Cruise*, starring Richard Dix and Lew Ayres. This was from Universal Pictures. It told the stories of a mixed bunch of passengers including a teacher, a salesman, a runaway and others, and someone who turns out to have murdered his wife. Greyhound buses featured again. Pacific Greyhound by now had a small fleet of Nite Coaches and parked one outside the Orpheum Cinema in San Francisco for the duration of the run.

Greyhound had operated its own terminals for many years. They had lunchrooms run by concessionaires. During the late 1940s concerns were raised about their quality and notably, the food they served. The decision was taken to open restaurants directly run by Greyhound using the new brand name of Post House. Eight were completed by 1940. Some were soon serving 2,500 meals a day for around 100 bus loads of passengers (Schisgall, 1985).

The Greyhound Corporation supplied a hundred specially designed buses for the 1939/40 New York World's Fair. As in the Chicago event, they transported visitors between peripheral transportation stations and the many pavilions of the Fair. The vehicles looked like streamlined, symmetrical trams, different from the articulated truck-based designs for Chicago. They had three entrances on each side, but no doors, to aid rapid boarding and exiting.

The level of bus-riding on the eve of World War II overtook that of Class I railroads (those having operating revenues of more than $1m) for the first time in 1935, at almost exactly 652m passengers.

California's Golden Gate Bridge, Opened in 1937

Chapter 8

The Automobile Revolution

The motor car in Europe is useful. The automobile in the USA is essential. James Akerman quotes Andrei Codrescu:

"An American without a car is a sick creature, a snail that has lost its shell. Living without a car is the worst form of destitution, more shameful by far than not having a home" (in Akerman, 2006:152).

Akerman himself puts it this way:

"The train endures in American culture and mythology as a symbol of continental conquest and modern humanity's mastery of nature, but the automobile's ability to infiltrate the landscape it occupies ultimately has made its geographical and cultural impact more far-reaching" (Akerman, 2006:152).

128

Again,

"The road map and the highway space it represented gave driving Americans the tools to explore the national territory in numbers and over distances without parallel in any other nation's experience. It widened the horizons of average Americans by leading them to and through radically different physical and cultural landscapes from those they knew at home" (p153).

A few pages later in his chapter Mr Akerman strikes a different note that counters the idealistic view expressed above. He notes the existence of the free automobile road map distributed by oil companies and others. In the USA there was no equivalent of Britain's Ordnance Survey which by the 1920s was marketing highly informative maps through ordinary retailers in most towns. These were maps that served walkers, cyclists, car owners and everyone else through their objective and comprehensive detailing. The Ordnance Survey was well behind the French *Carte Géométrique de la France* however, which had published the first multi-sheet topographic map series of the entire country by 1815.

Americans had to rely on commercial give-aways:

"The great irony of free automobile road map distribution was that while it worked in many practical ways to break down the barriers to personal geographical mobility, it also sought to regulate the movement of drivers, to bring their itineraries into conformity. At the simplest level, this meant directing motoring tourists to specific commercial establishments" (Akerman, 2006:156)

For example, the oil companies' service stations or accommodation providers paid for advertising spaces. Many of these maps were no more than schematic route maps between towns, omitting roads that did not serve their persuasive purpose. The backs of the maps often listed "the best hotels and motor courts … which we may assume have paid fees … or in some other way have sponsored the map's publication" (p157). Topographic maps of the USA would appear from the work of the United States Geological Survey, established in 1879. It brought together existing initiatives in surveying such as those by the army working in the Western States, etc. With a wide range of map-type responsibilities and a vast continent to cover, its productions were never going to be the go-to travel sources of the general public, however.

The invention of the motor car might look like the technological revolution that changed family life and work. Yet it was more than half a century after its invention that it really took on its modern dominance. Even that growth – in the 1950s and 60s – was most noticeable in the United States and the more affluent parts of Europe. In Europe, it was not the motor car but its power source, the internal combustion engine, that changed transport patterns first. Bus and road-coach services began to take passengers from railways, trams and trolleybuses. Motor taxis had a rapid effect on horse-drawn cabs. Even in the USA, as Bernard Rieger has described in his recent history of the Volkswagen 'Beetle' (2013), cars at first did badly in cities, but very well in rural areas, where the simple ruggedness of the Model T Ford and its ability to power farm equipment, made it a winner.

The Good Roads advocates, acting as campaigning groups in the USA, had to work hard to get any major roads built. Theirs was a widespread movement working at many levels. They argued the case for hard-surface tourist roads into the National Parks (Whisnant, 2006) and within and between the cities. Yet for a long time, the 'hard-surfaces' of many roads were made of dirt and stone rather than well-bonded asphalt. Weingroff wrote that "In 1912, the Nation's highways were just emerging from the Dark Ages of road building in the second half of the nineteenth century" (weblist: Lincoln Highway). Of 2.1m miles of rural roads, "only … 8.66% … had improved surfaces of gravel, stone, sand-clay, brick, shells, oiled earth, bituminous or, as a US Bureau of Public Roads bulletin put it 'etc'".

This was at a time when Europe had many roads built using any of three eighteenth-century methods devised by early civil engineers. A brief recap of the situation just prior to the period covered by the present book is needed. Post-1851 efforts sprang from the work of those early engineers. Influential European developments were those by the Frenchman, Pierre Trésaguet; a Yorkshireman, the blind John Metcalfe and two Scots, Thomas Telford and John Loudon McAdam. Each of them had invented methods combining techniques of layering stones of selected shapes and sizes. Trésaguet and Metcalfe began their first carefully designed roadworks in 1764 and 1765, respectively. The Frenchman used three layers of different sizes of stone to build up a solid, relatively smooth carriageway, convex in cross-section to drain away water. His Yorkshire counterpart did something similar by the use of two layers.

Thomas Telford trained as a stonemason working first on bridge-building and then on Somerset House in London. Telford had a remarkable career which took in not only bridges and buildings but docks, canals and even, late in life, preliminary surveys for railways. His work involved managing large projects, one of which was organising the London to Holyhead road with cuttings, embankments and bridges, his 1826 suspension bridge over the Menai Straits being the greatest of them. The organisational tasks took in the setting up of granite mileposts with cast-iron plates carrying destination names and distances, and the toll-house system that brought income to reimburse construction costs. Thomas Telford's canal projects were equally spectacular, the Pontcysyllte aqueduct on the Llangollen Canal, the Caledonian Canal in Scotland and the initial plans for the Göta Canal in Sweden being magnificent examples. Canals were not primarily made for the use of passengers but goods, even though some fly boats made trips along them as they were discovered by tourists. On the other hand, canals are all major tourist attractions in the 21st century.

John Loudon McAdam (1756-1836) was an almost exact contemporary of Telford and likewise Scottish. Having worked in New York at his uncle's counting house, he returned to Scotland a wealthy man. McAdam then operated a coalmine and had interests in an ironworks. 1783 saw him a trustee of the Ayrshire turnpike with increasing involvement in similar projects over the next decade. His method was similar to those of Metcalfe and Telford, using good foundations with crushed stone on top. His workmen had to break stones to a three-inch size (7.5cms) for the foundation layer and half that for the running surface. These stones had to be smaller than the 1¾in (4cms) width of the iron carriage tyres passing over them. McAdam not only built roads: he publicised his methods through two booklets of 1816 and 1819. His system became known as the 'macadam road' after him. It was used in the United States to complete the Baltimore to Wheeling road between Hagerstown and Boonsboro, Maryland. Incidentally, 'tarmacadam' was an invention of 1902, binding macadam layers together with surfacing made of tar and sand. Its variation name of 'tarmac' has since been widely used for other bound-together surfaces including modern asphalt concrete.

There were experiments in Switzerland and France using asphalt to bind stone aggregates into a smoothly rolled surface. Edward J de Smedt paved a street in New Jersey in 1870 with asphalt from Trinidad. His method was used by the US Army Corps of Engineers to pave part of Pennsylvania Avenue in

Washington DC for the US Centennial. After seeing its successful properties, seventy miles of the capital's streets were resurfaced with it [Petroski, 2016].

Railways were the key transport components of the successful Great Exhibition of 1851. They delivered exhibits and visitors. Better roads, such as turnpikes, played their part, from acting as feeders to railway stations to helping other visitors get to London in their carriages. While the show had entry prices enabling different classes of people to mix together, there was a distinct difference between the masses travelling by rail and the wealthy who went by road. Steam-powered buses had been making themselves felt and heard for some two decades. They could travel faster than horse-drawn carriages, were cheaper to run and were considered less damaging with their wider tyres than the narrow, rut-cutting wheels of horse vehicles. The way might have been open for an expansion of steam-operated road services. It was not to happen. Turnpike trusts had been failing. Tollgates were seen as impediments to trade and railways had had an immediate impact on turnpike revenues. Noisy, smelly steam vehicles and the new automobiles that followed did not mix well with horse traffic. Perhaps the prosperous with their carriages and the growing-wealthy railway companies imposed their new influences on government to limit vehicle developments. There were many attempts at electric cars including by Porsche, Edison and Ford. Batteries were not up to the requirements of road journeys, however.

During the last four decades of the 19th century, restrictive Locomotive Acts imposed speed limits and other rules on non-horse vehicles in Britain. That of 1861 stipulated, among other rules and restrictions, that vehicles must be manned by two people, plus an extra one if a train of wagons was being towed; a speed limit of 10 mph (16 kph) on open roads and 5 mph (8 kph) in inhabited areas was imposed. A Locomotive Act of 1865 required a crew of three plus an additional one if two or more other vehicles were attached; another, carrying a red flag, was to walk 60 yards (55m) ahead, stopping the vehicle if horses were encountered. Speed limits were tightened to 4 mph (6.4 kph) in the country and 2 mph (3.2 kph) in towns.

The first British auto exhibition was held in 1895 in Tunbridge Wells. Owners lobbied Parliament to remove, or at least make less restrictive, the speed limits. An Act of 1896 increased the speed permissible to 12 mph (19.3 kph), or between 8 and 16mph if the local authority preferred it. The man with the red flag disappeared. A celebration was organised by Harry Lawson who began the Daimler Car Company that year. On 14 November thirty-three car owners met for breakfast at the Charing Cross Hotel. Lord Winchelsea symbolically tore a red flag in two and then the group set off for Brighton. It was not a race, the new local speed limit of 14 mph (23 kph) being enforced. Seventeen automobiles arrived in the coastal town, where Lord Winchelsea presided at a grand dinner (Brendon, 1997).

Shorter runs were held over the next years until in 1927 the Brighton run was repeated. With a break during the 1939-45 war it became a major annual tourist event. The vehicles had to be ones built before 1905. Today, more than 400 automobiles set off from Hyde Park after a red flag is torn in half. The annual Veteran Car Run is organised by the Royal Automobile Club, which was formed in 1897, still imposing the 20 mph (32.19 kph) introduced in the 1920s. The 60-mile route would impose stresses on the elderly vehicles at higher speeds. Some of them take more than twelve hours, drivers and passengers wrapped up against the weather in the open cars.

The part played by Henry Ford in inventing the 'Tin Lizzie' – the Model T Ford – in 1908, and revolutionising auto-building by devising assembly-line production in 1913 is immensely important. But he did not invent the motor car. The Belgian, Étienne Lenoir, had built the first internal combustion engine in 1859 at his works in Paris. It used coal gas, as supplied for domestic lighting. 1863 saw him make a walking-pace journey of six miles with it fitted to a special, three-wheeled, wooden carriage. He took the development no further, however. Then came Karl Benz in Mannheim, Germany, with a petrol-engine car in 1885 and Gottleib Daimler, who built an internal-combustion car in Schorndorf, Germany, in the same year.

Karl Benz had built a successful car, but he lacked confidence in its engineering to promote it for sale. His wife Bertha was also his business partner, having put money into his workshop before they married. The law of the time said that as a married woman she lost her power to do things independently of him without his permission. Bertha had faith in his invention but saw his lack of confidence. What she did was to take an action well ahead of her time, more in line with a modern media+tourism stunt.

In August 1888, without telling Karl, she took their two young teenage sons and the latest model of the automobile for a long drive. They set off at dawn with Eugen at the controls, leaving a note for Karl who was not yet up and about. The vehicle would have looked fragile to modern eyes, with only three wheels, a simple bench seat and a tiller for steering. The destination was

Pforzheim, 104 kilometres away, where her mother lived. Bertha and her boys stopped in Heidelberg for breakfast. The car ran on a fuel called ligroin that was only available at pharmacies. When fuel was needed, they stopped in Wiesloch and filled the tank. The pharmacy is still operating today and has a modern steel sculpture symbolic of the journey in front of it.

Off they went again, finding trouble going uphill when Frau Benz and Eugen had to let Richard steer while they got off and pushed. Even downhill was a problem since the leather brake blocks wore out and they had to stop again to buy more. The carburettor became blocked: Bertha's hatpin cleared the pipe. An ignition wire lost its insulation: Bertha used a garter to replace it. People along the way were amazed by the spectacle. One story goes that two peasants had a big dispute about whether the vehicle was powered by clockwork or the work of witches.

At last they arrived in Pforzheim after a five-hour journey. Bertha sent Karl a telegram to announce their safe arrival. The trio stayed three nights in the town, waiting for a new drive chain that Karl agreed to send, then they returned by a different route that was shorter and less hilly. There was much publicity about the journey and Karl added a third gear at the adventurers' suggestion to help with hill climbs. In 2008 a 194-kilometre Bertha Benz Memorial Route was publicised to commemorate her exploit. It runs through both industrial and scenic countryside, taking in the stopping places of the original journey
.

Germany might have been the place where the automobile was invented and then publicised by Bertha's media work. But it did not catch on there, not straight away. Bernhard Rieger has recently drawn attention to this by comparing ownership ratios for four countries in 1927. In Germany, there was one internal-combustion engine vehicle (car, truck or bus) for every 196 Germans. In France and Britain, it was one for every 44 inhabitants. For the USA, the figure was one for every 5.3 inhabitants (Rieger, 2013). Henry Ford's assembly line production, geared up to the high demand of Americans for a workhorse vehicle, had been making the USA a gasoline-driven nation.

There had been other influences helping to popularise automobile use. While numerically small, a band of pioneers was showing the excitement that could be had with a good car. Bertha Benz did not stay the only overland adventurer for long. In 1902 Dr E E Lehwess set out on a planned round-the-world drive in a car accompanied by a fellow German driver, Max Cudell, an English barrister and journalist, H Morgan Browne, plus a professional chauffeur and a chef. The vehicle had been built for him by Panhard-Levassor, and Carrosserie Industrielle, both of Paris, at a cost of £3,000 (equivalent in 2017 to about £236,000). It was painted canary yellow and named 'Passe-Partout' ("All-purpose"). *Grace's Guide* website records Dr Lehwess as a "a rogue and fraudster" with several convictions to his name.

The colour would be like that of Toad's caravan in *The Wind in the Willows* and the name a reminder of Phileas Fogg's servant in *Around the World in Eighty Days*. At the time the motor caravan was described in the London *Westminster Gazette* as a 'travelling hotel'. It weighed nearly three tons. There was photography equipment on board. Dr Lehwess was said to speak German, French, English and Russian. He planned to supply accounts of the journey to the media in mainland Europe and Asia, and H Morgan Browne would handle the media in America and Britain. The journey started from London, reached Paris and took a six-week break to enjoy the city. After that, all went well across Europe until the vehicle broke down in a snowstorm near Nizhniy-Novgorod, after which the expedition was abandoned. Lehwess sold the 'travelling hotel'. It was rescued from Russia by a London motor dealer, Charlie Friswell.

There are conflicting accounts of the expedition in archived magazines such as *The Autocar* of February 1902, *The Automobile Magazine* of June 1902, and *Motor Sport* of June 1947. The website *Grace's Guide* details Dr Lehwess's chequered career [weblist: Lehwess]. The vehicle had been named *Passe-Partout*, a reference to Phineas Fogg's resourceful servant, but that was the nearest the expedition came to be emulating Jules Verne's inspirational account of world travel.

Some less ambitious adventurers had already been achieving successes. A manufacturer named Alexander Winton drove one of his cars from Cleveland to New York in 1897, a ten-day journey: slow compared with some methods, but speed was not the point – the reliability of his vehicle was what counted. [Schaffer, 2001]. The first transcontinental crossing by automobile was made in 1903 by Horatio Nelson Jackson and Sewall K Crocker. It took them two months and three days to drive from San Francisco to New York. More crossings followed – the first by a family and the first by an all-women group. Car manufacturers supplied vehicles in return for publicity, while photographs and accounts of the journeys reproduced in newspapers and magazines began to awaken the public to adventurous tourism.

On the Move

1919 saw a US Army vehicle convoy travel 3,250 miles from Washington DC to San Francisco. It was three miles long, decorated with red, white and blue bunting and even carrying a band sponsored by the Goodyear Tyre and Rubber Company. Its eighty-one vehicles were from the Motor Transport Corps, anxious to show its strength and mobility. Speed could not be its forte. The summer roads were often quagmires as well as being rough, with frequent creeks and rivers to be crossed by bridges of questionable utility. They averaged fifty-two miles in a day, or about five miles an hour. One of its officers was the young Lieutenant Colonel Dwight D Eisenhower, who became the US President in 1953. Soon after taking office, he initiated the new Interstate Highway system that, like the earlier *Reichsautobahn* system in Germany or the later motorways in Britain, provided the trunk routes so needed by the increasingly heavy traffic.

Better Roads

Motoring was unlikely to become popular as a recreation if the roads were as bad as Weingroff described them. State governments had realised the problem, with some states such as New Jersey and Massachusetts beginning to fund new road building in 1891 and 1893, respectively. Then in 1897 the US Secretary of Agriculture began to build short '*object lesson roads*' to show what could be done [Weblist: FHWA].

Object lessons were popular in teaching for many years. A common object would be used as the focal point for a classroom lesson. For example, an acorn might help to illustrate the growth of a tree, or plants in general. The method was central to many nature walks in the 19th century, with the acorn being displayed next to a mature oak. Children might be shown animals on a farm or the way that a church was designed. An adults' excursion leader would naturally point out landscape objects to help explain themes to people. The principle was one of 'Seeing for Yourself', perhaps the strongest argument for being a tourist. It was an easy step for Horatio Earle of the League of American Wheelmen (LAW) to devise a plan for promoting better roads that used the object lesson idea. An object lesson road had been built in New Jersey in 1897. Earle would use such a demonstration on a bigger scale.

'Wheelmen' was the term used for bicyclists. The League was founded in Newport, Rhode Island in 1880. The name was kept until 1994 when 'Bicyclists' replaced the earlier label. From 1880, the League aimed to protect the rights of its members and to campaign for better roads. Earle became the chief proponent of the LAW's Michigan Highway Improvement Committee, in 1896. One of his tactics was to organise an international good roads congress four years later (Weblist: FHWA). The event had elements of a festival with bicycle races, automobile tests, concerts, fireworks, speeches and a banquet. Hundreds of delegates, from the USA and Canada, attended the venue in Port Huron, Michigan. It was an echo of Thomas Cook's Loughborough event of 1841: a campaign wrapped inside a package of entertainment. A tourist event.

In fact, Earle's campaign attraction was something very unusual – a railroad train of flat cars and carriages. On the flat cars were road-building machines: a traction engine, road roller, sprinkler, dump wagons and farm wagons. Several hundred people rode in the carriages. They were delegates from many walks of life, who shared an interest in getting better roads built. The train took them and the construction gear to see the object lesson road, where a stone crushing machine and a grader were on show. The train and the machinery had all been loaned for the event by local operators. Road builders would, of course, benefit from contracts awarded for new roads. Railroad companies saw a benefit from roads that would make it easier for people and goods to access their services.

It was a successful enterprise (Weblist: FHWA). A mile of new road was built over three days as the delegates watched. New processes were explained. At the end of the event it was clear the benefits for cyclists, automobile users and transport companies were many. The congress adopted a resolution calling on the US Government to give plentiful assistance to new roads, to support more object lessons in every State and to use convict labour to help with the work. Other railroad companies and machinery suppliers began to operate their own promotional shows. Someone at the time described them as a cross between a travelling circus and a Chautauqua show (an adult education camp meeting named for a place in New York State).

The Southern Railway spent $80,000 on its train. It visited eighteen places across six States, over four thousand miles. An object-lesson road was built at each one with delegates to the conventions held at each watching the demonstrations. Similar work continued elsewhere. The successful road building that followed led to President Woodrow Wilson signing into law the first federally aided highway programme in 1916 (Weblist: Marriott). It made money available to those States which had established their own highways department.

On the Move

Paul Marriott writes that previously roads had been built for

> "either economic or military advantage. The introduction of the bicycle and later the automobile, occurring almost simultaneously with a new awareness for conservation and the first National Parks, was spurring Americans to take to the roads and explore the countryside and the wilderness" (Weblist: Marriott p37).

Maurice Eldridge of the Office for Public Roads Information had pointed to this happening, back in 1902:

> "It is far more pleasant for wealthy Americans to spend their summers travelling through Europe, where good roads abound. By the construction of good roads Switzerland has been made 'the pleasure ground of Europe', but if we should add good roads to all our other attractions and advantages over foreign countries we could turn the tide of pleasure seekers and make our country not only a garden spot but the pleasure ground of the whole world" (Weblist: FHWA).

Maurice Eldridge was seeing that kind of tourism in terms of leisure and pleasure. There were others beginning to go beyond that, adding both education and environmental management to the mix.

Taking to the Road in America

The boost in road building after 1916 when President Wilson established a federally aided highway programme was enormous, but progress was slow. Business people had pressed for improvements for decades before 1916. In 1912, an Indianapolis Speedway owner and car headlights manufacturer named Carl G Fisher hosted a dinner for friends in the auto industry. He proposed building a coast-to-coast road of high quality that would show what a good highway ought to be. It would help economic growth, but mainly boost the new motor industry. Private enterprise should build it. The dinner guests pledged a million dollars within a month, though when asked to join in, car-maker Henry Ford said no. He thought that the government should pay for roads and private enterprise would never be able to afford the engineering required anyway (Butko, 2013).

For many State legislators the idea of paying for road projects, which would be called 'internal improvements' was prevented by their constitutions: it was the job of private individuals or cities. A new association of businesspeople was formed to take on the task. They chose a route and a name – the Lincoln Highway, knowing how that name would resonate with citizens across the land. In 1913 a Trail-Blazer Tour of cars and trucks set out from Indianapolis for San Francisco. It took 34 days to get there, publicising the project in cities along the way and sending regular reports to newspapers. Theodore Roosevelt, Thomas Edison and President Woodrow Wilson personally contributed money to the fund – Wilson gave $5 ($\approx$$130), which earned him Highway Certificate #1.

The Lincoln Highway Association quickly found it could not itself afford to build such a mammoth project, so the money raised was used to whip up interest and support. Over the next few years, existing roads were incorporated, and new ones built using money from Federal Aid programmes, State Agencies (where they could legally help) and some commercial sources looking for publicity. An 'Ideal Section', 1.3 miles long (2.09 km), was built in north-west Indiana as an exemplar in 1923. It had a 40-foot (12.2m) wide paved core built using reinforced concrete, underground drainage, lighting, landscaping, a bridge and pedestrian paths. It is still marked by commemorative signs.

The Lincoln Highway was an idea, something to be shaped out of whatever could be brought together by way of existing roads and new builds (weblist: Lincoln Highway).

Shaffer quotes a set of promotional articles in the US *Travel Magazine* in the spring of 1915 (see Schaffer, 2001:131). These were by Newton A Fuessle. The current World War, he wrote, had confined Americans to their home country with positive effects, because they could take automobile tours along the Lincoln Highway, the subject of his three articles. The Highway was

> "teaching patriotism, sewing up the ragged edges of sectionalism, revealing and interpreting America to its people, giving swifter feet to commerce, gathering up the country's loose ends of desultory and disjointed good roads, and binding them into one highly organised, proficient unit of dynamic, result-getting force, electric with zeal, it is quickening American neighbourliness, democracy, progress and civilisation" (in Shaffer, 2001:131).

The USA had not yet entered World War I in 1916. The coming conflict would be one of the causes of the nation's move towards centre stage in world affairs.

Two of the others were the growth of Hollywood's film industry and the invention, not of the internal combustion powered motor car, which was largely European in origin, but the assembly line production of motor cars, which was American. The United States shared with other countries the newspaper industry, dominant in news reporting, and book publishing, incomparable in its presentation of the most detailed, comprehensive and authoritative information available on any subject at the time. Newspapers, books, cars and railroads carried the news across continents.

The USA had achieved its coast-to-coast railroad in 1869. Rail transport remained dominant beyond the World War I, but the automobile was beginning to attract attention. The Duryea brothers built their first 'motor wagon' in 1893, converting a horse buggy, bought elsewhere, by adding a single-cylinder gasoline engine. Some hand-built vehicles followed. Studebaker made their first auto in 1897. Ransom Olds introduced stationary production-line manufacturing in 1901, pushing up car production from 425 cars that year to 2,500 in the next.

Ford and Cadillac cars had their origins around the same time. Henry Ford's Model T auto dated from 1908. It became famous through skilful advertising and Ford's moving assembly line system begun five years later, increasing his car production from 82,000 to 189,000 within its first year. By 1916 it topped half a million; in 1921, 1 million (Watts, 2005).

Auto Adventures Promote Taking to the Road

The first adventure was one enjoyed by the splendidly named Horatio Nelson Jackson, who drove a Winton car from San Francisco to his home in Vermont. His co-driver, and mechanic, was Sewall K Crocker. The journey took place in 1903 and it was an epic in which flat tyres, breakdowns and mud-filled roads played a great part. Jackson and Crocker and a pit bulldog named Bud became celebrities for their coast-to-coast automobile crossing of the country. Six years later, Alice Ramsey became the first woman to drive across, from New York to San Francisco, using a Maxwell car. She had three travelling companions, one of whom was aged 16 (Ramsey was 22). None of them could drive. They used *Blue Book* guides from the American Automobile Association to decide their route, at least to the Mississippi. There was no guide available to cover the rest of the way to the Pacific until 1912.

Like Jackson, Ramsey had to learn much about automobiles and the handling of them. But she and the others also learnt much about their own country and its people. California's sugar pines and redwoods had been unknown to them. They also discovered a new form of prejudice when a farmer gave direction including turning left at his "yellow house and barn", which they could not find. It turned out he was critical of automobile travel in favour of horses and had painted the buildings green previously so he could annoy lost drivers. Even so, after 59 days and 3,800 miles, Alice drove them into San Francisco in triumph.

Neither Jackson nor Ramsey could drive the Lincoln Highway route in 1909, since it was not finally decided, signposted and publicised until 1915, the year of the Panama-Pacific Exposition. The Highway was announced by a dedication event in 1913, after which it existed as a route of variable quality, slowly metamorphosing into a road over several years. In the Western States it continued to challenge by its lack of good bridges and frequency of seasonal mud sinks. The first guide to the route was a folder paid for by the Packard Company in 1913. Brian Butko's detailed celebratory *Greetings from the Lincoln Highway* quotes some of the instructions contained: "straight ahead across sage brush mesa" and in part of Nevada "fill each ditch with brush before crossing" (Butko, 2013:20).

The Highway came about thanks not only to Carl G Fisher and friends, but businesses and city leaders the whole way across, helped by the obviously nascent demand by people like Jackson and Ramsey for a usable route. Marguerite Shaffer notes [2001] that a man named Fred Trinkle had made the journey seventeen times by 1908, and the family of Jacob M Murdoch had made the trip from Los Angeles in a month.

Establishing the Lincoln by 1915 was a valiant effort, though improvements to the route and the road would continue for many years. Publicity in newspapers and magazines achieved results, but there was a part played by movies and newsreels, too. A movie star, Anita King, set out in a Kissel Kar on the first stage of her solo journey West to East. She left the Lasky Studios in Los Angeles, one August day in 1915, to drive to San Francisco. That same day, a film crew arrived there after a four-month drive along the Lincoln Highway from New York. They had been shooting film for the Lincoln Highway publicity people. Their arrival was part of a Highway Day Celebration.

A 365-foot-long relief model of the Lincoln route had been placed in the Panama-Pacific Palace of Transportation. Anita King arrived after a 17-hour, overnight, drive. Publicity about her forthcoming attempt to travel the whole route along the Highway to the East had been intense, thanks to film studio publicity people and the Lincoln Highway promoters. After a few days' rest, King set off on her journey. Daily bulletins of her progress were arranged. Little flags were added to the relief map as news of her day-by-day position arrived. She was successful, arriving in New York after a 49-day journey (see weblist: Anita King).

There were other named roads including the Roosevelt International from Portland Maine to Portland Oregon, and the Dixie Highways, a series of interconnected roads from Michigan to Florida. The Yellowstone Trail started as an attempt to get a local road built between two places in South Dakota. Within a month of its original conception in 1912, it was being promoted as a coast-to-coast route running through the Northern States.

The sponsoring Yellowstone Trails Association issued a route map in 1914. It was something of a pious hope at that stage. James Akerman quotes text on the map that the sponsors needed help, as they were "lacking in accurate information and data ... We would appreciate several logs and ask those making the run to mark on a map the exact distance between towns as shown by the speedometer, and forward such maps to us" (Akerman, 2006:175).

Sinclair Lewis's *Free Air* (1919) was one of the first novels based on a road trip. Its heroine, Clair Boltwood, is the daughter of a prosperous railway supplies businessman. He overworks consistently. Claire "wanted to travel, but her father could never get away" (Lewis, 1922:11). Then he collapses from nervous exhaustion. Claire manages to get him to agree to her driving the family roadster to Seattle. It is a journey full of adventures with the car and the roads, but most of all becomes the romantic story of her leaving behind their business society for marriage with a motor mechanic.

This young man helps rescue them from the tribulations of travelling by car before accidentally-on-purpose following behind to the coast. *Free Air* symbolises her escape from an urban life to adventures in the open country, from a railroad world to a motor car world. Claire's pioneering spirit harks back to the 19th century, but showed it can offer people, especially women, the chance to seek the excitement of discoveries in the 20th century.

Steven Parissien thinks the automobile was so influential in tourism that it "revolutionised holidays – indeed, it almost created them." (2013:99). Historians of holidays would disagree, but for individual families in the early 20th century it was often true. If they could afford a car, it opened up possibilities that had never existed before. And they may have been expressing tribal cultures – at least, according to one trade journal. In 1929, the British *Autocar* magazine rather pompously claimed that "Public transport, no matter how fast and comfortable, inflicts a sensation of serfdom which is intolerable to a free Briton. It dictates the time of starting, the route, the speed and the stoppages" (in O'Connell, 2007:120). Car ownership was growing. A whole new infrastructure had to grow with it. A selection of the innovations to feed it on both sides of the Atlantic gives a taste of the changes:

The idea of white lines along road centres publicised in the USA: 'stay to the right of the line'; 1883. First used in Trenton, MI in 1917.
First multi-storey car park in London: Wardour St, with five floors, 1906
First UK roadside petrol pumps: Shrewsbury, 1915
First UK filling station built: Aldermaston, 1919
First drive-in restaurant, Jesse G Kirby's Pig Stand, Dallas, 1921 (pork sandwiches delivered to people in their cars - by 'carhops')
First motel in France is shown at the 1925 Paris Exposition: the Halte-Relais Hôtel
First motel in California, in San Luis Obispo, 1926
Drive-in movie theatre, Camden, New Jersey 1933 (there were some earlier experiments)
First elevated road in Britain: the Silvertown Way, London, 1934
Cat's Eye markers for road centre lines invented in Halifax, UK: 1934
(Sources: Margolies & Gwathmey 1991, Moran 2010, Parissean 2013, Petroski 2016; Wikipedia)

Thomas Dowler Murphy was an American who found touring Britain by automobile a pleasant way to spend a summer in Europe. It was in 1907. Having made a previous trip through the country by train, "Imprisoned in a dusty and comfortless first-class apartment – first-class is an irony in England when applied to rail travel, a mere excuse for charging double", he and his partner chose to bring their automobile over for the next trip. Writing his account of the tour in a book published the following year, he reported that driving was much superior: "This method of touring will give opportunities for enjoyment and gaining actual knowledge of the people and country that can hardly be attained in any other way" (Murphy, 1908:5).

Besides the appearance of new roads, new cars and everything that serviced them, the effects were already being felt in traditional industries. Sean O'Connell writes: "One estimate of the impact of this new trend suggests that during the 1930s Devonshire farmers derived up to 75% of their income by providing teas and accommodation to newly mobile holidaymakers." (O'Connell' 2007:120). There were cultural, social and educational effects, too: an anonymous contributor to *Harper's* magazine in late 1920s America wrote that "ten cars in a row may bear the plates of five different states ... The filling station is a rare spot, in a country of magnificent distances, for the cross-pollination of ideas" (Flowers & Wynn Jones, 1981:131). It echoed what Thomas Dowler Murphy had predicted in his 1908 book.

Critics of cars in the countryside soon began to make themselves heard in Britain. The philosopher, C E M Joad, would be an influential panel member of the BBC's *Brains Trust* from 1941. He was a frequent critic of the motor car. He called a set of motor cars interrupting a ramble a "pack of fiends released from the nethermost pit" (in O'Connell, 2007). Howard Marshall in *Britain and the Beast* – the Beast being uncontrolled urbanisation – wrote that "Beauty is sacrificed on the altar of the speeding motorist. Advertisements and petrol stations and shanties ruin our villages" (Marshall, 1938:164).

Aldous Huxley observed a powerful sports car treating Italian mountain hair-pin bends like a race-track: "It came up after us, like a wild beast pursuing its prey, bellowing ... It disappeared, carrying with it a load of hatred, envy and mixed uncharitable-ness of every variety" (Huxley, 1925:13). It has to be said that Huxley had become a car enthusiast after having bought his first car. In describing the encounters in Italy with the 'wild beast', - an Alfa Romeo – he admitted he envied it.

A love/hate relationship with motor cars was blossoming between the two World Wars. This was quite different from what had happened with trains, trams and motor buses, first because cars were private possessions and often considered as part of the family. Second, because they offered the potential for the family to have fun by making their own expeditions and discoveries.

"There was an explosion in car ownership [in Britain]. In 1918 there had been no more than 100,000 private motor cars but by 1939 there were two million.   Cars were at first a leisure accessory rather than a means of business conveyance.   Early motoring magazines focused not on cars but where to drive them, as the car took people to places inaccessible by railway and even motor bus" (Thurley, 2013).

It was all very well, but in an age long before satnavs, the motorist needed help to get to those special places.

A marker on the Lincoln Highway: Valparaiso, Indiana

Chapter 9

Helping the Motorist Find the Way

The difference between the origins of USA mapping and, for example, French and British mapping, is major. Both European countries set out strategies at central government level to map their whole territories. The French were much the earliest and visionary. Jean-Baptiste Colbert, minister-in-chief to King Louis XIV, established the Paris Observatory and the Académie Royale des Sciences in 1666. They were to advance the art and science of map-making, producing maps of France to encourage commerce, develop transport links and support military activities. Two members of the famous Cassini family, César-François and his son Jean-Dominique, guided the surveying of France in detail. Field teams used geodetic triangulation with theodolites ^(Withers, 2008) between 1756 and 1789. 181 sheets formed the published versions which were completed by 1815. Napoleon Bonaparte initiated a new survey in 1808 for a version suitable for battlefield use.

Britain's Ordnance Survey had its beginnings in military requirements. King George II agreed to the mapping of the Scottish Highlands in 1747. This was the result of the army needing to deal with Jacobite dissenters after the Battle of Culloden the previous year. Proposals for a survey of the whole of Britain were turned down on grounds of expense, but the French Revolution in 1789 raised fears of domestic unrest coupled with a possible French invasion. The Master of the Board of Ordnance was the 3rd Duke of Richmond, Charles Lennox, controlling military resources and supplies. Lennox initiated the Ordnance Survey in 1791 with precision methods carried out by newly appointed expert surveyors. They worked on what has been known as the Principal Triangulation of Great Britain, completed in 1853. While the maps made were primarily for military purposes, their usefulness for general development and, later, leisure, was obvious even then.

Part of the success of the Ordnance Survey was its use of a marketing strategy (see Owen & Pilbeam, 1992). It published maps at different scales by 1851. Large-scale maps were used by central and local government departments while others, notably the 1-inch to one-mile maps, were popular with the general public. The ¼ inch to one-mile map, which would be available for the whole country in its second edition by 1918, had begun preparation in 1859. The First Edition of the 1880s was criticised for both its standards and its design. In later editions, it would become a useful map for the general motorist and for a map-minded armchair public. Getting a government agency to act in a successful commercial way took time, but from the 1920s onwards it was becoming much more competent.

Map production in Britain has had a long history going back to Tudor strip maps and county surveys by specialist producers. One such general cartographer was John Cary (1754-1835) who was based in the Strand, London (Hewitt, 2010). His globes, atlases and regional maps at a scale of 1 inch to five miles gained him a solid reputation. This led to the Postmaster General commissioning him in 1794 to survey all the major roads of England and Wales. Another well-known business would be that of John Bartholomew & Son Ltd, founded in 1826 out of the practice first established by his father, George. The company was a rival of the Ordnance Survey but also enjoyed a friendly relationship. When competition led to disputes, they were usually sorted out before getting to court hearings (Owen & Pilbeam, 1992).

The Ordnance Survey reached the World War I as a successful agency. It coped with the many new demands placed upon it, which included having to have teams of surveyors working in France and Belgium. They mapped trench positions and supported the allied artillery by rapidly printing perhaps 10,000 copies of newly surveyed maps within as little as one week at the Southampton Headquarters. 32,872,000 maps, plans and diagrams were supplied during the war (Owen & Pilbeam, 1992:92).

Major wars have strong influences on the growth of tourism, though the world would be a far better place without the horrors that wars inflict. They alter human relationships and political geography while raising the awareness of places and almost certainly introducing new developments such as those in transport and communications. From World War I came aerial bombardment of cities, but soon after 1918, aeroplane development led to innovations in air passenger transport using converted bombers. Most forms of road transport were improved, but railways were overstretched as we saw in Chapter 4 and there were few technological advancements. The stresses of war on every mode of transport were made worse by the economic decline that rapidly followed.

The Ordnance Survey played its part supporting the national efforts, but it, too, was hit by the economic crisis. Staff had to leave, map revision schedules were slowed and new ways of raising commercial income had to be found. The need for selling more maps to the public revolutionised popular understanding of its work. In the long term, it led to marketing successes and helped to encourage outdoor activities, landscape awareness and every tourist industry. American production of popular maps was left to the commercial interests. British mapping was adopting the 'inform, educate and entertain' strategy discussed in Chapter 1. Greater topographic detail in new maps supplied information, their attractive design and usage entertained people and helped educate them. The information they contained about roads, railways, canals and ports in relation to centres of population was the solid foundation of the transport networks. It shaped economic life and showed the way to new developments in leisure tourism.

The Ordnance Survey appointed two salespeople, known officially as 'map travellers', from amongst men returning from the war (Owen & Pilbeam, 1992). At the start they had to use first class rail transport with a taxi into town centres, after which they visited potential retailers on foot. There were some problems at first in getting new orders delivered to the shops, but these were slowly overcome and after a while the salesmen were even supplied with cars. Equally important was the choice of another ex-serviceman, Ellis Martin, as a designer. He had worked with the newly created Tank Corps in making sketch maps of marshy ground to warn drivers of heavy transport what to avoid. Before the war he designed railway posters and other items for W H Smith's bookstalls. Martin became a full-time artist with the Ordnance Survey and indeed, the only one. Others would be men employed in OS departments like Arthur Palmer from the Photo-Writing Department who was brought in part-time to design more covers.

Martin's work was to design covers for maps and material to help at points-of-sale. His drawing of a cyclist sat on a hillside with an unfolded map became a classic illustration, executed in black linework on a pale-yellow background. Others followed that were in sunny outdoor colours. Owen and Pilbeam record his "flair and sheer artistic skill ... his work was the embodiment of that strange era of intense leisure pursuit which existed between the wars" (p100). The paintings and sketches of Martin, Palmer, J C T Willis and others evoke nostalgia and calm in a way much needed after the carnage of the 1914-18 war. Today the covers are mainly adorned with glossy, full colour photographs which stand comparison with the guidebook covers usually displayed nearby. Those of the '20s and '30s have an idyllic, gentler, artistic appeal (see Browne, 1991).

Meanwhile, John Bartholomew & Son continued to design and publish both sheet maps and road atlases for British users. From their base in Edinburgh they published the *Atlas of Scotland* for the Royal Scottish Geographical Society in 1895. Twenty-seven years later came the *Times Survey Atlas of the World* for the newspaper company in a partnership which continued into the 21st century. Bartholomew's became famous for large-scale maps including the Half-Inch to One-mile series of 62 sheets that covered the whole of Great Britain.

It should be noted that maps are never purely impartial. They take a selective view of the ground they represent and can deliberately affect the map-reader's quest. Only a few relevant features can be shown, by using symbols. The question, which features are relevant, means that someone will be controlling what the reader is to be shown. A stark example is Bartholomew's *Contour Motoring Map of the British Isles* (1907), which was aimed at leisure motorists and showed an inset map of 'industrial areas to avoid' (Moran, 2010:57; O'Connell, 1998). At a more prosaic level, Ordnance Survey maps do not, for example, show official Conservation Areas or the periods of buildings. They no longer show

149

the interior layouts of certain buildings as they did with early large-scale maps. More recently, they stopped showing woodland as coniferous, deciduous or mixed, as they once did. Where road junctions are given a certain amount of detail to help drivers, they have to be drawn bigger than their true scale. Cartographers have to prioritise the features they can consider including in crowded areas, missing out some that would be shown in other situations.

An Emporium of Maps

One of the world's great map retailers is the firm of Edward Stanford in London. Yet they are more than sellers of maps; they have been an important publisher of maps. Maps had been sold in London for decades. In the half century to 1719, the London Gazette published advertisements for over four hundred map sellers who existed at one time or other in that period (Garfield, 2012). Stanford had begun his career in 1852 when he was accepted as a partner in the existing business of Trelawney Saunders in Charing Cross. Within a few months Saunders handed the business to Stanford entirely. It may have been a pre-planned arrangement to allow Saunders to move on into semi-retirement (Whitfield, 2003). The two men collaborated in later projects. Trelawney Saunders became the librarian and map curator of the Royal Geographical Society, which would have been an excellent contact for Edward Stanford. Saunders had been a seller of maps. Stanford became a publisher of them. He had been for a while an apprentice printer but had no skills in map-making, which was the field of the Ordnance Survey or commercial interests.

Having realised through the Trelawney Saunders shop that there was a demand for maps, he concluded better money could be made by publishing them as well. He bought the printing plates and the remaining map stock of the Society for the Diffusion of Useful Knowledge, which had ceased publishing in 1848. By selling atlases, individual maps (9d (≈£3) coloured) and map selections, Stanford built his business. The first map collection was of 29 in an atlas for Harrow School (Whitfield 2003).

The Ordnance Survey completed its First Series 1" to 1-mile maps of England and Wales on 1 January 1870, eighty years after those maps were first ordered to be made. Rachel Hewitt notes that 150 agents across Britain were selling the maps by 1870, while six publishers in London, Edinburgh and Dublin, including Stanford, sold them in their own shops. A comment was made at the Paris Exposition of 1868 that the Ordnance Survey mapping on show there "is a work without precedent and should be taken as a model by every civilised nation" (in Hewitt, 2010). Hewitt writes "by 1870, English and Welsh citizens owned a lifelike cartographical mirror of their countries, whose sheets were then retailing at the modest price of 2s..6d" (≈£7.83). It would have been more accurate to say they "might have owned" since 2s..6d was beyond the available buying power of most people then, and the set of 108 map sheets covering their countries would have come in at over £13. That would have taken a skilled tradesman of 1870 some 65 days to earn. Still, most buyers would only have wanted one or two maps and the half-a-crown price was not a bad investment for something useful for years. If they could read it.

Stanford's business expanded, thanks to the expertise and care with which they looked after their customers. Among these were government departments, prominent individuals such as Florence Nightingale and John Ruskin and ordinary members of the public. Ruskin, like William Wordsworth, indirectly helped to build tourism through writing about the attractiveness of travel, from the Lake District to mainland Europe. It is one of the great ironies, therefore, that both men retreated into elitist positions after raising interest in such places. They objected to the railways which started to democratise travel. Ruskin wrote to Stanford's in 1887, asking for an atlas – "without railways in its maps ... Of all the entirely odd stupidities of modern education, railroads in maps are the infinitely oddest to my mind" (Whitfield, 2003:21). William Wordsworth claimed members of the working classes did not have the capacity to appreciate the rural beauty of the Lake District.

Stanford's bought out Murray's Handbooks in 1910 but sold that popular business to James and Findlay Muirhead only five years later (Garfield, 2012). They became map publishers on a large scale, besides being retailers and wholesalers. Peter Whitfield describes Stanford's own output as offering

"a rich and detailed picture of the Victorian world – of political changes, geographical exploration, colonial affairs and patterns of travel. All these maps were published for fundamentally the same reason: to satisfy public interest ... There is no doubt that Stanford was more strongly drawn to political mapping than to physical or scientific mapping. There was no counterpart in Stanford's output to the graphic presentation of physical geography which was typical of the new German school of cartography" (Whitfield, 2003:46).

As far as the general map-reading public was concerned, Stanford's maps were like accessories to newspaper reports. They showed places that were being described in press reports as explorers and armies, traders and tourists, moved across the globe. Theatres of war from the Crimea to Afghanistan were mapped with details of troop deployments and movements. Competing European colonies in Africa and the growth of the British Empire were laid out for the public's instruction. To help spread knowledge in family homes and public reading-rooms, the firm began to supply 'map screens', display units designed in the style of popular folding room dividers onto which maps could be hung. Flat maps were supplied to schools, colleges and government offices for wall mounting. Britain was not ignored. Stanford's produced map atlases of London, maps of the River Thames and atlases of counties showing economic production, parliamentary divisions etc.

George Philip & Son Ltd

The business set up by the Scotsman, George Philip (1800-1882), in Liverpool, had parallels to that of Edward Stanford, but was aimed more at the schools and colleges market. In due course, 1947, it would take over the Stanford business though the two would separate in 2001. Philips still exists, though at the time of writing is part of Hachette Livre. George Philip was born in Aberdeenshire, but moved to Liverpool, aged 19, where his brother was a nonconformist minister. Philip found employment in a city bookselling business. In 1834 he branched out on his own as bookseller and stationer. He added the publishing of books and maps and a wide range of educational goods and materials. His son, George Jr, daughter Jane and nephew Thomas Dash Philip all worked in the business.

George Philip used work by leading engravers to produce maps on copper plates from which he printed monochrome sheets. These were then hand coloured by his own staff. By using people like John Bartholomew Jr., one of the leading cartographers of the time, to supply the engravings, he ensured high quality. Bartholomew had spent time with the German cartographer, August Petermann, who in turn had been influenced by Alexander von Humboldt, the immensely important German explorer and cartographer. Four generations of Bartholomews studied with German map makers. The quality of their work thus flowed through to George Philip, enhancing not only Philip's published maps of newly surveyed places such as Northern Canada, but his atlases, being used by government departments and educational institutions. Britain trailed Germany in the teaching of geography in the years before the World War I. However, the work of the Ordnance Survey in mapping and then supplying maps through high street bookshops, combined with popular travel by rail, hiking and bicycling, and increasing use of geographical studies in schools, produced a new national culture of exploration after 1914-18.

Early United States' strip maps

The first road atlas in the USA had taken the form of a series of ribbon or strip maps describing the road from Philadelphia to Annapolis, Maryland, in 1789. It required a book of 83 plates, each of which showed three segments of the route. The cartographer/publisher was Christopher Colles. He had little interest in showing anything more than the roads to follow, indicating some of the landmarks that could be seen from the roads. Often, just a line of tree symbols by the route showed the existence of woodlands. Thirteen years later, S S Moore and T W Jones produced a better strip map, for the road from Philadelphia to Washington DC (Rumsey & Punt, 2004). It was a leather-bound, pocket-size atlas, neater in appearance and shown with side turnings labelled to other destinations. Towns were indicated by a few symbolic rows and columns of squares representing buildings.

Mathew Carey published a second edition in 1804 under the title *The Traveller's Directory, or, A Pocket Companion Shewing the Course of the Main Road from Philadelphia to New York and from Philadelphia to Washington* (Rumsey & Punt, 2004). Rivers and canals appeared and there were "descriptions of the places through which [the route] passes ... illustrated with an account of such remarkable objects as are generally interesting to travellers". Mapping the route was still diagrammatic. Strip maps reoriented winding roads into vertical columns, so the important Compass North indicator was seldom at the top of the columns. *The Traveller's Directory* boasted it was made "from actual survey", though that information was only concerned with the roads and immediate vicinities.

Roads were important, but so were navigable rivers. Coloney, Fairchild & Co of St Louis published a ribbon map of the Mississippi in 1866. It covered the river's length of 2,600 miles from Lake Itaska in Minnesota to the Gulf of Mexico. The ribbon map was not in the book form that strip maps usually occupied. It took the form of a printed series of seven-centimetre-wide sections, joined into a single, three-metre-long roll, wound into a paper-covered holder by a small handle. On the part-coloured ribbon were shown features important for river-boat captains – towns, landings, tributaries (including the Ohio River) stagecoach roads and landmarks to help navigation. A revised edition of a now-lost earlier version, it had much information about towns along the river supplied by William Bowen, President of the Pilot's Association of St Louis (weblist: Rumsey).

There were few clues as to the nature of the wider topography through which the traveller passed on either road or river strip maps. These were maps targetted at travellers with narrowly defined requirements. General reference maps to be used by all kinds of customers from armchair browsers to professional planners would come about from specialist agencies.

Drivers needed information once they ventured beyond the familiar territory of home. Unlike in Britain, where Ordnance Survey maps with huge detail could be bought relatively easily, in the USA most give-away maps showed cities and railroads with little else. Bicycle clubs had combined to form the League of American Wheelmen in 1880, and it became an important pressure group. Some map publishers were pressed to make available maps showing roads and topography, since knowing where steep hills threatened riders with great exertion was important. As the twentieth century got under way the rapid growth of car ownership by better-off citizens created a new market. In 1900 there were only eight thousand automobiles in the USA: by 1913, there were 1,190,393 (weblist: US transport). Map producers began to overprint their stock rail maps with roads in a contrasting colour (see Yorke & Margolies,1996).

A different approach was to supply guidebooks describing where to go, which route to follow, and where to turn left or right or go straight on. One of these was the work of *The Automobile,* a popular new US magazine. In 1901 it issued the *Official Automobile Blue Book* with four maps and guidance on 'blue routes' – the best to take between cities, with details of major hills and gas stations. It became an annual production. From 1906, it appeared in conjunction with the Automobile Club of America, covering the nation in a series of leather-bound volumes. The 1907 Section 2 book was devoted to New England, for example (Class Journal Co, 1907). In almost five hundred pages it showed city maps and used ribbon maps to depict key routes. These were then described, eg on page 36 (retaining the original spelling and punctuation):

"Poughkeepsie to Danbury, Connecticut – 45 miles

An important thorofare between the Middle Hudson River and western Connecticut: fair-to-good running except for about thirteen miles between Stormville and Carmel. Heavy grades and rough narrow roads on this portion, including over a mile climb (East and Southbound) over the

"Mountains" after leaving Stormville. However, the Blue Book car made this ascent without difficulty in December 1906, and we do not consider it a bar to the trip. From hotel or garage take the most convenient streets into Hooker Ave (trolleys). Follow car-tracks, winding past Hudson River Stock Farm (on right), 1½ miles out; just beyond (where trolleys turn left for Vassar College), keep straight ahead on good road".

The journeys needed the work of both drivers and navigators by the look of those instructions.

The *Blue Books* also carried advertisements for hotels, inns, garages and car accessories. There were details of the requirements of each state and the "principle European countries" regarding variations in legal requirements. American States had different laws regarding automobiles, for example the need to be registered for Connecticut, which might have made crossing State lines present problems. The speed limits in Connecticut were 12 mph (19.3 kph) in cities and 15 mph (24.1 kph) in the country, whereas Massachusetts allowed 20 mph (32.1 kph) in rural areas, but all curves and intersections had limits of 8 mph (12.8 kph).

Later guides had photographs replacing sections of text, with arrows and captions overprinted for directions. The pioneering example was published by H Sargent Michaels in 1905, a $5 (≈$114) collection of 350 photographs with notes showing the route from Chicago to New York: good, but expensive.

Rand McNally had produced the first maps to help cyclists in 1894. Ten years later they printed the first automobile map of New York city. Having taken over H Sargent Michaels in 1910, Rand McNally issued their own photographic route guides, as we will shortly see. Other maps, by other publishers, were quick to follow [Yorke etc, 1996]. Finally, after World War I, as the federal and state governments began to produce numbered roads, the first route maps appeared. Some were strip maps like those of Tudor cartographers in Britain. Others were road maps of selected areas or whole states, given away by gasoline suppliers or sold by companies such as Rand McNally, the General Drafting Company or H M Gousha.

On the Move

United States Geological Survey

The near-equivalent of the British Ordnance Survey and the French *Institut National de l'Information Géographique et Forestière* is the United States Geological Survey (USGS), founded in 1879. As noted earlier, its brief was wide. It was not, unlike the Ordnance Survey, given the single job of producing a topographic map of the country. It never served the touring public directly in the way that the Ordnance Survey did. US companies such as Rand McNally & Co fulfilled that role, working from USGS data. The clue, of course, is in the name. The Act of Congress of 1879 gave it the responsibility for "the classification of the public lands, and examination of the geological structure, mineral resources, and products of the national domain" (weblist USGS1).

Military reasons – and staff – drove the early Ordnance Survey. 'Ordnance' referred to artillery and the government department controlling its logistics. The Ordnance Survey was given the job of mapping the whole of the British Isles – Ireland was entirely within its remit in those pre-Republic days. It worked on a landscape that was already known, at least topographically. It was therefore making a map – a series of maps – with a high level of accuracy. Each presented a snapshot of its district which might be undergoing change but was otherwise relatively established as part of the nation. Its character had been largely decided, so the Ordnance people were mapping the result.

The American situation was different. Much of the Western half of the country was generally unknown or little known in 1879. The Federal Government (and the nation) did not know what existed in much of its Western States. There were still major changes as the century-old nation continued to absorb places once in French or Spanish hands, with continued reorganisation of what had been Native American lands. The early surveys had to explore and then aid the Federal and State legislatures in deciding who would now own the land. It required great detail, allocating farming, ranching, mineral extraction, forestry activities, town and city development, transport networks and more over vast areas. The country was in the early stages of recovery after a destructive Civil War. The old South and the old North needed reconciliation while the new West had to be integrated within the post-War situation. These things impacted on tourism as US citizens explored and began to exploit their new opportunities, both as travellers on business and at leisure. To benefit from what the nation had decided would be its Manifest Destiny would require, in a very literal sense, the road maps that the USGS would be producing and which were of more use than the simple strip maps of roads.

156

Economic reasons drove the American organisation – mineral and water resources primarily, but in addition the composition and underlying structure of the rocks that configured the landscape and its character. The latter helped to determine settlement and infrastructure patterns such as transport networks, and that meant the surveys of the USGS provided information so important to the development of tourism. The Survey Agency took on, from 1926, the supervision of oil and mining operations on land leased from the Federal Government. Operational functions like these have never been part of the Ordnance Survey's brief. Four surveys had been at work in the USA before 1879, either in the field or in their offices preparing the maps. Setting up the USGS brought existing survey work under the one organisation. Its mapping developed in many ways, turning out thematic maps on geology and water resources and topographic maps showing landforms, settlement, transport networks, water features and the like, similar to Britain's Ordnance Survey.

Cartographica Extraordinaire by Rumsey and Punt [(2004)] is a treasure-trove of information about mapping the USA. The surveys carried out before the USGS was formed were ambitious and skilful. The authors pick out work by John C Fremont and Charles Preuss with their *Topographical Map of the Road from Missouri to Oregon* of 1846. 'Road' meant route in this case, although the map had been drawn with a double line looking to us like a well surfaced road. "Fremont's second expedition produced seven sequential maps, which collectively could be considered America's first traveller's maps". They contained "descriptive excerpts from Fremont's reports, a commentary of the Continental Divide, and practical information such as water, fuel, game availability; and tables of meteorological observations for emigrants travelling westwards in their footsteps". (Rumsey & Punt, 2004:28).

Another example shows how the early surveyors benefitted both resource exploration and tourism. The army engineers of the USA had surveyed the best route for the Transcontinental Railroad opened in 1869. One of the leading surveyors of the day, Clarence King, had suggested what the best rail route should be. King was an accomplished mountaineer, spent time learning field geology with the California Geological Survey and later surveyed the rim of the Yosemite Valley. He persuaded Congress to appoint him as geologist to a survey wanted by the Federal government along the Fortieth Parallel. The Transcontinental Railroad had opened, joining tracks laid by the Central Pacific and Union Pacific companies, meeting in the State of Utah. It not only brought the West Coast into contact with the Middle and Eastern US states; it presented many opportunities for developments along its route. Clarence

King spent ten years mapping a swathe of territory a hundred miles wide and several hundred miles long that contained the railroad, from the Rockies to the Nevada Basin. He used up to date surveying techniques and drew the maps using similarly innovative methods. These included rejecting the cruder hachuring used to show mountain slopes in favour of brush-stroking that gave much subtler results (Rumsey & Punt, 2004). He was an excellent choice as the first head of the USGS on its formation in 1879.

It is useful to summarise the nature of the work of the USGS to show how different it was from that of the Ordnance Survey. The US organisation developed different series of topographic maps, from County to State and National Park series, at various scales, today ranging from 1:24,000 to 1:1,000,000. Most USGS maps became based on quadrangles defined by two lines of latitude and two of longitude. So-called 7.5-minute maps used lines 7.5 minutes of latitude and longitude apart; 15-minute maps at those 15-minute measures apart. The stock would run to millions of maps, all to be updated periodically. A surprising feature of the maps still is that they can be very out of date as a result of the workload imposed by the tasks in hand. For example, I bought, online – now the usual method of purchase – in 2001, large-scale maps of the Disney World area in Florida to use in degree teaching. The resort was not shown, even years after it opened in 1971. On the other hand, the scale, scope and quality of the United States Geological Survey mapping, as each is completed, is high, ambitious and valuable.

Rand McNally & Co

Prominent among mapping companies in the USA, Rand McNally & Co had its origins in the railway hub of Chicago. William Rand had opened a printing works in 1856. He was joined by Andrew McNally in 1858. The following year saw the men taken on to run the printing works of the *Chicago Tribune*. 1868 saw them set up Rand McNally & Co, buying the *Tribune*'s printing business and printing timetables and tickets for railroads serving the city. Business directories, a weekly newspaper and a Business Atlas of North America were added within a short space of time. Educational maps, globes and textbooks expanded the output, with general book titles from 1884. We have already mentioned their first road map of New York City, published in 1904. Such maps would be a mainstay of their cartographic output, and still are today.

An excellent overview of the range of maps made by Rand McNally can be had by looking over the website of the David Rumsey Historical Map Collection (davidrumsey.com). It is free to view and contains thousands of maps that can be examined in detail. The collection covers national mapping agency work of several countries as published at different dates. There are atlases included as well as thematic maps and large-scale examples. Rand McNally work spans US State maps of the 19th century, Perry's Mining Map of West Kootenay, British Columbia (1893) with broad details of the landscape marked with words such as gneiss, schists, galena, copper etc, to a total eclipse of the sun poster-map advertising a New Haven Railway excursion programme (1932).

Other examples that were specifically aimed at tourists included Rand McNally's *Official Auto Trail Maps* and *Auto Road Maps*. They covered two or three states at a time. They often carried a standard image of a Native American drawing a horse, rider and arrows on a rock face, as if giving directions. On a road below him is seen an open-topped automobile with tourists. The booklet-map carried advertisements for gasoline, motor oil and hotels along with route maps of the region and city centres. Guidebook entries described the cities. As was often the case with US road maps, they showed merely city locations connected by networks of straight or curved lines representing the highways, with relevant mileages for the distances between centres.

An interesting series of guides for automobile drivers was that of the *Photo-Auto Guides* invented by G S Chapin and sold by H Sargent Michaels to Rand McNally in 1910 (Akerman, 2006). These were books of photographs taken at every road intersection along chosen routes, printed four to a double page spread, with arrows added to indicate the turns the driver had to make (weblist: Rand McNally). Andrew McNally II took the photos for the Chicago-to-Milwaukee guide while on his honeymoon. The books were innovative but not ultimately an easy publishing deal. The Chicago-New York and back guide needed 796 photos. Frequent photo-updates were needed as landmarks were replaced or routes were redesigned. Drivers really needed a passenger to handle the guide and announce the necessary turns, as was the case with the *Blue Guide*-type of production mentioned earlier. Yet the books answered a demand every auto user had for detailed guidance on how to get from one place to another.

For more detail on USGS maps, see weblist: USGS2.

On the Move

Attempts at Auto-Navigation

The basic principle by which navigation aids could be made more automatic, freeing the driver or passenger from handling a guidebook, was suggested by a US patent obtained in 1880. Surveyors had long used measuring devices to check road distances. They used a long handle to push or pull a wheel along the ground and a simple, geared, mechanism indicated the distance moved. The Ancient Greek and Ancient Chinese surveyors used them, and modern automobiles have mechanical or electronic versions known as odometers, from the Greek *hodos* ('way') and *métron* ('measure'). Britain, and other anglophone countries, traditionally used the term 'milometer'. From the principle of a wheel driving a meter it was a relatively simple step to make a device driving not a meter but a scrolling public display.

The American, William Johnson, proposed an automatic railroad car indicator which would show passengers their train's current location [Monmonier, 2017]. It suggested a canvas scroll inscribed with the names of the stops along the train's route. The scroll was to be fitted into a box displaying one name at a time, placed at the end of the passenger car and large enough to be easily read by customers. A series of rods and gears was to connect the scroll's feed and take-up spools down to the nearest railroad carriage axle. Carefully calculated spacing of the names along the scroll would make it show each stop as it was reached. It would have been possible to display paid-for shop names related to the stops as they were approached. The Johnson idea effectively cut out the human being in the vehicle-to-display operation. If applied to the automobile, that meant freeing the driver from doing more than glancing at a display unit. It would be decades before it could come to reality, and even then the 'glance' would be a long one.

Two US patents were granted in 1909 to different versions of route guide. One was to Frank Lindenthaler and John Protz for their 'Route Indicator for Automobiles'. A punched paper roll held in a metal box would be linked by an odometer cable to an automobile wheel. A chosen route would have been shown in strip form on the paper roll, advanced automatically as the automobile moved along. At the edge of the roll were small holes relating to each part of the journey. As the roll reached the appropriate point, the hole allowed electric contacts to meet, sounding a bell to warn the driver of next instruction. Mark Monmonier claims one intention was to deskill chauffers' jobs to save money – "an early warning of deskilling as a consequence of automation" – rather than having to employ men well versed in knowledge of route details [(2017:71)]. Auto owners would also be able to make their own paper strips – even sell them. But Monmonier has not found any evidence to say the inventors ever exploited their proposal commercially.

The second device was William Jones's 'Live-Map Meter' of 1909. It, too, operated automatically, this time from the auto's odometer. The driver had a kind of turntable in a holder to which he attached a celluloid disc. This carried instructions about the route round its edge. The disc was placed so the starting point – usually the nearest city centre – was against a pointer. As the vehicle moved, so the disc turned, very slowly. Each disc carried up to a hundred miles of instructions. After that, a new disc with the next required details had to replace the older one. The Touring Club of America compiled the route information and sold the celluloid discs from 1912 onwards. William Jones was the Club's Director. His company made the discs, which by 1919 were available for more than 500 routes.

The *Saturday Evening Post* carried an advertisement claiming that "To have it with you is like having a man in your car who knows every road, every corner, every crossing, every landmark, every puzzling fork and crossroad in the entire world" [(Nilsson, 2012:np)]. Even allowing for the exaggeration of the last four words, Monmonier's point about the expense of such a man is very understandable. On the other hand, chauffeurs cleaned the cars, did the driving, ran errands in the cars, kept an eye on necessary repairs and were status symbols. Automatic route guides could not replace those things.

The problem was, once again, changes on the routes, making the discs out of date and impossible to use. The Jones Live-Map went out of production sometime in the 1920s.

The 'long glance' needed to read the Live-Map must have proved a problem at times. Drivers probably stopped on more than one occasion to read the disc or relate the instruction given to the view around. George Boyden's 1916 'Vehicle Signalling' system attempted to do away with the need to read in favour of listening. He proposed a phonograph on the dashboard with a loudspeaker playing the instructions in response to the odometer reading of the distance travelled [(Monmonier, 2017, 2018)]. The idea of a phonograph working happily as the automobile bounced along the poor roads of the day was a brave one. It was never put into production.

On the Move

By the 1920s there were not only plentiful maps available – and for free if they were given away by oil companies – but motoring organisations tailored instruction cards in response to motorists' enquiries. The American Automobile Association, known as Triple-A, was formed in 1902 and began to issue road maps in 1905. In 1937 it launched 'Triptiks', a title that was a play on the name of the 'triptyque' temporary import permit issued in many European countries.

State automobile clubs supplied their own route planners tailored to the needs of individual enquirers. These were based on simple advisory cards prepared for chosen routes, just as the Live-Map discs had been. The Automobile Club of Michigan, for example, had supplied a card 9"x7¾" (22.8cm x 19.5cm) , folded once into a tall, narrow, pocket format. The four panels listed the US Route number, the distance of each junction reached from the start and the instruction to be followed. A 1934 example for Cleveland, OH to Harrisburg, PA ("327 miles-All Paved-65 miles Macadam-Balance Concrete") showed at 53.3 miles out "MECCA, keep right halfway around traffic diamond and continue ahead with State Road No 88". The card was printed by letterpress, presumably because it was in high demand. Other examples were prepared by typewriter and probably run off on an office duplicator. It was a reminder that nascent tourism businesses depended on the development of small office services as well as great highways and expensive automobiles.

The Triple-A's Triptik, folder was more ambitious. It had strip maps with additions like rivers as landmarks. In due course, towns were described in brief paragraphs while facilities like hotels, motels, restaurants and service stations were listed with indications of prices. Information about speed limits and homilies about safe driving were added. Front covers carried the name of the Triple-A member who had requested the guide, hand-written and with the name of the Travel Consultant shown. The latter might have assembled the guide from standard route sections to make up the whole thing while the customer waited. Due regard would have been used by the Consultant to the preferences and interests of the member by choosing route sections as appropriate. Road maps were marked with the exact highways to be used shown with an inked line. The pages were bound in card covers to make the finished guide. Each was a little bigger than the cards that the Automobile Club of Michigan had issued (see image on p172).

Signs of the Times

The pre-motor car world had roads designed for walkers and wagons making short journeys, and with stagecoaches moving from one inn to another. Roadside information gave the distance from one town and the distance to the next in the shape of a milepost. Some of them therefore solved the question of which of two or three routes should be taken to the required destination. They were usually made of stone pillars or blocks set at heights for the walker to read. There were examples of wooden posts, much higher, with finger-boards to show directions. A UK example exists in replica form on the modern A44/B4081 junction near Broadway in Gloucestershire. It is said to be at a height suitable for stagecoach drivers to have read easily. Not far away on the B4077 outside Toddington is a much lower fingerpost sign with 'hands' pointing out three directions. This region of England has some interesting mileposts. Just outside Wroxton in Oxfordshire is a decorative stone column erected in 1686. It marked a point on the route from London to Wales that was used by salt merchants and others. Signposts like these were often one-off designs with variable road information and plenty of details about the local powers-that-be.

As roadbuilding became better organised through the work of Thomas Telford and turnpike trusts, mileposts and signposts became regularly spaced, distinctive devices with a certain element of artistry in many of them. This made them easier to spot. They worked as branding on behalf of the different trusts. General Turnpike Acts in 1766 and 1773 required those roads to be measured accurately and markers erected at distances of one statute mile apart. They had to be inscribed with the name of the next town or important place to which they were leading. The 1773 Act stipulated that highway junctions should have their own marker stones or posts to show where each road led.

The coming of rail transport took over much of the way people moved around the country. Turnpike trusts lost business and became economically unsustainable, so what had been good roads deteriorated. The trusts were gradually wound up, with the last going in 1885 (weblist: turnpikes). The new County Councils took over the maintenance of main roads in 1889. Local roads became the responsibility of Rural District Councils in 1894, though in 1930 they were transferred to the care of the County Councils. In 1909, central government had begun to give grants to local authorities for road maintenance.

163

On the Move

Motor transport introduced much more than just a new way to travel. Owning horses to enable people to make long journeys was expensive and required equipment, stabling, skills and – if more than a solitary rider were to be involved – a suitable carriage. The horses that worked farms were not ideal for making journeys, especially as they were needed on the farms. There were serious problems caused by horses by way of pollution. Horse manure had to be removed by the ton from roads, especially in cities. Rain or other surface water spread the manure like an even skimming over rough roads that could trap particles easily, dirtying footwear and clothing and causing a disease hazard.

In 1894 *The Times* newspaper predicted "In 50 years, every street in London will be buried under nine feet of manure" (weblist: manure). There were 11,000 hansom cabs in London and thousands of horse-drawn buses, each needing twelve horses per day, according to contemporary reports. This meant 50,000 horses for transporting people, daily. Many others delivered goods. Each animal produced between 15 and 35 lbs ($\approx$ 6.8-15.9 kg) of manure a day, plus urine. The result was a daily mountain to be removed. And since horses lasted for only a few years on average, often dying in harness, carcasses also required removal as soon as possible.

Motor vehicles were smelly but their exhaust fumes in those days could be ignored. They were expensive to buy, needed maintenance and new skills, they sometimes frightened the horses (and people) but could carry the same number of passengers as a light carriage for a very considerable distance with few stops. During the period we are looking at, their growth in numbers and reduction in price made them much more popular with families. Motor cars began to replace horses in urban areas.

The demands of the World War I helped ensure trained men were more plentiful. After 1918 they could act as chauffeurs or family excursion drivers. In 1919 there were 100,000 cars on British roads. Twenty years later, as war broke out again, two million Britons owned automobiles (Brendon, 1997). The Parliamentary Acts of the 18th century had stipulated mileposts and signposts at junctions, but motor buses and cars in large numbers on the roads needed a better system of management and guidance.

An important step forward in helping motorists was a reorganisation of how roads were identified. For many years some had been known by names like 'Great North Road' in Britain and 'National Road' in the United States. French roads were using numbers around 1910, but in confusing fashion. "In a given *Département* one might find the same number attributed to different and totally unconnected roads" (Ribeill, 1991:7). There was also a maintenance problem connected with levels of traffic usage. Georges Ribeill draws attention to points raised at the First International Meeting on Roads held in Paris in October 1908.

At that time, roads were maintained according to their status – national, county or local – in which the higher status roads got more help than the others. A speaker asked if it might be better to identify the routes that got heavier use and concentrate more on those. The actual routes taken by drivers, he suggested, might use combinations of those three levels of use categories. Rationalising the way numbers were used and using them in a system to identify routes would help motorists by better employment of signposting and map labelling. It looked like only a step towards an ideal method.

The need for a better labelling system was dear to the heart of André Michelin, who had founded the famous tyre company with his brother, Édouard (Harp, 2002). Their first *Michelin Guide* in 1900 had been given away free to motorists. It was entirely about the care and maintenance of cars. Articles explained how to change tyres. There were lists of towns with details of repair shops. As new editions appeared, they carried more city maps, 13 in 1900, 600 in 1913 (Ribeill, 1991:15).. More general information was added, such as where to find doctors and pharmacies. Hotels were listed. Places were described. The book was changing from being a repair book to a work on historical geography, from an education about auto mechanics to an interpretation of the national environment.

André Michelin had advocated improvement for several years. His text for an advertisement in *Le Plein Air* played the tourism card:

> "Why do rich foreign tourists hesitate to visit our country that they love and admire? Because it is very difficult to get their bearings on our roads that are so poorly marked. It would be different if they were numbered. France would then see the development of automobile tourism take off, and she would become like Switzerland, rich and prosperous, as a result of motoring" (Harp, 2002:83-84).

In 1912 he started to write a weekly column in *Le Journal*, pressing for better numbering and better signposting. He was not alone in this. The Touring Club

165

de France, which in 1906 had had 104,000 members, the smaller, but wealthier Automobile Club de France, and the Association Générale Automobile, had all been working to improve automobile touring since their founding in the early 1890s [Harp, 2002].

His article of 2 September 1912 advocated giving every road a name, showing the name on maps and using it on signs of all kinds along the road itself. His ideas would only be partially adopted. Roads would become labelled with either a name or a number. Michelin maps would show the road numbers, distances between important junctions and even which routes were scenic by edging the roads shown in green. However, where he had hoped all mileposts would have the labels added, he was disappointed. Where they are shown, he would say, they are "indicated on a very small number of milestones. When they do exist, they are practically illegible from the road, and the driver must stop and get out to see the numbers" [Ribeill, 1991:8].

Michelin's campaigning was vigorous. It apparently included getting the French President to sign the first page of a petition demanding road numbering, under the impression he was adding his name to the visitors' book of an international air show. It was in April of the following year that a bill was enacted numbering all the major roads of France.

Work classifying United Kingdom roads began in 1913 but was interrupted by the War. The definitive list of the principles was published in 1923. The country was zoned using a system of radial segments spreading from London, with three other zones in Scotland and a more *ad hoc* method in Northern Ireland. It was, in fact, a pattern that André Michelin had recommended to the Ministry of Transport [Moran, 2010]. The USA approved a national system of numbered highways in 1925 using a framework based on a grid.

Stephen Harp considers Michelin to have been immensely important in French life far ahead of being a tyre maker:

> "Michelin claimed to be helping tourists to discover France, to be assisting in the economic growth that would result from greater tourism. In the process, the company contributed as much as any institution, and a good deal more than the French state, to the creation of a culture of modern touring in France" [p56].

Britain's national cycling clubs led the way towards improved safety by erecting their own hazard warning signs. It was a recognition of cyclists as tourists – people unfamiliar with new locations where steep hills and tight bends could be among the problems of which they had to be aware. The clubs persuaded the government to have county councils made responsible for signs showing directions and distances to places. During the early 20th century, organisations like the Automobile Association [Keir, 1955] and Royal Automobile Club [Brendon, 1997] in Britain joined in with their own signs in corporate colours.

The infrastructure of exploration had reached epic development. Besides the AA and RAC, there were the publishers of guidebooks showing routes, hill gradients and things to see and marvel at. The spread of filling stations and repair garages, mileposts, road signs and parking places not only served motor buses and coaches but a mass of individual travellers choosing their own times and places to go exploring. They might well have started out by following the persuasions of the marketing people, but they began choosing for themselves from an ever-growing set of possibilities.

The AA had adopted the colours of its first president, the 5th Earl of Lonsdale, whose coat of arms had black circles on a yellow background. The RAC used royal blue and white. Both organisations began to operate motorbike and sidecar patrols who could be sent to help members with car problems. Just before the World War I they both started to install roadside telephone boxes that members could open with a key to summon help. The keys worked for both the AA and the RAC boxes, phone messages being passed on to the member's own service if necessary. The origins of the AA did not lie in the need for breakdown assistance, however. David Keir [1955] recalls how a letter in the March 1905 edition of *The Autocar* suggested a club made up of cyclists wearing a badge and paid for out of club subscriptions should be created to note where police speed traps existed and to warn motorists.

The AA had taken up the idea in October of the same year, with bicycle patrols who observed passing automobiles and estimated their speeds close to certain areas. The areas in question were those monitored by police constables with stopwatches. It was hoped their evidence when needed might counteract that of the constables. The first speeding prosecution to call a cyclist patrol to give evidence did not go in the motorist's favour, however, resulting in a fine of £5 plus costs. His subjective opinion as to the motorist's speed held little weight with the legal system. However, the system continued for some time, with motorcycles replacing ordinary bicycles after 1912.

A map of police speed trap locations appeared in *The Autocar* in May 1907. Readers were invited to send in corrections and additions, just as users of satnav systems would be invited to do a century later regarding speed cameras [Keir, 1955]. AA members had badges on their vehicles. Patrols were told to salute these vehicles as they passed. But in 1909, members were told that if a patrolman did not salute, they must stop and ask why. The answer should be (assuming the patrolman had not missed seeing the badge) that there was a police speed trap ahead. The law stated that any patrolman signalling to a speeding motorist about policemen operating a trap would be obstructing the officers in the execution of their duty. The practice grew of drivers noting the failure to salute, slowing down, but not stopping. Patrols could hardly be prosecuted if they forgot to salute.

The Association merged with the rival Motor Union in 1910. The MU had been vying with the AA for the nine years of its short existence, with similar services on offer. Having three national motorists' organisation had been seen as too many. After negotiations in 1910 the AA and the MU became one. The MU name was kept alive until the inter-war years when it was quietly dropped.

The Automobile Association put into place 6,500 directional signs and 15,000 village signs by 1926. During the 1930s, local authorities were made responsible for all signage, so both motoring groups stopped providing them. Most signs of all kinds were removed during the Second World War in case of invasion, when it was thought dangerous to give any sort of help to invaders. The AA and RAC began to supply guidebooks, route leaflets and other services within their first decade. They also developed teams of inspectors of hotels and restaurants, supplying their members with annual handbooks with encyclopaedia-style information about Britain and later, Europe.

For example, an archived *Automobile Association and Motor Union Handbook for 1914-15* is a small pocket size, hard backed volume, with pages of details about where AA/MU patrolmen could be found on roadside duty. They were able "to undertake minor roadside repairs to members' cars and motorcycles; they are all qualified to render first-aid services, being equipped with wallets containing comprehensive first-aid outfits." [AA/MU, 1914:14]. Patrolmen could supply information on the state of roads in their district and help to call medical or mechanical aid. Much of the *Handbook* consists of a gazetteer of towns with garages listed and in some cases, hotels. "The list of hotels is not yet complete" tops every page. Illustrations show AA/MU signposts with one or two words below a triangular arrangement of the organisation's title:

'School', 'Cross Roads', 'Dangerous Corner' etc. Services were already becoming available in continental Europe which were similar to those in Britain. Lists of shipping costs across the Irish Sea are given: eg Fishguard to Cork, three times a week, for £2..10s to £3..3s depending on size (equivalent value in 2017: £140 to £186).

The equivalent Handbook for 1931-32 had more of the same, expanded with more garage and hotel listings, tables of lighting up times (issued in those days as guidance on the use of headlights); the AA service whereby buyers of used cars could have them checked for problems, or old cars looked over to see if maintenance was needed, and a new aviation department "to give assistance to the growing number of members who are owners of aircraft" (AA Handbook, 1931-32:81). This included obtaining all the necessary documents for flying abroad, waterproof maps that could be written on and later washed clean, and message bags for dropping from the air at AA roadside phone boxes. They were for messages for patrolmen to forward by telephone or telegram.

John Bartholomew & Son published a twelve miles to the inch map of England and Wales for the AA at 6s..6d (≈ £9.44). It had no obvious date, but the roads are not numbered so it would be pre-1923. Ordnance Survey maps could be bought in 'dissected' versions in which panels were cut out and mounted onto a canvas backing sheet that was easy to fold and hard wearing. The Bartholomew map was the same, though it was also big enough to make a wall display.

An example of an OS map mounted on canvas but not dissected is the Tourist Map of Exmoor at a scale of 1 inch to 1 mile. Its survey with corrections date was 1929. The cover bears a monochrome version of the royal coat of arms with the initials 'GR' flanking it. That might explain the note on the back reading "Published by Authority of the Ministry of Agriculture and Fisheries" who presumably gave permission, but it is not clear why the coat of arms was added. Was it published in 1935 at the time of King George V's silver jubilee?

An article in the Edwardian journal *Nineteenth Century* by B H Thwaite had a proposal for a 'carway' from London to Birmingham. It would have been a four-lane road taking a straight line across country, starting in Edgware and arriving at Bickenhill outside Birmingham (Parker, 2013). It was well received, though was never built. Car enthusiast John Montague MP said London to Brighton was a better idea. "He far preferred the idea of one running from London to the ritzy playground of Brighton over one to grimy old Brum .. 'I doubt whether there are sufficient automobiles in Great Britain to justify such a scheme' he wrote in *The Autocar* in August 1902'" (Parker, 2013:100). The British term 'motorway' would be used for the first time in 1924 (Moran, 2010:21). It would be 1959 before the tiniest stretch of motorway, the Preston bypass, opened as part of the planned M6.

Britain was slow in building new roads after World War I. Between 1918 and 1927 it managed only 127 miles of new road (Parissien, 2013). Italy began to construct *autostrade* in 1921 and its dictator, Mussolini, took up the cause immediately after coming to power the next year. The Italian government hosted the fifth International Road Congress in 1926, making much of its new transport network, which by 1939 would reach over 400 kilometres. Hitler's Germany authorised 4,300 miles (6,920 kms) of *Reichsautobahn* after he came to power in 1933 (Parissien, 2013).

British interest was then sparked. A German film, *Schnelle Strassen*, was launched in 1937, showing 'British tourists' (played by German actors) being delighted by the new roads (Moran, 2010). A large delegation of Britons crossed the Channel to Germany to see the *Reichsautobahn*. Some people in Britain began to imagine a British motorway system, but the war intervened, followed by unavoidable austerity.

Some of the people who saw Hitler's network had been doubtful about its real purpose. Steven Parissien is one writer who notes contemporary beliefs that the high-speed roads were for military use rather than domestic or tourist activities. But right up until the fateful year of 1939, British (and doubtless, other) commercial operators were liaising with their German counterparts promoting tourism. Germany was on the British destination list. The *Reichsautobahn* did give access to scenic splendours and they were equipped with picnic sites.

Hitler's strategy was to boost the national car industry by subsidising and producing grand cars for the wealthy at home and abroad; and a 'peoples' car' to bring ordinary Germans together while enabling them to explore, admire and understand their country – especially as it was being 'improved' by Hitler. In addition, Grand Prix cars like Mercedes' W125 of 1937 would aim to dominate international circuits, showcasing German motor leadership. The new motor roads were part of a social tourism campaign that, as we shall see in *Making Sense of Tourism: 2 Bright Prospect*, was itself embedded in a strategy of German rebirth as envisaged by the Nazi Party.

Managing the Traffic – USA and UK

Signposts in the USA were largely a matter of interest to automobile clubs who wanted to advertise local businesses along the roadside. The result was often a plethora of signs erected by different groups. A seven-year-old boy from a family with a business in New York City in the 1860s became fascinated by the lack of traffic management in the city. Horse-drawn vehicles became snarled in traffic jams, difficult to untangle "since neither drivers nor police, if there were any around, knew anything about the control of traffic or the proper thing to do (Petroski, 2016:63).

He was William Phelps Eno. He and his family travelled to London and Paris, where he incidentally observed what was happening on the streets. Eno entered the family real estate business but continued to observe traffic and think about its management. He published an article in *Rider and Driver* magazine in 1900 calling for urgent action to solve problems. 1903 saw him design, pay for and have erected, a hundred signs in New York telling slow moving vehicles to keep close to the right-hand edge of the road.

Eno published *Rules for Driving* which he distributed, and in 1909, *Street Traffic Regulation,* praised by the *New York Times* for helping New York traffic reach "its present satisfactory condition" (Petroski, 2016:65). The book stipulated that traffic moving easterly and westerly should give way to vehicles moving northerly and southerly. Eno is also credited with publicising octagonal stop signs, made first by a Detroit police sergeant; pedestrian crossings, traffic circles (roundabouts), one-way streets, and pedestrian safety islands. His ideas were instrumental in London and Paris adopting the measures.

By the early 1920s, the situation was becoming seen as a problem. A group of concerned individuals from Indiana, Wisconsin and Minnesota toured several states and passed on their opinions to the Mississippi Valley Association of Highway Departments (Petroski, 2016). They proposed using signs recognisable by their shape – circular for a railroad level crossing, diamond-shaped for general caution and the already-adopted octagonal for stop signs. Different colour combinations, shapes and wording were in use by independently minded cities by then. Some standardisation followed the 1924 First National Conference on Street and Highway Safety and a concurrent recommendation of the American Association of State Highway Officials.

On the Move

Some colours faded more easily, and paint technology had to advance further to solve that problem. More coordination would await post-World War II activity. As for traffic lights, in 1912 Salt Lake City took the lead in replacing policemen operating mechanical traffic signals at the centre of junctions. Officer Lester F Wire dipped bulbs in red and green paint, put them in a plywood structure and used a switch at the roadside to change the signals. He had felt very vulnerable with the old signs, stood in the middle of the road to operate them in busy traffic.

Britain had motoring organisation and cycling club signs. The Motor Car Act of 1903 added four national advisory signs using shapes – a white ring for speed limits, as shown in numbers on a plate below it; a white or red diamond for, eg weight restrictions; a red disc for prohibitions and a red, open triangle to warn of hazards. Oddly, these last sometimes gave the details on a separate plate, but at other times the motorist just had to guess. From 1933 the signs were given legal force. Out of these beginnings came the range of signs familiar to an older generation until the reorganisation imposed by the Worboys Committee of 1963. At that point, UK signs began to follow European practice in using only symbols and no words, cutting out possible language problems. Whether the new 1960s versions were as pleasing as the older signs has sometimes been disputed. It again goes to show what a range of expertise is required for good transport management and good tourism development.

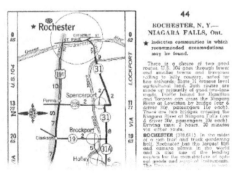

From an Automobile Association of America: A Triptik Guide extract

Chapter 10

Life on the Road

The Caravan

Having a home on wheels is popular today in the form of a caravan, motorhome or 'RV', the American shorthand for Recreational Vehicle. It is not a modern idea. Shepherds and roadmenders used them for shelter or overnight sleeping in Victorian times. Roma peoples lived in tents made of bent saplings covered in cloth or canvas up to the mid-19th century, and then began to use wooden caravans pulled by horses. Travelling showmen adopted them around the same period. Mrs Jarley, in *The Old Curiosity Shop* by Charles Dickens, lived in one when touring her waxworks show. "A smart little house upon wheels, with white dimity curtains festooning the windows ..... [with] a pair of horses in pretty good condition" (1840-41). Later in the century, Salvation Army men used large caravans as what they called forts. These were horse-

On the Move

drawn sleeping and preaching units moving from village to village. The men sold their magazine *War Cry* and preached from a platform at one end to whoever could be induced to listen. No fewer than thirteen young men and a Salvation Army officer could be based with the vehicles.

Dr William Stables

The attractive world of caravan adventuring was in its early horse-drawn phase that produced more accounts of real journeys and fictitious ones. George Nugent-Banks wrote *Across France in a Caravan* (1892) that proved popular. A delightful children's story, beautifully illustrated with full colour pictures and pen-and-ink sketches, was *Happy Days by Road and River* (1912) by Alice Talwin Morris. It had a pair of stories, one about a caravan holiday, the other about a canal boat trip. Towards the end of our period (1926), Gertrude Metcalfe-Shaw described a journey: *English Caravanners in the Wild West*.

It was a children's book author who pioneered real leisure caravanning. Dr William Gordon Stables was a prolific writer of adventure stories. One of his books was about a real-life adventure that Stables undertook in the 1880s (Stables, 1886). Gordon Stables had been a Royal Navy surgeon, born in Scotland but, on leaving naval service, was living in Twyford, Berkshire. Stables got interested in caravans while passing through Great Marlow in a pony and trap one summer. He saw a row of showpeoples' caravans where some fairground swings startled his horse, who "shied, and made a rather thoughtless attempt to enter a draper's shop." (Stables, 1886:4). The owner of a pretty little caravan invited him in to look around. Stables was hooked. He sketched out ideas for what he wanted and got the Bristol Wagon Company to build it. There is an excellent cut-away drawing by Max Millar of the finished vehicle in *Gypsies and Gentlemen* by Nerissa Wilson (1986:46-47). Dr Stables' caravan has survived to the present day. It is now owned by the Caravan and Motorhome Club and is stored in a specially converted goods shed at its site in Broadway, Worcestershire.

It is a leisure caravan, but not like a modern touring van. It is solid mahogany for a start with an interior lining of softwood. It measures 20 feet in length, 6 in width and 11 in height, or about 6 metres by 1.8 metres by 3.35 metres, weighing two tons when loaded, or 2,032 kilos. The wheels are rim-and-spoke, wooden, carriage wheels. Two horses are used to pull the caravan. It is divided inside into a kitchen or pantry area and a saloon, with a driving seat out at front. An unusual mix of furnishings and equipment was carried in

174

Stables' day, ranging from an oil burning Rippingille stove to a harmonium, a marble washstand to a bookcase with favourite books, a Persian rug to 'a good revolver'. There is a storage bin holding two bushels of corn for the horses. There was a folding wooden framework with a canvas covering that fitted up outside as a tent, usually used for Dr Stables' morning bath. Cold, of course.

The real contrast to today was staffing. Gordon Stables was accompanied by a valet, Albert Foley, who cooked, cleaned and generally served his master. He was carefully chosen for honesty, competence, and an ability to sleep without snoring. He slept in the rear kitchen compartment, closed off by a curtain. A second servant was the coachman, recorded as 'John G', who looked after the horses, taking them to nearby stables at night and sleeping near them. There was a parrot and a dog. While on the move, Foley rode on a Ranelagh tricycle ahead of the caravan, checking the chosen route was clear.

Caravanning with a valet and coachman to serve his needs suggests Dr Stables was a man of superior means and attitude. His previous naval life showed through. He liked to call his caravan 'the Land Yacht Wanderer'. Foley was described as sleeping 'athwartships' across the kitchen space. When Stables published the account of his main journey, to Scotland, he called it a 'cruise'. He mentions a wife and family, who hardly figure in the story beyond the trial trip made with the newly acquired caravan. His valet and coachman are largely part of the vehicle's fittings, who in the book are occasionally asked a question and whose respectfully brief answers are noted. There is a chapter part way through the book about 'the crew', which has a positive attitude towards them, but is written rather like a naval officer completing an annual review of the ratings. The parrot and the dog get longer descriptions. People met along the route are quoted sometimes at length, often in a representation of their accents. Dr Stables is always the focal point of the story: what he does, what he sees, what his opinions are.

Caravanning in those days was for the rich. Their 'homes on wheels' were usually custom-made unless they managed to buy, or hire, a van from a gypsy or traveller family. The custom-made vehicles came from railway carriage works. Some enthusiasts built their own, with varying degrees of success. There was even at attempt by a car maker to build a motorhome. It was Marshall of Manchester in 1903. They placed a 20hp engine into a chassis, then added a five-bunk accommodation. The result was not successful. It was too slow. *The Motor* magazine thought it an idea for "misguided folk who imagine motoring has something to do with carrying your home about with you" (weblist:

The Scotsman). It would be the type of comment of the car enthusiast about the caravanner for ever afterwards.

The result of increased interest was a desire to swap ideas and share the enjoyment of caravan life. The Travel Exhibition of May 1907, held at the Royal Agricultural Hall in London, had caravans on show. L C R Cameron's *The Book of the Caravan* appeared that year, the first book on the subject. J Harris Stone brought together Mr Cameron and others with the result that the Caravan Club was formed in June 1907, by ten men and one woman. By 1912 it had 267 members, of whom a third were women. Today it is known as the Caravan and Motorhome Club.

Rallies of caravans and their families were immediately key activities. May 1908 saw the first at Ockham in Surrey. Two years later, one was held in Hounslow and another at Cane Hill near Coulsdon in Surrey. London was clearly the focal point of the early membership. More followed quickly. Caravan sites were being registered with the Club. 450 pitches were recorded in Britain and Ireland by 1912, about one in nine being in leafy Sussex. The caravans were quite different from those of today. Their owners were prosperous and able to have their vehicles custom-built. "The larger ones [were] equipped with running water, flush sanitation, libraries and even, records show, a piano" (Ellis, 2006:16). Strong elements of romance were suffused into the appeal of caravanning, distilled from elements of escapism and rural freedom. They chimed well with the ideas of the Arts and Craft Movement of William Morris & Co, rejecting for a time the increasingly modern industrial world in favour of an imagined one of an arcadia that it supposedly replaced.

The years between 1900 and the World War I were important for countryside awareness, conservation and new forms of rural tourism. Most forms of transport developed in symbiotic relationships with these interests as books, magazines, newspapers and printed advertising spread their messages on both sides of the Atlantic. People took advantage of camping and caravanning to escape urban life. At the same time, movements like the Garden Cities campaigns and model villages projects were trying to show how urban existence could be made better. Travellers being inspired by better rural qualities returned home and were hopeful of improved conditions around them. We will deal with these developments in the next book in this series, *Bright Prospect*.

On the eve of the World War I, about a hundred club members gathered in a field at Cadnam near the New Forest. They had horse-drawn caravans. It was June. War was declared on 4 August. The mechanical age of warfare brought motor vehicles to the fore with the result that leisure caravanning after hostilities ceased would begin to look to the petrol engine as its source of power. Philippa Bassett [1980] describes the Caravan Club as almost dormant during the interwar years, with horse-drawn vehicles becoming things of the past. Only one rally was held, in 1920 at Maidstone. Motor caravans were appearing, but slowly, as the ordinary family car took first place for those who could afford one.

With the 1930s, rallies began to be held again, spurred on by a sense of competition among their builders. The Camping Club, started in 1901, began to take a serious interest in caravans. It became the Camping and Caravanning Club in 1933. Mit Harris started *Caravan and Trailer* magazine that would prove highly influential in sharing information. The Caravan Club had only about 80 members by the mid-1930s and was struggling, run virtually single-handed by its founder, J Harris Stone [Bassett, 1980:iii]. Mit Harris and his magazine's co-owner Bernard Dolman supported the relaunch of the Club for caravan trailers. Stone agreed to step aside from the Club, which was becoming too much for him [Ellis, 2006]. The Club was relaunched by Harris and Dolman. Their publicity campaign led to a rally at Leamington Spa in 1936 with some hundred caravans. Trouble flared again, however, the following year. There was internal rivalry between owners of horse-drawn caravans and motor-hauled vans. Local authorities campaigned for more control of where camping sites could be opened. Many Club members resented the influences exerted by commercial members. During this period, Harris and Dolman split up, Harris starting a new magazine, *Caravan World*, and the Club again came to a stop. For a while, it became a subsidiary company of Link House Publications, with its members keeping control of policy, membership and social activities [Bassett, 1980:iii]. It remained that way until the 1950s when moves were made to turn it into a self-sufficient members' club. As in so many parts of the tourism world, politics and ideologies shaped everything. Understanding the mechanisms and issues involved at the grass roots as well as the party-political level is essential.

Manufacturers

Several homes-on-wheels builders before the 1914-18 war tried fitting internal combustion engines onto chassis used as the basis for living accommodation.

Andrew Jenkinson [2003] mentions the wayward Dr Lehwess as a pioneer, whose failed round the world trip is described in Chapter 8 . Jenkinson adds that a motorhome was built for M Collin Dufresne of Grenoble. It was a two-ton giant sleeping eight people, including a chauffeur. It was divided into compartments, had washing and toilet facilities and a kitchen with a paraffin stove. A 40hp engine gave it a top speed of 25 mph (40 kph). Jenkinson's choice as the first commercial motorhome in Britain was a 21 ft (6.4 m) bus-like vehicle by the Belsize Motor Company of Manchester. It was used by a Liverpool businessman, Mr Mallalieu, to tour Britain. The cruising speed was very low compared with today, at 9 mph (14.5 kph), though at the time the legal limit was between 8 and 16 mph (12.8 - 25.7 kph) depending on the local authority of the area being visited. This size of motorhome was not suited to soft ground. The Belsize was a four-tonner. Trailer caravans were a better prospect for parking in fields. Motorhome owners used car parks. Such vehicles were the playthings of the wealthy unless people could build their own.

An alternative idea was to use an ordinary car to sleep in. An American supplier, the Outers Equipment Company, advertised folding beds designed to fit various automobiles [Gellner & Keister, 2003]. They weighed only 13-14 lbs (5-6 kilos) and could be fitted within a few minutes. Andrew Jenkinson [2003] includes a photo of a 1930 Austin Seven "converted for two girls to go camping" by a bedding arrangement on the rear seats. Such methods left no room for any other gear. Resourceful Americans did develop the automobile-as-home idea by carrying a tent or simple stretch-out awning. With a luggage trailer, they could carry cooking and eating equipment and other domestic items.

It led to gatherings of what were called 'Tin Can Tourists' in new resort destinations like Florida. These were often large camps of autos, tents and luggage trailers spread across fields, by open water and woodlands, perhaps untidy but with a strong sense of togetherness and delight in the open air.

"World War I also ensured that thousands of vehicles [such as staff cars], declared surplus when the war ended, would find their way into the hands of individuals around the world ... the automobile became the symbol of a 'New Generation' of Americans that delighted in the mobility and anonymity it provided ... throwing a tent in the back or strapping it on top of the car, thousands of Americans set out to explore the backroads of the United States" [see Wynne, 1999].

From 1919, two annual gatherings took place, one in Michigan and the other in Florida. The Tin Canners (who probably took their name either from Henry Ford's 'Tin Lizzie' or their love of canned food) continued their travels and gatherings. One group set up the Camping Tourists of America at Braden Castle Point, Florida, in February 1924. It bought a 34-acre plot which it divided into 40ft x 40ft (12m x 12m) lots on which CTA members could build. Since some townships regarded Tin Canners as badly behaved and noisy, the Braden Castle project adopted strict rules which also reflected their own views. Purchasers of lots had to be over 55, with no children or pets allowed on sites.

Several American suppliers sold goods to the devotees of youth group pioneers Robert Baden-Powell, Ernest Thompson Seton and Daniel Carter Beard. They promoted a love of the outdoor life and wilderness exploring. Abercrombie & Fitch, in the United States, dealt in a wide range of goods from tents to clothing to cooking gear, in extensive catalogues. These carried advice on the kinds of food to take into the great outdoors, with suggested quantities. There were self-cooling water bags, aluminium cooking pans that nested together and metal box lanterns using candles and folding flat when out of use. Americans looking to equip their trailers and caravans could rely on the Sears Roebuck or Montgomery Ward catalogues.

Britons had the Baden-Powell tradition of relying on utensils that could be made from sticks and logs. Caravan owners often took kitchen items from home. The French-born chef, Alexis Soyer, invented a kerosene-fuelled 'magic stove' that he had marketed from 1849. It could be placed on a table – even a study table or ladies' craftwork desk (weblist: Soyer). A spirit lamp heated fuel and delivered it under pressure to a metal hob on which a pan could be placed. The adventurous Marquis of Normanby took one to Egypt where he had a hot meal served to him and some friends at the top of one of the pyramids. The stove could be used in camping and caravanning with ease. The Marquis was only one of a strong tradition of adventurous tourists that continues today, a sub-sector that inspires others to get out of their comfort zones and try something unusual. Other stoves, by Francis Fox Tuckett in the 1850s, Fridtjof Nansen in the 1880s and Frans Wilhelm Lindqvist in 1892, followed. The last-named was the inventor of the famous Primus stove used by early caravanners and generations of campers.

Many needs could be met by taking from the household store of pots, mugs and cutlery. Other things could be obtained from commercial suppliers. Many firms were well established as suppliers of extras beloved of army officers. The

Army and Navy Store in London published a catalogue in 1883 that listed *The Handy*. This was "A most convenient holdall … capable of carrying a complete Change of Clothes" (p1170). It was made of waterproof canvas forming a kind of roll-up pack with a carrying handle. The cost of an empty holdall was £1 1s 6d (≈£71). For 15s 6d extra (≈£51) it could be supplied fitted with hair, clothes, tooth and shaving brushes, a shaving glass, shoehorn, button hook, razor, pocketknife, nail scissors, comb, soap box and housewife. The last name was, in fact, a sewing kit, displaying a shining example of Victorian men's views of women. British soldiers were still using the term for a sewing kit post World War II. The caravanner, camper or indeed, any kind of traveller, would have found *The Handy* useful.

Thomas Hiram Holding was a great leisure camping pioneer and founder of the Camping Club that in the early 1930s became the Camping and Caravanning Club. In 1909 he published *Refined Camping,* a catalogue of useful accessories that he sold from his premises in Maddox St, London. It included kit useful for caravanners as well as the users of tents. He supplied Primus stoves, pans and kettles, carrying bags, quilts and canvas buckets and bowls. The Club later ran its own Supplies Department based on catalogues sent to members (Constance, 2001).

The author of an article in *The Windsor Magazine* in 1922 described both horse-drawn and motor caravanning in detail. Clive Holland was writing at the time when horse-drawn vans were facing competition for attention against motor caravans and trailer caravans. He even described a collapsible trailer caravan attached to a motorbike and sidecar. It erected with canvas sides from a base frame on two wheels, looking like a modern lightweight trailer. Holland gave useful information on hire prices:

"Small motor caravan sleeping 4, per week in August: £7.00 (≈£203)
Large ditto, sleeping 4 but carrying 10, 6 using tents: £10-20 (≈£290-£580)
Cost of petrol per week: not much more than the hire of a horse
(Don't forget the cost of a chauffeur/mechanic if required)"

The modern camping and caravan book *British Caravans Vol 1: Makes Founded Before World War II* by Roger Ellesmere gives a detailed survey of the many makers and models on the market. Ellesmere makes 1919 the starting date for commercial production, noting that only one owner, Frederick Alcock, scratch-built a van before then in 1914 for his own use. Others built their own in the early 1920s "and after loaning or hiring this built more vans for hire before progressing to building for sale" (p7). Spending a few pounds sterling a week on hiring was better than a couple of hundred on buying. Most customers would have had little knowledge of the caravanning experience. Trying out by hiring made sense. "As late as 1932 at least 14 manufacturers were still running hire fleets. The practice, before the Second World War of selling new vans with full domestic equipment including china, cooking utensils and cutlery, probably had its origins in the necessity of providing these items for hire vans." Andrew Jenkinson notes that the Alcock van was way ahead of it time, with sweeping roof and windows all round. It could have "hastened the coming of trailer caravanning" (Jenkinson, 1998:7).

World Wars never have silver linings, though new opportunities may be found when they end, including some in tourism. World War II made available aircraft, pilots and infrastructures suitable to launch new transport links. World War I made available road vehicles, spare parts and trained mechanics and drivers. Businessmen such as Richard St Barbe Baker, George Hay-Moulder, R E Gash, the Piggott Brothers, Alfred Ensor, Clifford Dawtrey and many others took up the commercial opportunities (Jenkinson 1998, Ellesmere 2012).

Baker's *Navarac* of 1919 was the first caravan put on sale. It used aircraft materials bought from the Government Disposals Board in Croydon. The result looked like a four-wheel gypsy caravan made of timber with an iron cooking range, hanging wardrobes, a water tank in the roof and lockers with spare awnings, tents and camp beds. The windows let down into wall slots like railway carriage windows of the day. Ellesmere tells how the business launched. When the van was taken out for the first time in May 1919, it was filmed by a newsreel man. The next evening saw the launch was shown widely in cinemas. An exhibition by the Government Disposals Board at Olympia showcased the van as an example of building from ex-military materials. Other businessmen took up the idea. Lighter, two-wheeled caravans were soon produced. Richard Baker's own interest was really in forestry. He gave up building vans and sailed for Africa in 1920, where he worked as a forest conservator with great success.

Jenkinson and Ellesmere illustrate the hundreds of early caravan builders. Some owed their looks to shepherd's huts, like the popular Raven *Dominion*. Others owed their ancestry more towards gypsy vans, though on two wheels and of plainer design, such as Arthur Gardner's *Cheltenham*. The famous Eccles Company did make luxurious four-wheelers for showmen. Streamlined vans were soon common. W R Earl was successful with his Carlight series, from the

Light Four through the *Continental* to the *Colonial Minor*, the last-named, of 1939, reducing the strict aerofoil shapes of the others in order to get more internal space. By that year, war was breaking out again, closing mainland Europe to would-be tourers and then closing down caravan building for more urgent needs. The end of the war in 1945 would bring a boost for ownership as a way of supplementing destroyed housing stocks. "At least ten manufacturers for everyone who was in business before the war" [North, 1952] would presage the rapid growth of the later consumer era..

Prestige Parkways for Tourism

The United States had its resourceful tourists. Besides motoring and staying overnights in motels it was developing a caravan tradition, generally under the title 'travel trailer'. Arrol Gellner and Douglas Keister ascribe those many developments to important cultural and demographic changes in the late 19th and early 20th century [2003]. Between 1879 and 1916, twelve National Parks were designated. 1916 saw the National Parks Service founded. It would be influential in many ways, notably in attracting visitors to its six million acres and supplying on-site information about what visitors would see. The proportion of the American population living on farms dropped below fifty per cent by 1920. More city dwellers were owning automobiles. Getting out into the countryside was becoming literally a driving force behind cultural changes. There had been fifty and more years of sometimes violent agitation for an eight-hour working day. It took until the Roosevelt New Deal of the early 1930s before it was well established, but it brought leisure possibilities of all kinds.

The New Deal was primarily intended to improve the economic situation of the nation, battered by the 1929 Wall Street Crash, itself following earlier downturns. President Franklin D Roosevelt initiated federal programmes of public works and financial reforms. Construction projects were intended to provide work for the unemployed and to set longer-term economic stimuli. An example of the strategy can be found in Appalachia. Local chambers of commerce and tourism businesses in North Carolina and Virginia had been seeking ways of boosting their economies. Pigeon Forge in Tennessee had been an iron-working centre and from 1870 it had a health resort at Henderson Springs.

Nearby Gatlinburg grew as a logging town. As it thrived in the period before the World War I, residents offered lodging accommodation to workers in the lumber industry and tourists who explored the mountains known as the Smokies. A hotel opened in 1916. The Great Smoky Mountains National Park opened in 1934 after extensive campaigning by promoters in Asheville, North Carolina and Knoxville, Tennessee. June of that year saw 41,000 visitors to the park. In June of 1935 there were over 128,000 (Williams, 2002:297).

Local promotional interests wanted to build a parkway similar to the successful Shenandoah National Park's Skyline Drive. It would give employment while building and again when open. Local businesses could finance and operate accommodations and retail outlets. The idea was taken up by New Deal officials as the Blue Ridge Parkway. The Appalachian people had in mind not only a tourist route but a utilitarian transport road serving their towns and cities. They found that the Federal rules defined a parkway as "an elongated park ... to contain the roadway" (Whisnant, 2003:90). Only cars were allowed to use it – not trucks or buses. Parkway land could not have direct access from individual properties, only at limited intersections serving important highways. The local trade 'boosters' could only accept that. They concentrated for much of the 1930s on the route the Parkway would take and other details to do with land acquisition, concessions policies and the average one thousand feet (304.8m) width of the right-of-way Political debates like these are always the nitty-gritty of tourist developments. In the case of the Blue Ridge Parkway they affected the costs and benefits along the 469 miles of the route. The project embraced so many commercial, State and Federal activities besides affecting the lives of ordinary folk. Anne Whisnant calls it "the complicated and messy process of identifying and pursuing some version of a public good" (Whisnant, 2006).

Beyond the economic aims there were educational hopes about introducing visitors to wildlife and Appalachian culture. This included not only exposing city dwellers to the ways of mountain people, but those same mountain folk to what National Parks staff thought of as better attitudes to conservation. Those living near the Parkway included Cherokee Native Americans and Whites. The *Asheville Citizen* reported ahead of discussions about the project that the Great Smoky Mountains National Park wanted to promote Cherokee and native White people as part of its tourist offer. Cherokee dances, games, sports, art and crafts "are tremendously interesting to the average tourist" (Whisnant, 2006:200). The Parkway plans led to building interpretation centres, information panels at key locations and a spate of guide and history book publishing.

On the Move

The Parkway was opened in sections with the last being the Linn Cove viaduct, delayed by many years because of difficulties in acquiring the land necessary below Grandfather Mountain. It was completed end to end for traffic only in 1987. The Blue Ridge road remains the most popular part of the National Park Service with over five million visitors noted year by year.

Regular Resting Places According to Transport and Coming of the Motel

Accommodation for tourists in the period 1851-1941 will be covered in *Making Sense of Tourism: 2 Bright Prospect.* It is useful to mention the first motel ever in this chapter because it came about through the needs of road travellers on the West Coast of the United States. It was like a staging post on the journeys north and south through California as much as it was a city hotel – hence the new name coined from motor + hotel, or motel. Britain had its inns on roads where there was a need for overnight stops; indeed, most European countries had had them of one kind or another ever since the Romans set up their *mansiones* about every fifteen miles (24 km) apart on major roads [Tucker, 1922].

When the Spanish spread north from present day Mexico, they set up a series of missions at frequent intervals. These were the centres of evangelical work among local Native American peoples and places where travellers could stay at night. It was the old European monastic practice of offering hospitality and a safe place to stay. Between 1769 and 1833 21 missions were established along what became known as the *camino real* or 'royal road'. They also became places of economic production and export, of leather, tallow and textiles. The missions were roughly the distance a horse could travel in a day, or people by foot in three days [see Forbes, 1925]. This has usually been noted as approximately 30 miles (48 kms).

It is also worth including as an example the Cold Spring Tavern near Santa Barbara between that town's mission and its farm in the Santa Ynez Valley [weblist: Cold Spring Tavern]. The Tavern was on the San Marcos Pass over mountains at a point where the road had to follow the contours of a valley, up one side, down the next. The road became a turnpike operation in the 1860s with stagecoaches along it. Motor traffic and a fine new bridge straight across the valley at Cold Spring ended the tavern's main utilitarian phase. It became a noted and popular restaurant occupying its wooden shacks, shaded and cool during the tourist summer, and is well known today. Similar taverns, spaced apart to suit the needs of travellers, were dotted across the roadways of the Western states.

Cold Spring Tavern near Santa Barbara, California

Railroad hotels in the South West of the USA in the 19th century were often spaced a hundred miles apart. They made sensible places for locomotive tenders to be refilled with water, passengers to be fed and where appropriate given overnight accommodation. Fred Harvey's restaurants on the Atchison, Topeka and Sant Fe railroad were built at these places, replacing the dreadful earlier diners with restaurants with good food and proper standards of service (Fried, 2011). Judy Garland's song titled by the name of the railroad in the 1946 movie *The Harvey Girls* would publicise Fred Harvey's staff and tell a story.

The San Luis Obispo Motel

Motels, a distinctive feature of American history and tourism, were different from those earlier stop-over places. They were often individually owned and set up by 'moms and pops', couples who built perhaps idiosyncratic places and gave their guests homely service. Poor roads and low speeds in many places meant that an excursion out of forty miles and then back home again was about the limit in the 1920s unless there was somewhere to camp or sleep in the car overnight. Hotels were relatively expensive and upscale for weary travellers. Something rather better than a car seat or tent – a hut, basic but comfortable, would be better.

The first motel appears to have been the Milestone Mo-Tel, afterwards called the Motel Inn, on Monterey Street on the outskirts of San Luis Obispo in California. It was located halfway between Los Angeles and San Francisco. The road connection was better than most: the drive of nearly four hundred miles could be done in two days. Janet Penn Franks in *San Louis Obispo: A History in Architecture* dates it as 1925 and writes of it as "one of San Luis

Obispo's best steakhouses and most popular watering holes" ^(Franks, 204:121). It was styled as a Mediterranean building, a nod presumably to the Spanish influence in the area. A courtyard was surrounded by separate bungalows facing inwards. The rooms had their own bathrooms, telephones and many had a garage attached. There was a laundry area, grocery shop and restaurant. Franks notes that guests were encouraged to pick oranges from the tree growing outside every bungalow. For this, the travellers paid $1.25 for the room. The motel closed in 1991 but has been scheduled for restoration.

In contrast to the way the United States is often characterised, the country has a long history and a landscape rich in the resulting legacy. There is more for the interested tourist to unlock, especially from the era before Europeans began to arrive. Railways and aircraft speed by. The road is the better way to find and savour the detail.

A Roadside Café in California,
Now, as Then

Chapter 11

Wings Around the World

Flying is so accepted as a feature of tourism that it is easy to forget human flight has only been common for fifty or sixty years. Before that, it was mainly an indulgence by wealthy inhabitants of Western Europe and North America. It is common to think that package holidays arrived as aircraft began to carry tourists abroad. Package deals of organised holidays with transport, accommodation and organised leisure activities were a feature of the later 19th century. The transport was usually by train, with coach services added during the 20th century. Aircraft were what turned those packages into mass tourism events, dominating media publicity like never before.

Before World War II, travel by air was for individuals making their own arrangements through operating companies. Long haul travel by plane was more about business travel or was undertaken as part of a change of occupation or residency. Being able to fly was several stages on from travel by boat, train or coach. Whole new theories, practices and skills were needed before flight could be achieved. It took efforts over a couple of thousand years to enable people to fly, with most of that time spent hardly achieving anything.

People-carrying vehicles on land merely needed a source of motive power and a surface to move along. Roads, snow and ice, rails or stretches of water could use animals, human effort, steam power or internal combustion engines to travel. Flight required the third dimension to be conquered, by applying lift. A lot of lift was needed before a suitable craft could carry people and goods into the air. While dragging things along the ground was second nature to human beings, working out how to make a vehicle lift itself must have appeared like using magic. No wonder that villagers finding an early balloon descending to earth thought it the work of the devil and destroyed it. Nor that others welcomed an aeroplane with religious ceremony because they thought the occupants were gods. A balloon belonging to a Monsieur J A C Charles landed in Gonesse, France in 1783. Villagers thought it a ferocious monster and destroyed it [Rolt, 1985]. Islanders in Vanuatu in the South Pacific during World War II began to worship the aircraft that they saw for the very first time. The planes were delivering freight. The villagers thought it the work of a Messiah, so they developed cultural rituals to attract more planes with goodies for them [weblist: Cargo].

These stories are not just about technological change. They have significance for the worlds of tourism, education and the mass media. Gonesse is only fifteen miles from balloon-pioneering Paris, yet the sight arriving in the village was entirely alien to its inhabitants. The mass media had not been used to learn about Monsieur Charles' demonstration. Education had not told them about hydrogen balloons, nor enlightened them about myths and monsters. No-one had travelled in the balloon, but its owner made a rapid excursion to see for himself what had happened. Explanations would have been made to the good folk of Gonesse about the event. The Vanuatu flights will have followed a similar course of later explanations. Lessons were learnt all round.

A recap of attempts at flight before the 1851 start date of this book is important. Early ballooning was not included in *The Beckoning Horizon* and is better recounted here as background to later developments. Many of the first flights were tourist events, spectacular forms of entertainment. They often had to be, so that financial support could be attracted through sponsorship or the sale of tickets for the best places to view what was taking place.

Simple daily observation brought useful ideas to the great pioneers of flights by balloon, the Montgolfier brothers. Joseph and Etienne would inspire many experimenters by their own spectacular efforts. They were part of the family running a Royal Manufactory in Annonay in southern France before the Revolution of 1789. It might have been the sight of a cone of paper thrown onto a fire floating up the chimney without burning that gave Joseph thoughts of flying by using hot air balloons. After smaller-scale experiments they flew a large balloon from the town square on 5 June 1783 (Rolt 1985, Payne 1992). News of the successful flight reached Paris. The next flight was not one of theirs. It took place from the great public venue of the Champ de Mars that August. The event was the one set up by Jacques Alexandre Cesar Charles, with the balloon which finished up scaring the people in Gonesse. A viewing enclosure had been arranged where spectators could pay one crown to stand with a good view of the event.

The Montgolfier brothers experimented with their hot air balloons. A flight in September 1783 took a sheep, a cock and a duck aloft to around 1,700ft (518m) (Rolt, 1985) - international practice is to quote all flight altitudes in feet. It was a magnificent occasion in front of King Louis XVI and Marie Antoinette at Versailles. The 17m (56ft) high, 12m (39ft) diameter balloon was made of paper covered in cotton cloth. It was decorated in blue and gold and carried the royal insignia. It might have been an experimental flight with passengers, but it was presented like an upmarket tourist spectacle. Three cannons were fired in succession to mark the release, which took place at the third report. The balloon sailed away on an unexpectedly short journey of about three kilometres to finish at the forest of Vaucresson. Small tears in the fabric had leaked hot air. Even so, everyone was satisfied with the flight.

Jean-Francois Pilâtre de Rozier became the first man to ascend in a tethered balloon, in October 1783. A free balloon flight took place the next month with the Marquis d'Arlandes, flying for almost half an hour over 9 kms. Lee Payne (1992:7) describes the event and notes that half a million Parisians watched it happen. Among the crowd was the American ambassador to France, Benjamin Franklin. Across the Channel, Londoners saw their first flight in September 1784, by Vincenzo Lunardi. Jean-Pierre Blanchard and Dr John Sheldon made a 115 kms (71.4 miles) flight from Chelsea to Romsey in Hampshire, in a hydrogen balloon. They touched down in Sudbury where Sheldon got out and was replaced by ballast before Blanchard continued. In January 1785, he crossed the English Channel with the American, Dr John Jeffries, from Dover to Guines. The Frenchman made the first American flight eight years later from Philadelphia.

Charles Green and two friends made an epic 480-mile, 18-hour flight in 1836 from Vauxhall Gardens to Weilburg in Germany. Astonished local people could not at first believe that the aeronauts had left London only the previous afternoon. Green and Co were feted, dined and entertained by concerts. An elaborate ceremony changed the balloon's name from *Royal Vauxhall* to *Nassau*, the name of the Duchy where Weilburg was situated. Everyone who was present or who read about the flight in newspapers must have begun to imagine the days when fast aerial journeys would become possible, leaving every other form of transport behind.

Meanwhile, Charles Green returned to London and Vauxhall Gardens. The renamed balloon was owned by Messrs Gye and Hughes, the proprietors of the popular Vauxhall entertainment venue. They must have valued Green and the very many balloon ascents he made from their property for the publicity value. He was left to fly as and when he chose, and they apparently were not worried that their balloon was no longer carrying the *Royal Vauxhall* name. Henry Mayhew, the writer, reported in the *Illustrated London News* in 1852 about the panoramic view now possible from flying at height, something which would be increasingly enjoyed by air passengers – so long as cloud did not interfere:

> "And here began that peculiar panoramic effect which is the distinguishing feature of a view from a balloon … the earth appeared literally to consist of a long series of scenes, which were being continually drawn along under you, as if it were a diorama beheld flat upon the ground, and gave one almost the notion that the world was an endless landscape stretched upon rollers, which some invisible sprites were revolving for your special enjoyment" (Payne, 1991:14).

Mayhew was referencing (and mixing up) two popular forms of theatrical presentation that had been exciting audiences for over half a century. Dioramas were giant paintings on muslin watched by people as, first, lights shone on the front, which had one view, and then from behind on another view painted on the back of the muslin. The result was a slow transition of one scene into another, say a peaceful mountain view into a dramatic appearance of a storm. Panoramas were exceedingly long paintings on canvas of a continuous scene. They were slowly wound past the audience's view. A common panorama show depicted a journey with the many changing landscapes encountered. Mayhew's description seems to blend the journey that he was taking, opening its views of the earth, with moving cloud shadows passing across them. Travellers had always seen the visual narrative of their changing surroundings as they moved, made more dramatic if they were lucky enough to have made a fast train journey. The flight of a balloon showed its passengers the even more spectacular moving panorama of the world below them.

Charles Green's 480-mile flight was eclipsed by one made from St Louis to Henderson in New York State in 1859. John Wise, with another balloonist named John LaMountain, his sponsor, O A Gager and a reporter flew 826 miles (1,329 km) in almost exactly 20 hours [Rolt, 1985]. Their balloon was named *Atlantic* in the hope of a later ocean crossing. It had a lifeboat suspended below the balloon's basket, with the ocean attempt in mind. As they passed over Lake Ontario a violent storm nearly forced them onto the water. Instead, they cut the lifeboat away, gaining height as a result. The reporter had an excellent story, Wise gained publicity, but the ocean attempt was quietly forgotten. LaMountain and many others made more balloon journeys, some of great distances.

For example, Gaspard-Félix Tournachon, known as 'Nadar', travelled 400 miles (644 km) from Paris to Neustadt am Rübenberge in Germany. Nadar was the most celebrated French photographer of his day. He took the world's first aerial photograph from a balloon in 1858, of the valley of the Bièvre.

He had a balloon, *Le Géant*, built in 1863. It was a giant, 60 metres (196 ft) high, holding over 6,000 cubic metres of hydrogen and able to lift 4.5 metric tons [Rolt, 1985]. Three hundred seamstresses had been employed sewing the layers of white silk forming the gas-tight balloon. It had a wicker work, box-like, construction below divided into six compartments with a balustraded balcony on top. There was a store for provisions, plus three sleeping berths, a lavatory, photographic store and printing press. Eight people joined Nadar in an excellent dinner on the balcony during their evening flight from Paris. The next day they attempted a landing in Germany, but strong winds at ground level made *Le Géant* tear along at speed, being narrowly missed by a locomotive before crashing into a wood where the balloon burst.

Much smaller than *Le Géant* was James Glaisher's balloon of 1862 in which he rose to some 35,000 feet, the present-day domain of international airliners. It was a flight made popular by the 2019 movie *The Aeronauts*. Glaisher was a founder of the new science of meteorology, a pioneering balloonist and a prominent photographer. His UK flight helped to establish knowledge of upper atmosphere weather conditions. In the film he is accompanied by a female balloonist, 'Amelia Rennes', seen as a crowd-pleasing exhibitionist, contrasting his scientific researching with her own practicality and sheer daring. During the high altitudes reached, Glaisher passed out, having insisted they continue to fly as high as they could. Amelia frees the frozen gas-release valve by climbing the balloon's ropework – without any safety gear – bringing them down to earth again. In reality, James's co-pilot was Henry Coxwell, who saved the balloon, the unconscious Glaisher and himself by releasing the valve just in time. The movie depiction of a dashing young woman suits 21st century aspirations at the expense of acknowledging a real pioneer.

Balloon exploits were exciting, drawing crowds to watch and bringing publicity. They were only reliable forms of transport if they could be steered. "I have profound faith that the screw will be our aerial motor", Glaisher wrote in 1863, envisioning a machine using screws to lift it off the ground with others for forward flight (Rolt, 1985:145). Perhaps he had absorbed one of Leonardo da Vinci's flying machine proposals that had a wide helical screw to provide lift. Screws, in the more elegant shape that we would call propellers, needed power, for which steam engines and electric motors were both tried but with only minor success. They lacked the level of power needed. Steam needed copious fuel and water, while firing was dangerous under a gas balloon. Electricity needed large batteries. Charles Renard and Arthur Krebs achieved some success in *La France* of 1884. They were able to fly from Chalais-Meudon on a five-mile route and back to their starting point (Payne, 1991). It was steerable under its own power so was not just a balloon but an airship or dirigible. However, their batteries and motor could only provide sufficient power to succeed on calm days.

It was in 1888 that an internal combustion engine built by the Daimler company powered an airship flown by Dr Karl Woelfert. It handled well but was underpowered. A bigger craft was finally funded and took off from Tempelhof Field, Berlin, in 1897. Kaiser Wilhelm had ordered the army to help. The dirigible climbed to almost a thousand metres (3,280 ft). Expanding hydrogen vented through a valve just as Woelfert decided he could ignite the Daimler engine that used an open flame. The hydrogen reached the engine and exploded in flames, killing Dr Woelfert and his mechanic, Robert Knabe (Payne, 1991). Just a few months later, an aluminium airship built for David

Shwarz crashed at Tempelhof. The pilot survived uninjured, but the airship was destroyed. One of the spectators that day was Count Ferdinand Zeppelin.

The lighter-than-air fliers built by Count Zeppelin's company (1900 onwards) were by far the most important once ballooning was considered practicable. They were relatively luxurious. Passengers were carried thousands of miles. Military versions caused great destruction in the World War I. The sight of a wartime Zeppelin looming overhead caused fear because of its bulk and slow, relentless movement. Zeppelins were the first flying craft to carry tourists and business travellers, crossing continents and oceans. One of them, LZ-127, *Graf Zeppelin*, circled the globe with eighteen passengers and reporters for German newspapers and those of William Randolph Hearst in America. They dined at tables set out as if in a large house. They typed up their reports at the tables and spent time relaxing, eating, chatting or viewing the world below. They could retire to their cabins where daytime sofas converted into night-time bunks.

Guillaume de Syon summarises the intense pride felt by Germans for their achievements in peace and war:

> "Only 119 Zeppelin rigid airships were built between 1900 and 1939, yet Germans celebrated them with countless kitsch pieces – mass-produced collectables that, just like battlefield souvenirs or mementoes of Queen Victoria's golden jubilee, illustrated their subject's hold on the popular mind … Zeppelins may have transported thousands, but they enchanted millions" (de Syon, 2002:3)

Count Ferdinand Zeppelin (1838-1917) had joined the army of Württemberg, from where he was given leave to study engineering in university. In 1863 he took leave to go to the USA to become an observer for the Union army in the Civil War. Zeppelin met a balloonist, John Steiner, when in St Paul, Minnesota. Steiner gave him a flight in his balloon, leaving Zeppelin with a memory that years later turned into the origin of a new career. Another influence was a lecture he attended in Berlin in 1874 by Heinrich von Stephan on the subject of *'World Postal Services and Air Travel'*. The carrying of airmail would become a major source of income for fledgling air services. Zeppelin began to consider how a steerable dirigible could be built. Drawing on the work of aeronauts of the day and his own engineering knowledge, he noted in his diary on 25 March 1874 his design. It was for a cigar shaped and metal-framed outer envelope with a number of hydrogen-filled gas bags inside, as first proposed by Jean Baptiste Meusnier in 1783.

Count Zeppelin left the army as a General in 1890. He set up in business to build airships, employing engineers to work with him on the designs. Raising finance proved challenging when the Prussian Airship Service agreed to provide funds but withdrew the offer only weeks later. A lecture by the Count to the Association of German Engineers provided the key to a solution. The Association took a patriotic view in a report saying "France, North America and England have overtaken us [in the field of flight] with considerable resources. Should not German technology participate too in the solution to this problem?" (de Syon, 2002:19). They organised a public appeal for funds which helped considerably. 'Crowd funding' is nothing new, even if in those days it was rare.

With Zeppelin's own investment, the result allowed building Zeppelin LZ-1 which flew for the first time on 2 July 1900 over Lake Constance near Friedrichshafen. It used a floating hangar that could be turned to the best angle for bringing out LZ-1, whatever the wind direction. Media interest began to be taken in the vast structure: reporters and casual visitors hired boats to get closer, but openings in the hangar were draped with cloth. At last the airship was brought out and released to rise some 300 metres. Then an engine crankshaft broke, LZ-1 veered round and bent part of its metal frame. It flew for twenty minutes before returning to the hangar. The press was ecstatic. "A building-sized machine led by a veteran hero of the Franco-Prussian War had successfully defied gravity" (de Syon, 2002:23).

Even so, further progress was still hampered by a lack of funds. For a time, the whole project was shut down and employees paid off. It was 1905 before new funding allowed work to restart. The next airship, LZ-2, flew once but crashed after mechanical failures and strong winds brought it down. LZ-3, however, made good flights that changed the attitude of the German government. It granted Zeppelin 500,000 marks to help him continue. Two airships were to be delivered to the military. This was done, but no more such contracts were forthcoming. There was one more, unsold, airship doing nothing.

The solution this time came from Alfred Colsman, the business manager of the Zeppelin company. Colsman persuaded the Count to set up DELAG, the acronym for the German name of the 'German Airship Travel Company'. It became the world's first passenger airline, using the unsold dirigible to get going. Strictly speaking, it was not at that time an airline as defined today, as it never operated regular, timetabled flights and routes (see Botting, 2001). But Zeppelin was becoming a tourism pioneer. Colsman did a deal with Albert Ballin, head of the Hamburg America Line. Ballin put up 100,000 marks a year to promote DELAG, and in return was given the exclusive rights to sell tickets for journeys by airship (Payne 1991, de Syon 2002). The unused LZ-6 found its new use as an excursion airship flying over German cities.

Colsman and Ballin tapped German pride in their country and their pioneers of flight, though Zeppelin thought it all a bit beneath him (Botting 2001, Syon 2002). LZ-6 played its part by flying to Berlin on 29 August 1909 to be greeted by a claimed two million people in the streets and a hundred thousand at the Tempelhof Field. Several city mayors joined the enterprise by building airship hangars in their cities, the first municipal airport facilities anywhere. Dusseldorf completed its hangar first and a newly built airship, LZ-7, arrived at it on 22 June 1910 (Payne, 1991). The flight path had been announced with the planned timings, which meant excited crowds at every possible point. By July 1914 DELAG had carried over 34,000 passengers on more than 1,500 flights.

World War I switched airship attention to military uses. The passenger Zeppelins were taken over by the military. Other Zeppelins, including newly built craft, went to war, notably carrying out bombing raids on Britain. These exploits raised pride amongst the German nation for Count Zeppelin and his machines, but he was not to enjoy his fame for long as, at the age of 78, he died in 1917. The next year, his country lost the war. The peace conference that took place at Versailles imposed damaging provisions on Germany (see de Syon, 2002). It had to accept blame for the loss and damage suffered to its opponents in the war, a verdict that not only caused its people resentment but confirmed the feelings of enmity by its victorious opponents towards Germany. Zeppelins were destroyed in their hangars by their own aircrew rather than have them handed over as reparations to the Allies. At least, the company plant, archives and key personnel survived, and limited new constructions could be taken on – for a while.

A new airship, *Bodensee,* was built and began regular flights between Berlin and Friedrichshafen. Now the company was becoming a real airline. It made it possible for Berlin people to get to the tourist destinations of the German south. The airship was fast, reaching 132 kph (82 mph), cutting the journey time from 24 hours by train to six by air. A second airship, *Nordstern,* was added for a proposed Friedrichshafen-Berlin-Stockholm run. The Treaty of Versailles had stipulated only flights to wartime neutral countries were to be allowed. Then the Allies ordered Germany to hand over the two airships in compensation for the Zeppelins destroyed by their aircrews. The company turned to making kitchen pots and pans out of aluminium and even gearboxes and automobiles, in a desperate attempt to earn money (de Syon, 2002).

Crossing the Atlantic Ocean offered the best cost/benefit ratio for air travel. The first successful flights were made in 1919, led by aeroplanes. A Curtiss NC-4 flying boat of the US Navy made the west to east crossing over five days in May, using two stops in the Azores. Two weeks later, RAF pilots Alcock and Brown flew non-stop from Newfoundland to Ireland, taking 16 hours and 27 minutes. Almost immediately, the British rigid airship, R34, crossed from Scotland to Long Island, New York, against the prevailing winds. It was a flight of 108 hours. It was notable that the reception party had no experience of handling airships, so Major J E M Pritchard parachuted from the R34 to supervise the work. Eight days later, R34 flew back to its base in Pulham, Norfolk (Botting, 2001). In 1927, Charles Lindbergh would make his solo flight from Long Island, New York to Paris. Aeroplanes were competing with airships and their future prospect looked bright.

The Zeppelin company was kept going by its head, Dr Hugo Eckener, who succeeded Ferdinand Zeppelin on the latter's death in 1917. Eckener was different from Zeppelin: pragmatic, skilled at business planning and an experienced airship pilot. He investigated the possibilities of foreign sales of passenger-carrying airships – the Treaty of Versailles banned German military craft – to the USA, clinching a deal for LZ-126. This was a twenty-passenger training ship for the US Navy. It was the first to have sleeping accommodation, plus radio room, electric kitchen, washrooms and toilets. It had five engines by Maybach, giving it a top speed of 126 kph (almost 80 mph). Less well known is the fact reported by the UK's *Independent* newspaper of 23 August 2013 that the intestines of 250,000 cows were needed to make the gas bags that held the hydrogen providing the lift.

LZ-126 was test flown in 1924. Eckener flew it with German crew and American Navy observers to the naval air station at Lakehurst, New Jersey, after making a circuit about New York City with a climb to over 3,000 metres (5,000 feet) to the amazement of crowds far below. It had been the first Atlantic crossing by a Zeppelin. The airship, named *Los Angeles*, proved highly successful, with a total of nearly 5,000 hours flown in its eight-year working life (Botting, 2001).

The Atlantic flight marked a turning point in German-US relations and a new high point in Germany's own view of Dr Eckener. He was lauded at home and in the United States. The Zeppelin company entered into a close relationship with the Goodyear Tyre and Rubber Company of Akron, Ohio, itself strongly interested in developing airships. Hugo Eckener returned to Germany to a hero's welcome. On the face of it, however, Zeppelin had built its last ship. It took another public funding appeal to raise money for whatever was to be built next. Eckener travelled the country, delivering illustrated lectures about the American exploit. Then the Treaty of Locarno, 1925, allowed Germany to build big airships again. LZ-127 was born. It was named *Graf Zeppelin* after Count Zeppelin. LZ-127 was the longest airship to date, with a crew of 36, destined to make nearly six hundred flights totalling 1.7 million km (over 1 million miles) over its nine-year life.

After a test flight over Germany and the Netherlands it crossed the North Sea to Harwich, England and then back to its Friedrichshafen base. Three weeks later, the airship set out to cross the Atlantic. It was a flight aimed at showing commercial passenger flights to the USA were possible – and profitable. Twenty passengers made the trip, a mix of German ministry people, reporters, photographers and artists who would record aspects of the life on board. One of the reporters was Lady Grace Hay Drummond-Hay, the vivacious widow of a much older man, a multi-surnamed diplomat and adventurer. Her travel writing for the Hearst newspapers helped to show her readers some of the magic to be gained from flying: "The golden ball of the sun sank lower and lower toward the horizon. The shores of Spain took on gleaming clusters of sparkling lights as one by one the tiny fishing villages illuminated themselves against the darkness" (Botting, 2001:118). Less romantic was one of the methods of checking the altitude of the airship. The duty officer would fire a gun loaded with a blank cartridge out of the control car window. The time taken for the echo to return from the sea below was measured automatically by an electric meter. Firing a gun with a mass of hydrogen close overhead did not reassure the passengers. Smoking, of course, was forbidden.

An emergency situation arose when a storm combined with a helmsman's error to send the airship up at a sharp angle, creating chaos as furniture and kitchenware were thrown around. One of the ship's stabiliser fins had part of its doped cotton cover ripped off. Hugo Eckener sent a radio request for ships to stand by. Volunteers from the crew had to climb out of the envelope to make repairs while the ship slowed down so much that its wind-powered generator failed, cutting off the kitchen's electricity and the radio room power. But the emergency call was not needed. It was a pity Eckener had to send it, just in case, because bad publicity could have been harmful. A temporary repair sufficed, and the airship continued. Bad weather made progress slow and erratic. American radio stations during the radio silence had assumed the Zeppelin lost. When at last it crossed the coast, people began to pour into the streets of cities as soon as it appeared, Hugo Eckener deliberately taking a course over Washington, Baltimore and New York to show off his ship before turning to Lakehurst Field in New Jersey. They landed after 111 hours and 44 minutes' flying time on 15 October 1928 (see Botting, 2001).

America went mad over the exploit. Lady Hay was feted as the first woman to fly across the Atlantic. There were dinners, speeches, theatre shows, more speeches, press shows, and meetings, it seemed, with anyone who was anyone on the Atlantic coast. A writer in the Viennese *Arbeiter Zeitung* declared the exploit greater than that of Charles Lindbergh who had flown an aeroplane from the USA to France, solo, the year before (de Syon, 2002).

Round the World

It was exciting, triumphant, even pioneering – but airships were fighting a rear-guard action against the progress of aeroplanes. By 1928 there were scheduled, reliable, aeroplane passenger services across Europe and beyond. They operated from London to Moscow, into the Middle East and as far as India, using multiple stops along the way. In 1919 there had been some 5,000 passengers carried, worldwide. In 1929 the number reached 434,000 (Botting, 2001). Airships represented luxury but they were difficult to handle. Airports could only cope with one at a time. Around 240 men were needed to manoeuvre them on the ground (Davies, 1991). Bad weather caused problems since they presented such a large profile towards the wind. The gas needed to lift them took a long time to assemble and load into the gasbags. If it was helium it was safe, but it came from the United States and was banned from export. If hydrogen was used, it was a deadly threat.

No new contracts had come from the Atlantic jaunt. Eckener needed to set up more publicity flights. The first was a non-stop flight across the Mediterranean to Greece, Crete, Palestine, Egypt and back via the Danube valley. Over Jerusalem and the Dome of the Rock the airship hovered with engines stopped as a mark of reverence. At the Dead Sea, Eckener and his crew took the Zeppelin almost to the surface of the water, revelling in the idea that they were actually flying a thousand feet (305m) below sea level.

Next, another Atlantic crossing. It nearly ended in disaster. The Zeppelin's chief engineer had altered the propeller couplings on the engines. Before they had left the coast of Spain, two engines failed. They turned back. Two more failed. They were just able to reach the French airship base near Toulon. It was two months before new engines could be fitted and LZ-127 could return to Friedrichshafen.

Hugo Eckener still wanted publicity for Zeppelins as worldwide passenger transports. "'We knew we had a good and capable airship', he was later to inform an audience of six thousand members of the National Geographical Society in Washington DC, 'so we conceived the seemingly fantastic idea of a world cruise'" (Botting 2002:156). A route was chosen that suited *Graf Zeppelin's* range between refuelling and re-provisioning, that gave relative freedom from high mountains and bad weather. It ran across Russia to the Siberian city of Yakutsk, then turned south to Tokyo before heading for San Francisco and Los Angeles, Chicago and New York, ahead of spanning the Atlantic to North West Spain and on to Friedrichshafen. The story has been told in detail by Douglas Botting (2002) and in cinematic form by Ditteke Mensink's film *Around the World by Zeppelin,* originally called *Farewell.* Lady Grace's diaries were quoted at length, read by Poppy Elliott. The film has been made available in its entirety on YouTube.

Financing the round-the-world trip was a problem. Hugo Eckener had calculated a total of over $250,000 (Payne, 1991:175). Apart from the direct costs of the Zeppelin there was a major support expense required: shipping 883,000 cubic feet (25,000m³) of *Blaugas* to Tokyo. This was the gaseous fuel used by the engines. A team of technicians had to go with it to supervise the ground crew handling the fuel.

That was solved by William Randolph Hearst, whose reporter, Lady Grace Hay, had been on that first Atlantic trip and the cruise to Egypt. But Hearst wanted exclusive rights to the story in return for supplying two-thirds of the total budgetary need. Eckener knew he dare not exclude German reporting, so agreed finally with Hearst to let the media mogul have US and UK story rights alone in return for meeting just under half the total cost - $100,000 (Payne, 1991:175). The German newspaper and newsreel people would pay and the third amount would come from passenger tickets sold at $9,000 (≈ $133,000) each for the round the world trip, and payments by stamp collectors for special commemorative stamps and first day covers. These were always very lucrative items for the Zeppelin company.

Eckener wanted the start and finish to be at Friedrichshafen. Hearst insisted on New York and specifically with a flight around the Statue of Liberty. Eckener agreed. He knew the *Graf* would go from Germany to the USA to fulfil Hearst's demands, while at the end of the circumnavigation in New York would make a return journey to its European base. It would be like having two orbits that began and ended at whichever point you acknowledged. The German route would be the more important of the two, of course (Botting, 2002).

Lady Grace would again be one of the reporters for the Hearst media. Another was to be Karl Wiegand, also reporting for Hearst. He had been on the famous Atlantic pioneering trip and on the Egyptian cruise. Wiegand was a married man. But he was having a romantic liaison with Lady Grace, the young widow. Other reporters represented France, Spain, Japan, Russia and Germany. There were both stills and movie photographers. Sir George Hubert Wilkins, the Australian explorer, was taking part. William B Leeds was an American multi-millionaire, the only traveller to have bought his own ticket. The officers, crew and passengers totalled 61, with Lady Grace the only woman. The Zeppelin flight to New Jersey began on 1 August 1929. On 7 August it took off for Germany, making a crossing coast to coast in fifty-five hours. On the 15th it left Friedrichshafen, photography and filming taking place at every available opportunity. A particularly prominent shot showed the passengers gazing at a map of the world (Botting, 2002).

Graf Zeppelin crossed into Poland at a height of 400 metres (1,300ft), flying over Danzig to a welcome by aeroplanes and the sounds of "ships' sirens, factory hooters, locomotive whistles, church bells" drifting up to them (Botting, 2002:163). Bad weather over Russia prompted a change of course that omitted Moscow, to the angry disappointment of the Russian reporter on board. Later, the Kremlin delivered a note to Berlin denouncing what it called a clearly political snub, routing the *Graf* closer to the aristocratic city of Leningrad rather than the city of the new USSR, Moscow.

They began the long crossing of the USSR. The appearance of a giant airship could have an unsettling effect on people who had not, like those in the western cities, been kept up to date with such futuristic technology. "Suddenly

I spot a couple of peasants in a field. They must have been sleeping there, because they take one look at the airship then run in panic across the meadows to a little log cabin and disappear inside", wrote one of the passengers (Botting, 2002:167). After the Urals came the long flight over Siberia with its monotonous forests, lakes, rivers and swamps. Eckener recalled "the impression of a dreadful waste, uninhabitable for man or beast" in a speech to the National Geographic Society later (Payne, 1991:176).

More scattered villages. In one of them, a panic-stricken horse on seeing the airship bolted and the cart it dragged demolished two huts. At last, the Zeppelin turned south and headed for Japan. After another long flight they landed in Tokyo. They had flown non-stop over 11,200km (7,000 miles) in just under 102 hours, a new distance flight record. The Trans-Siberian Railway would have taken more than fourteen days.

Vast crowds watched the airship arrive. There were great celebrations. "'The Graf Zeppelin has conquered Japan' commented Lady Grace. Tokyo is Zeppelin mad'" (Botting, 2002:186). It prompted "stunning displays of enthusiasm for all things German, and even a rare imperial reception" (de Syon, 2002:136). There were tea ceremonies and banquets. Meanwhile, a hundred Japanese mechanics overhauled the ship, revictualled and refuelled it and topped up the gas bags. After days of junketing, the airship took off for San Francisco. It would be the first non-stop crossing of the Pacific Ocean. Hugo Eckener chased a typhoon in the hope of gaining more speed, then found the ship between two thunderstorms with lightning playing around them. They were fierce storms but over within half an hour. Following winds pushed them along at around 100 mph (160 kph), covering the 5,400 miles (8,690km).

Their route on a great circle course from Japan to North America lay over the North Pacific, through banks of fog. Then, after three days flying, the coast of the USA came into sight just south of San Francisco. They continued down the coast to their landing point at Mines Field (the future LAX), Los Angeles, and the usual excited welcome. On the face of it, flying the broad Pacific showed a bright prospect for the airship industry. Douglas Botting (2002) summed up international opinion: The Chief of the US Bureau of Aeronautics predicted round the world scheduled service would soon be a reality. The Japanese government said it would welcome a German-Russian-Japanese service using airships. The director of the German Lufthansa airline thought aeroplanes could work closely with airships in commercial services. Despite a minor problem taking off again from Los Angeles, Graf Zeppelin flew on to Lakehurst,

New Jersey and after a short stay it returned to Germany. It arrived after a total time in the air of slightly under 300 hours and an average speed of 70.07 mph (113.7 kph) (Payne, 1991:178).

Hugo Eckener stayed in the United States for two weeks, discussing with Paul W Litchfield, President of the Goodyear-Zeppelin Corporation, plans for a network of airship services linking continents round the globe. The success was a boost for German technology in general. "From Leica cameras to Krupp crank-shafts, anything associated with the trip was offered for sale, thus indirectly confirming Eckener's claim that the airship would help world trade" (de Syon, 2002:136). The idea of tourism flights, notably sensational ones like that of the *Graf Zeppelin*, was spread wide. "Some of the more enthusiastic accounts of its trip around the world actually appeared in the form of adventure books published abroad" (de Syon, 2002:136).

It is probably not pushing an idea too far to say that World War I, while a subject of humiliation for Germany, was seen elsewhere in the 1920s as a force unlocking people's realisation that the world was open for travel. Millions had suffered and resentments were common, but millions had spent time abroad. It was now much easier for ordinary people to overcome fears of different cultures. Tours of battlefields were made with tour operators. As we have already seen, cars, coaches and their operators had drawn on wartime resources and training. To some, wartime had been an adventure time. To the better-off, boating and even flying were more accessible. Seeing the world from on high was exciting. Zeppelins were a shape of things to come.

It was not to be. Airships represented the end of a line in flying. They used hydrogen instead of helium, the latter being only available in the USA. The disastrous burning of the airship *Hindenburg* on arrival at Lakehurst, New Jersey, on 6 May 1937 ended all but some minor flights by other airships. A spark of static electricity is believed to have ignited the hydrogen bags. Thirty-six people died.

The arrival of the *Hindenburg* was filmed, but it was a radio broadcast that seared into the memory of the public and which still resonates today. A thirty-two-year-old reporter from the Chicago station WLS, Herbert Morrison, had been assigned to cover the arrival with a recording engineer, Charlie Nehlsen. They had no facilities for live broadcasting so could only record. Morrison described the *Hindenburg* coming down to its mooring mast in the rain and then "It's burst into flames! ... and it's crashing! It's crashing, terrible! ... this is the worst of the worst catastrophes in the world. Oh, the humanity! " (transcript in Wikipedia: 'Herbert Morrison'). The recording was rushed to WLS in Chicago and broadcast with its chilling, agonising, message to the world.

The effect of the Lakehurst tragedy was immediate. It marked the death of the airship dream.

Aeroplanes

This chapter started with the frequent myth that package holidays date from when aircraft were used to fly tourist groups to their destinations. Another misleading myth is the thought that it took only sixty-six years to go from the Wright brothers' successful Kitty Hawk flight to landing a man on the moon. The premise seems to be that a single, simple, line of development took the required technology from the one to the other. It is very misleading.

The Wrights were aircraft men. The NASA teams were rocket men and women. Much was learnt and shared by the people who developed each line of work, but there were big differences between them. And both technologies date back hundreds of years at least. For the moment, we can leave rocket tech to one side, with passenger flights using them a long way off from our 1851-1941 period. Making military rockets that were powerful on liquid fuels was the obsession just before World War II, when they proved how terrifying they could be. Meanwhile, vast progress was being made with aircraft from the first real flights up to scheduled services carrying tourists. But it really got serious over a century before Kitty Hawk.

Sir George, and the Dragon

There were many experiments by people wanting to fly. Some tried to emulate birds, by making wings of feathers or cloth to attach to their arms. They did not understand power-weight ratios that were in favour for birds but not for humans. Some used kites, but kites did not go anywhere. Others used balloons, as we have seen. There were experiments with gliders. Some got no further than proposing ideas, some built models but failed to produce a full-size version that could carry a pilot. One that was fanciful, but only successful in the form of a model, was that of Tito Livio Burattini. He devised a strange glider shaped like a flying dragon, with four wings, a *Dragon Volant* (Harrison, 1996). It was said to have lifted a cat on a short flight in 1647. Burattini supposedly built a full-size version to carry three men. It apparently had operating wings giving lift and forward motion, but it never actually flew (Cynk,1963). The problem with Burattini and others was that they knew little about the science involved in flying.

Sir George Cayley (1873-1851) set out to change all that. He was the 6th Baronet Cayley, inheriting Brompton and Wydale Halls near Scarborough, North Yorkshire. Cayley was a scientist, engineer and inventor, responsible for developments in lifeboats, theatre safety curtains, the caterpillar track (known by him as the Universal Railway) and tension-spoke wheels. Above all these, his work on aeronautics was outstanding, leading to him being called the 'founding father of aviation' (Harrison 1996, Crouch 2003). Cayley's lifetime fascination with flight dated back to his childhood. He not only built a model glider in 1804 that flew, but a version later that lifted a stable boy on a short flight in 1849 along Brompton Dale. Other versions of this story exist, suggesting someone else as the timorous passenger, but a flight did take place and it contributed to Cayley's knowledge..

A replica of the craft is on display at the Yorkshire Air Museum at Elvington. Cayley had published accounts of his earlier aeronautical work in three papers between 1809 and 1813 in a well circulated science and arts journal. They covered wing shapes and angles in connection with lifting powers; the phenomenon of air streaming over a cambered wing producing low-pressure on the upper surface and high-pressure underneath. The benefit of wings being angled upward slightly helped lateral stability. He included other discoveries. Cayley could have explained to Tito Burattini some of the reasons why the dragon idea would not work.

Although it was more than eighty years before the Wright brothers experimented with their aeroplanes, Cayley's work helped them progress. Other inventors attempted successful model glider tests, following a tradition set out by Sir George Cayley – John Stringfellow, William Henson, Augustus Herring, Karl Jathro, Ponton d'Amecourt and Enrico Forlanini among others (Harrison 1996, Crouch 2003). Samuel Pierpont Langley flew a steam-powered model plane with a 4.5 metre (15 ft) wingspan across the Potomac in Washington DC. It travelled more than 1,200 metres (0.75 miles). His theoretical discoveries added to those of Cayley. Clément Ader made a 200-metre 'hop' near Paris using a steam-powered engine in a simple aeroplane. It rose about three metres. James Harrison (1996) has written that a gas-powered engine might have made the hops turn into flights. In Britain, Percy Pilcher glided 250 metres in the grounds of Stanford Hall in 1897, reaching height of 60 metres (197 ft). Otto

Lilienthal, from Pomerania, made two thousand flights in sixteen glider types (Crouch, 2003). Both Pilcher and Lilienthal would be killed in flying accidents.

Gustave Whitehead claimed he made flights in 1901-02 using a steerable aeroplane in Fairfield, Connecticut. He was an accomplished mechanic with much knowledge of aviation ideas. Newspapers reported his flight, based on a report by one Richard Howell, a journalist. Whitehead's claim has been supported by some specialist researchers, including Paul Jackson of *Jane's All the World Aircraft* in 2013 (weblist: Whitehead). There has been a long controversy over this story which, at the moment seems to conclude he did not fly successfully. On the other hand, there are websites offering vigorous support to his case.

There is an important issue for modern tourism here, by way of a case study. So many heritage attractions celebrate past events in ways which raise feelings of pride. There can be stirrings of national or regional leadership, or perhaps suggestions of racial, cultural or other group pride. The same applies to the stories passed down from one family generation to another, through the productions of the mass media and the even the teachings of formal education. Museum displays are researched, written and presented with just as much risk of bias as any other art form. We will see how this might have affected the Smithsonian Museum's attitude towards the Wright brothers' aircraft.

The Wright brothers

Orville and Wilbur Wright's story has been told in detail in many works (eg Ash 1974, Howard 1988, McCullough 2015). As with the history of balloons and Zeppelins, what is important to this book is the development of aeroplanes used to carry travellers and tourists. The Wright brothers were dedicated to achieving man-carrying, powered aeroplanes. They had business and technological skills from running their bicycle shop in Dayton, Ohio. They shared an interest in one of the great ambitions of the day, the emulation of birds' ability to fly, soar to great heights and twist and turn in any direction they chose. What they did not have, in the mid-1890s, was knowledge of how to solve the problems of human flight. Orville wrote to the Smithsonian Museum in May 1899, requesting information on the subject. The Museum responded quickly with annual reports, papers and extracts of books, plus a list of other books which were then promptly all ordered by Orville and Wilbur (Harrison, 1996). Within a month they had built a biplane glider that they could pilot by twisting the wings enough to cause a change in direction – wing warping.

They realised the importance of locations with steady winds to help them get airborne. Rather than inland Ohio, it became clear that coastal places were better. A copy of *The Monthly Weather Review* noted Kitty Hawk in North Carolina as somewhere with steady winds [Harrison, 1996]. They wrote to the area's County Commissioner with details of what they needed and their aims. Back came the reply: "If you decide to try your machine here … you will find hospitable people when you come among us" [Crouch, 2003]. Wilbur went on a 'scientific vacation', ordering pine timber in Norfolk, Virginia on the way, finding smooth hill slopes and yielding sand at Kitty Hawk – ideal for their efforts – and building a kite-like glider, ready for Orville to join him from the bicycle shop. Tourist vacations like this one could be the precursors of scientific progress!

The brothers spent a long time reading, building, testing with their own-built wind tunnel, flying models and then, over six years, a series of seven full-size craft. These included a kite, three gliders and three powered machines [Crouch, 2003]. Every tiny variable they could test was tested, from the materials used to the angle of attack of the wings, the vertical separation distance of the two sets of wings, the speed of the wind at different times and so on. There were times leading up to 1903 when Orville and Wilbur almost gave up because of the effort needed. They persevered, however, with a single, shared, determination that returned quickly after each setback.

In February of 1903 they began to build their *Flyer*. It had an engine machined by their bicycle shop engineer, Charles Taylor, based on a simplified automobile engine. It was not until December that they were ready to fly at a site in the Kill Devil Hills near Kitty Hawk. They laid a rail into the wind blowing over their chosen take-off area. The *Flyer* would run along it under its own power, fly and land on skids, since it had no wheels. It was a blustery day, the 14 December. A crowd of onlookers was on hand. Wilbur Wright took the first attempt after winning the toss of a coin. The plane moved forward under power, but Wilbur tried to make it rise too quickly. It stalled, crashed and needed repairs.

On the 17 December Orville climbed aboard. The take-off rail had been aimed into a 27 mph (43.4 kph) wind. This time, the *Flyer* flew, for about 120ft (36m). One of the onlookers, John Daniels, took a famous photo of the plane a mere two feet off the ground, with Wilbur visible to the right where he had been steadying the wing. It was a small elevation and a short flight, but it was the success they wanted. Three more flights took place. Wilbur took the plane 175 feet and Orville 200 feet. Then Wilbur achieved almost a minute in the air and a flight of 852ft (260m), before a sharp gust of wind caused a crash which smashed the front of the *Flyer* (Harrison, 1996). It would never take off again.

The Wrights would continue to research, build and fly, sometimes struggling to gain the recognition they deserved. This was partly due to newspapers misunderstanding what they had done, and in what way they differed from other pioneers elsewhere. The brothers were not effective self-publicists. They returned home for Christmas, reticent for some time to talk about their successes since they were anxious to protect their patents and methods. On 6 January they gave details of the flights to the Associated Press. Slowly, the word would spread, aided by the Wrights supplying new aircraft to take part in events like the Rheims Aviation Week in August 1909 and a series of exhibition shows, each of which was a tourist-attracting event. We have already come across Wilbur's 'scientific vacation', as recorded by him, noting it today as a tourist event. Soon would come the 'history by contract' episode with the Smithsonian, which, as a national United States showcase, gained one of its most important artefacts, displayed for tourists to see.

One of the reasons they had chosen Kill Devil Hills near Kitty Hawk was its remoteness from popular coastal resorts, so that they were not overrun by inquisitive tourists. That was the situation for three decades. There was nothing there to commemorate or describe the flights. The dunes were not easy to reach – Wilbur's first visit was made with the help of a leaky fishing boat crossing Albemarle Sound and accommodation was not easy to find. Kitty Hawk had a population of only 300 at the time of the first flights. The nearest railway station then was 46 miles away in Snowden NC. Shooting wild fowl and fishing were attracting wealthy northerners, but there was little other tourism and local people often disliked those visitors (weblist: Kitty Hawk tourism). Highway 64, running right across North Carolina 'from Murphy to Mateo' in a popular phrase, was designated in 1934. Ferries had to continue plying, crossing Albemarle Sound to take the route to Mateo and then the Outer Banks where the Kill Devil Hills stand. Bridges began to replace ferries from the 1930s.

As aeroplanes became more sophisticated and the part played by the brothers appreciated, moves were made towards commemorating the success. The Wright Brothers National Memorial was dedicated on Kill Devil Hill in 1932. Orville was still alive to see the event. Wilbur had succumbed to typhoid fever long before, in 1912. In November 1948, Orville Wright sold the Kitty Hawk aeroplane to the Smithsonian Museum for a nominal $1. The plane had been at the London Science Museum for some years after a dispute with the Smithsonian. Returning it to the USA was on condition that it be permanently on show with an information panel stating

> "The world's first power-driven heavier-than-air machine in which man made free, controlled, and sustained flight".

The terms of the sale contract stipulated that, should the Smithsonian decide another aeroplane flew under power before the Wright brothers, the Kitty Hawk machine would revert to the ownership of the brothers' estate. The Museum would therefore lose an important, original, artefact. It could be that the Smithsonian, arguing, as it has in other places, against the possibility of the Gustave Whitehead aeroplane having flown first, might be guilty of wrongly promoting its star exhibit, the Wright brothers' plane. It might therefore be misleading its visitors admiring the Wrights' achievement. This was called 'history by contract' in a book under that title by William O'Dwyer and Stella Randolph [1978] published in Germany. Gustave Whitehead was a German immigrant to the USA and originally known as Gustav Albin Weisskopf. To date, at least, the balance of opinions gives primacy to the Wright brothers.

The Kill Devil Hills site now has a visitor centre that was opened in 1960. It displays machinery and tools used by the Wrights, a replica of their 1902 glider and another of the 1903 aircraft. The wind tunnel they used for testing has been replicated. They built a hangar for the *Flyer* and a hut as living quarters. Both originals had been demolished years before, but they have also been replicated. Each of the famous flight paths used by the brothers has been marked out along the ground.

The Replica Workshops at Kitty Hawk
Part of a Popular Tourist Attraction

After their success at Kitty Hawk, Wilbur and Orville worked on making an aeroplane that would be fully controllable and dependable. They did so at a place known as Huffman Prairie near Fairborn, Ohio. It was easily accessible by rail from their home in Dayton, Ohio. Many test flights over two years led to the *Wright Flyer II*, considered by them as their first 'proper' aeroplane. It has been restored and put on show at the Carillon Historical Park in Dayton. A replica of their 1905 hangar and their launching catapult are at the Huffman Prairie Flying Field Historical Site. There is also an interpretive centre about their work. Their home and bicycle shop from Dayton were acquired in 1937 by Henry Ford and re-erected at his Greenfield Village open air museum at Dearborn, Detroit. Kitty Hawk, Huffman Prairie and Greenfield Village tell the Wright Brothers' story in more immersive ways than any book could do.

Flying People

More adventurers were trying their luck, for a high level of luck was what was needed in aeronautics. The London *Daily Mail* in late 1908 offered a prize of £500 (≈£40,000) for the first aeroplane flight across the English Channel. It was not claimed, so the next year it was doubled. The Channel represented a real challenge. A flight would have to cover over 33 km (21 miles) with no chance of landing on the way in an emergency. Proving a crossing made economic sense because of the potential demand for business travel between England and France. Delivering air mail, even by dirigible or balloon, had not yet been officially organised anywhere, though it was clearly going to be a profitable activity once planes were reliable enough.

Hubert Latham attempted '*La Manche*' on 19 July 1909, flying from Sangatte. Within 10 kms (6 miles) of Dover, his aircraft suffered engine failure and he had to pioneer a different skill – landing on the sea, from where he was picked up by a French destroyer. Louis Blériot made his attempt on 25 July, escorted by another destroyer from which he took his course, but quickly overtook the warship. He reached the English coast and landed near Dover Castle. The site is marked out now by an outline of his aeroplane in granite (see cover photo).

1909 saw two attempts at international aviation meetings. The first, according to David Wragg [1978], was spread over three months from 24 January in Monaco, but no-one attended at first, so another month was added. Wragg does not record any success brought by the extension. Then, in August, the first widely recognised meeting took place in Rheims. As often the case, a major tourism event provided a boost to a new industry. Up to 250,000 visitors took part over 22-29 August 1909, many brought by special trains from Paris. A race track at Bétheny, 5 km outside Rheims, was used as airfield, exhibition area and aerial racing circuit. It was equipped with aircraft sheds, 5,000-seat grandstands and public enclosures, a scoreboard, a 600-seater restaurant and even an airship hangar (weblist: Rheims). There was space for aircraft to manoeuvre and to take off. Four tall pylons marked the turning points in an oblong flying circuit, one lap of which measured 10 km (6.21 miles).

The spectators could inspect the planes taxiing before them, watch the races round the flying circuit and see aircraft take off on attempts to break records making long-distance flights. Most pilots at the time preferred to fly when there was no wind. So, a system of flags was displayed in Bétheny and along the road to the field to let potential visitors know if there would be flying that day: black for none when winds were too strong, white for possible flights, red for times when aircraft had already taken off (weblist: Rheims).

21 aeroplanes flew, with 17 others attending but only being displayed on the ground. The majority of the pilots were French, one was British and another British-born though permanently based in France. The Wright brothers looked upon it as a frivolous event, as usual missing the value of displays and races as publicity achievements. Glen Curtiss was the only American pilot, though there were six 'planes built by the Wrights. The Gordon Bennett International Aviation Cup was presented for the first time, for the fastest completion of a 20 km (12.4 m) course round the circuit. It was won by a margin of a few seconds by Glen Curtiss. Henry Farman, the Anglo-French pilot, won the *Grand Prix de la Champagne* endurance flight around the circuit by covering 180 km (112 miles). Hubert Latham took the altitude record by reaching 510 ft. Farman won a prize for making a flight with the most passengers – two. The flexibility, ease of ground and aerial handling and speeds achieved contrasted with what airships could do. Passenger capacity was another matter, however.

The First Passenger Aeroplanes

Little happened by way of regular aeroplane passenger services before World War I. 1913 saw the first service being established close to the end of that year in Florida. It flew between St Petersburg and Tampa with a Benoist Type XIV flying boat. The service was small, but perfectly formed, with a contract with St Petersburg that gave operators Tom Benoist and Paul Fansler a subsidy. From 1 January 1914 two round trips per day were made from St Petersburg, cutting out either a two-hour boat trip or a 12-hour railway journey to the shopping centre of Tampa [Chant, 1980]. Only a single passenger could be carried at a price of $5. It was a successful service so by the end of the month a larger Benoist flying boat was put into use. By then, the subsidy had been repaid and the business was making a profit. The contract was for only three months. From 1 April onwards they operated independently but the tourist season – one that was reliant on winter escapees from the North East – was ending. The service closed down.

The period between the pioneering flights of the Wright brothers and the end of the 1914-18 war was one of experimentation, publicity-seeking and then aerial warfare. Europe began to fight in 1914, the USA in 1917. By the end of hostilities technical progress and industrial organisation offered great potential for passenger flying. Services began in several places, often using converted bombers that gave appropriate engine power and cabin space. The trouble was, however, that the economic stresses of war began to hit hard. The brave new world of flying had not quite arrived, as events in the 1920s showed.

Kenneth Hudson and Julian Pettifer [1979] contrast European and American developmental services of the period as being based on passenger flights in Europe and mail delivery in the USA. America turned to passenger businesses late in the 1920s, but then forged ahead at speed. We have seen how Zeppelin airships operated by DELAG carried passengers in Germany from June 1910. German military services flew airmail in Eastern Europe during the war. The country's first airline was Deutsche Luft Reederei, in 1917, later to gain fame as Lufthansa. Britain was not allowed to start passenger flights across the Channel until 14 July 1919. Aircraft Transport and Travel Ltd took a single passenger, W H Pilkington of the St Helens glass business, from London to Paris early the next morning. He had missed his boat train and had an important meeting in the French capital. AT&T charged him £50 ($\approx$£1,453), flying him in an open cockpit. It took 2 hours 45 minutes [Hudson & Pettifer, 1979].

Scheduled flights to Paris began the next month, flying from Hounslow Heath, on the edge of where Heathrow now stands. Then, in March 1920, the British start of the route moved to Croydon. A wartime aerodrome had been established there in 1915 as part of London's defences against Zeppelin and aeroplane raids. Training squadrons were based there, and one of three National Aircraft Factories was built close by in 1918 [Learmonth et al, 1977]. When the war ended in November, only nine months after the first aircraft had been delivered from the factory, 1,500 employees were dismissed and 600 had their wages cut. Thousands of aircraft had been built there and so were put up for sale, either complete or as separate engines, instruments and materials. This was the source of wood mentioned earlier in describing how businesses were set up to manufacture caravans.

Croydon had become the Customs Airport of London with the move from Hounslow. It grew quickly with numerous huts, hangars and workshops. Trust Houses Ltd set up a hotel. It consisted of two parallel, single-storey buildings connected by two linking units, one being the reception area. Major expansion plans led to new buildings including a passenger and freight terminal designed to handle smooth flows of arriving and departing travellers. Alastair Gordon describes its symmetrical layout in his cultural study of airport design, *Naked Airport* (Gordon, 2004).

AT&T had moved its base from Hounslow to Croydon. John Pudney (1959) describes some of the navigation problems facing pilots, especially in an emergency, or, in a phrase used by George Holt Thomas, the boss of AT&T, 'an involuntary descent'. Thomas had proposed a 'ten-mile chain' of emergency landing grounds along the route between London and Paris. Some were arranged, but nothing like the suggested sequence of ten miles/16 kms apart. Radio communications between planes and ground facilities did not exist. Only the telephone linked the two main cities. There were what were called 'aerial lighthouses' – beacons – at the start and finish points. Along the route, some railway stations had their names painted large on rooftops. Following railway lines and occasionally large rivers was a prime navigation aid.

In May 1920, AT&T leased one of its De Havilland DH-16 aeroplanes to a newly formed company, which employed Jerry Shaw as pilot, flying between Croydon and Amsterdam. Shaw was the pilot who had flown Mr Pilkington to Paris. The new company was KLM. Although the pilot and the aircraft were British, Amsterdam was its base. Another experimental flight was made from that city to Bremen with a German aeroplane and crew. The next year saw them use their own crews and German-built Fokker F.II planes on the two routes (Hudson & Pettifer, 1979). F.IIs carried four or five passengers in some comfort. Their inter-continental service from Amsterdam to Batavia (now Jakarta), in the former Dutch East Indies, began with a one-off flight in 1924 using a Fokker F.VII. A regular scheduled service began in 1929, making the longest-distance scheduled service by an airline, at 9,500 miles, with stops at eighteen places over the twelve-day journey. Fokker aircraft were used at first, then from 1934 the Douglas DC-2.

Deutsche Luft Hansa was formed in 1926 through a merger of Deutsche Luft Reederie and Junkers Luftverkehr. Its Junkers F13 planes carried four passengers in seats fitted with safety belts and there were two pilot positions in the cockpit for safety and taking turns on long haul flights.

Meanwhile, AT&T ran into financial difficulties and closed down at the end of 1920. Others came to the fore. S Instone and Company was a coal-shipping company whose first vessel had been bought in 1914. It thrived during the war and had ten ships by 1918. It operated a private air service from 1919 on a route from Cardiff to Paris. 1920 saw it open up to the public as Instone Air Line, flying on the London to Paris route. In May 1922 it added a London to Cologne service, but competition on the Paris route forced it to close that service in the October.

Another company, Handley Page, had supplied heavy bombers with which to attack German bases. After 1918, it converted some planes for passenger use. It also produced its first dedicated passenger design, the W8. Handley Page Transport operated passenger flights on the London to Paris route. The competition that forced Instone to close a similar service also applied to Handley Page Transport. Foreign competition by French and German airlines undercut the efforts of British companies, thanks to their government subsidising them heavily. The trade journal *The Aeroplane* of March 1923 reported "The ding-dong struggle for the target number of passengers carried was won this week by the Air Union [forerunner of Air France] who carried 76 passengers to Handley Page Transport's 61" (Pudney, 1959:65).

The Handley Page service soon closed. The British government realised something had to be done. On 31 March 1924, Instone, Handley Page Transport, Daimler Airway (flying London to Manchester, Paris, Amsterdam, Hanover and Berlin) and British Marine Air Navigation (Southampton to Cherbourg, Le Havre and the Channel Islands using flying boats) were merged into a new body, Imperial Airways. All four had lasted only a few years.

Imperial Airways

The new airline concentrated on European routes, but it struggled in the face of continued competition from nationally subsidised airlines (Higham, 1960). The British government would not pay it a subsidy. Imperial began to abandon European routes and look at long-haul Empire services. The government took the opportunity to announce in 1928 that those would form Imperial's mission.

213

The strategy adopted was the creation of two major international routes, one to the Far East and Australia, the other down the eastern side of Africa to Cape Town. The routes were in common as far as Alexandria in Egypt, flying across France and Italy, with stops at Paris, Brindisi and Athens. Imperial had already taken over an RAF service in 1926, joining Cairo and Basra.

1929 saw Imperial begin an extension of the Cairo-Basra service, from Cairo back to Britain and from Basra forward to Karachi and later, Delhi. From April the route ran from Croydon to Basle by plane, train to Genoa, flying boat to Alexandria and land plane to Karachi – seven days for £130 single (≈£6,000). It was top-of-the-market activity – diplomats, senior politicians and company directors. However, political problems with the Italian government of Mussolini led to variations that included route points in Germany and Yugoslavia instead, and another advising passengers to use the Simplon-Orient Express from Paris to Athens. A variation of 1931 cut out Cairo in favour of Haifa, and which used Delhi Aero Club to operate between Karachi and Delhi. It was three years after that that a stable route took shape.

A 17-passenger Short S23 Empire Flying Boat
Operated by Qantas from 1938 (Wikipedia Commons)

After 1934 [see Davies, 2005], a traveller from London could fly by Handley Page 42 as far as Paris, then take a train all the way to Brindisi in the south of Italy. A Short S17 Kent flying boat took him or her to Cairo. Next came a Handley Page 45 via Gaza and Baghdad, Basra and Sharjah to Karachi. An Armstrong Whitworth Atalanta of Indian Trans-Continental Airways could fly the traveller to Delhi, Calcutta, Bangkok and Singapore. Imperial had so upset people in India by high-handedness that the government there insisted on operating the Karachi to Singapore section itself through Indian Trans-Continental Airways [Higham, 1960]. Qantas Empire Airways could take him or her to Batavia, Darwin and Brisbane.

Elsewhere, Cape Town had been served from 1932 using a similar combination of aeroplanes and railways. Between Cairo and Cape Town there were organised 27 main aerodromes and 30 intermediate landing places along 9,012 km (5,600 miles), with radio station contacts the whole way and a new

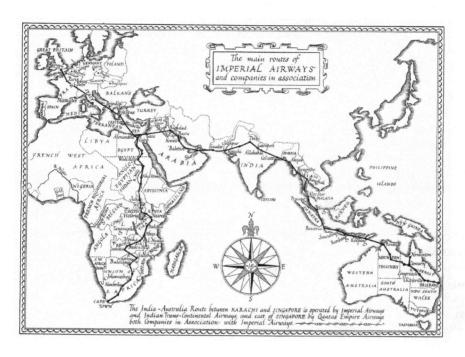

meteorological service to cover the route. London to Cape Town represented nearly 12,890 kms (8,000 miles) and ten and a half days' travelling (Pudney, 1959). The aircraft historian, Ron Davies, wrote of it as an interesting journey, "with scenic views of the Nile, Kilimanjaro, and the Victoria Falls, this would constitute an attractive inclusive package tour today" (Davies, 2005:40), though apart from some frequent safari hunters it was the travellers on business who largely made up the passenger lists. They represented "perhaps two per cent of the passengers" said one of Imperial's managers. They were people who still thought "Africa … a mecca for the safari business" (Hudson & Pettifer 1979:79; also see Bull, 1992).

As with KLM, whose early services to Batavia always started from Croydon, serving the needs of business and the administration of the Empire came first, with tourism a chance addition. Gordon Pirie analysed a sample of data from Imperial Airways about passengers in the period 1927-39. His conclusion put 64% as on work trips and 28% on recreational trips with 8% apparently unclear (Pirie, 2009:53). The implication seems to be that only the recreationists were tourists. The UK Tourism Society agreed definition of tourism in 2012 states that "A visitor is someone who is making a visit to a main destination outside his/her usual environment for less than a year for any main purpose [including] holidays, leisure and recreation, business, health, education or other purposes" (see Machin, 2016:28).

Previous definitions would have supported the clear distinction used by Pirie, but our views about what tourism is have changed markedly. A second problem arises: Pirie's figures do not record how many travellers would be away from home for more or less than a year, a key criterion under the Tourism Society definition. There is a third consideration. Even someone away from home in a full-time job would have recreational time, occupying an excursionist category. Most people are, in other words, tourists at any time when away from home for less than a year, moving between different *categories* of tourism. Even the one-year criterion is debateable. As pointed out in *Making Sense of Tourism: 1 The Beckoning Horizon*, and as suggested earlier by Chris Rojek and John Urry (1997), the question becomes – 'is there such an entity as tourism any longer?' None of this is to discount the value of Gordon Pirie's work – far from it. It shows the problems of understanding 'tourism' in the past, against the shifting sands of its definition.

Foreign travel from Britain after the 1914-18 war was no mass-market business. In 1921 only some 700,000 Britons ventured abroad, with most of them "in the service of the Empire and Empire trade" in Edmund Swinglehurst's words (1982:151) and few went by air. Even when, in the mid-1920s, air travel began to grow, tickets were expensive, having to cover the flights, meals and overnight stop accommodation on long-haul journeys. The aircraft used were larger, with between twelve and twenty passengers. This helped to spread the costs and reduce ticket prices, but they were comparatively high even so. The Handley Page W aircraft was the first designed as an airliner, though it was basically a version of one of the company's wartime bombers. It did have comfortable (but flimsy) wicker chairs, meal services and the first in-flight lavatory.

A few European services were added when suitable new aircraft offering a better cost/benefit ratio could be purchased. Airline market segments were at the top end of the scale, but prestige services and innovations were needed in the competitive world. A London to Paris service of April 1925 introduced the first use of an in-flight movie, *The Lost World,* not yet on general release. Kenneth Hudson [1972] notes the quality of the lunch menu on the French Air Union's Paris to London service. It included Langouste Parisienne, Poulet Sauté Chasseur, Jambon d'York à la Gelée and more, with champagne, red and white Bordeaux, whisky and other drinks. Imperial was not in the same league. A lunch menu of 1938 offered hors d'oeuvres, Fried Snapper au Citron, Roast Leg of Pork or Cold Buffet, followed by Apple Tart and Custard or Biscuits and Cheese or fruit. Perhaps the choice of those days was between Being Traditionally British or Trying Gallic Exoticism.

It was a world apart. Hudson quotes the French author of text in an Imperial Airways guide to the Paris-London service in 1924 who wrote: "At Le Bourget, introduce yourself to your pilot ... he will shake you by the hand and give you a brief idea what the flight will be like" [p28]. The author, Laurent Eynac, waxes lyrical about flying:

"Life expands in an aeroplane. The traveller is a mere slave in a train, and, should he manage to escape from this particular yoke, the car and the ship present him with only limited horizons. Air travel, on the other hand, makes it possible for him to enjoy 'the solitary deserts of infinite space'. It allows him to look around him freely and at never-ending variety. The earth speeds by below him, with nothing hidden and full of surprises, with its clear waters, its peaceful forests, its patient roads, its welcoming villages and fields" [p28].

We might read the above today with a touch of disbelief, even if remembering lower flying altitudes might have dodged clouds for a better view.. Others were promoting the new airline industry in similar terms. The travel journalist, Lowell Thomas, wrote a book called *European Skyways: The Story of a Tour of Europe by Aeroplane* based on a trip in 1927. "A new visionary world unfolds before the eye of the modern traveller who hurries from cloud to cloud ... We spiral down past cliffs of glistening mist, turning shell-pink on their edges as they are touched by the setting sun" [in Gordon, 2004:14]. Alastair Gordon points out that Thomas made "little mention of bad weather, air sickness, forced landings or engine failures", though it was an authentic account of the passenger's perspective at that early stage".

217

So much travel by air, at least in temperate zones, offers nothing more than a skyscape of dense clouds. But we are used to flying at thirty thousand feet. In the decades between the wars the ceiling for flying was about three thousand feet. Long journeys, such as to Africa or Asia, had to be broken by frequent landings for fuel and overnight stays, since night navigation was generally unknown until Luft Hansa began using a system of beacons to help its Berlin to Königsberg service in 1926. Going from London to Cape Town with Imperial required around thirty intermediate stops, let alone any that were caused by emergencies. Gordon Pirie notes that there were 72 hours spent in the air, there were four changes of aircraft and 2,000 km (1,243 miles) of rail travel (Pirie, 2009:55). There was at least the chance of scenic gazing, especially during the take-off and landing phases. Evenings and early mornings at each stop-over offered an encounter with a different climate, physical surroundings and cultures, not to mention different people.

Care would be taken to calm the anxieties of first-time fliers. "The pilot will not loop the loop or perform any other spectacular but useless and dangerous stunts" assured Cook's brochure *Aerial Travel for Business or Pleasure* (Swinglehurst, 1982:162). The corollary of anxiety was the adventure of the exotic experience.

"At Sharjah in the Persian Gulf, passengers were accommodated in a Beau Geste fort with watchtowers, parapets, iron-spike railings and barbed wire. Three dozen retainers of the local sheik stood guard" (Pirie, 2009:56).

Sometimes, the refuelling stop had to be built as a fortress. The Cairo to Baghdad section had to be provided with a fuelling stop halfway along its length, at Rutbah Wells. The Iraq government was persuaded to build a fortified compound, safe from possible predation by local tribespeople. It contained storage for food, water and fuel, aircraft spares, some hotel accommodation and a house for a manager and his wife. Apart from water from its oasis, everything had to be brought by road from Baghdad, 240 miles away. The British Director of Civil Aviation, Sir William Sefton Brancker, made an overnight stop. "The only detail that the architect had forgotten was the provision of fireplaces. Rutbah Wells must be nearly 3,000 feet above the sea and is often bitterly cold in December; we dined in overcoats and had a very shivery night in the hotel" (in Pudney, 1959:103).

At Cairo, the airline used Shepheard's Hotel and the Continental Savoy Hotel.

"Shepheard's was legendary, the epitome of style and sensation, a playground and watering hole for the aristocracy ... Many Imperial [Airways] passengers must have felt they were the new agents of Empire" (Nelson, 1960).

The special nature of making an early aeroplane flight was shown by an Australian lady speaking to author Julian Pettifer in 1978. She recalled travelling by QANTAS in the 1920s. Everyone put on their best clothes, she said, "after all, it was a very big event. You didn't turn up in any old thing" (Hudson & Pettifer, 1979:30).

Perhaps it reflected the upmarket nature of air travel. Railways and passenger ships might have had more than one class of accommodation. Until the boom in air travel after World War II, aeroplanes had just the one class. There was a measure of exclusiveness, of enjoying a special status when flying, that tempted the passengers to dress accordingly, carry appropriate accessories such as hand luggage, cameras and the like, and to behave in some suitable fashion. Hudson & Pettifer (1979:90) mark the importance of the 1939-45 conflict in a well-informed way:

"The Second World War, so far as civil aviation was concerned, was the Great Divide. During the decade which preceded it flying was becoming steadily safer, faster and more comfortable, and in the Western countries, about ten per cent more people each year were choosing to travel in this way. But the numbers were relatively small and, socially, passengers were a fairly homogeneous group. By modern standards, they were cosseted to an extraordinary degree. They expected good service, and, on the whole, they got it ... After the war ... [the airline's] business, as it now appeared, was to learn the new art of moving large numbers of people about the world fast and contrive to make a profit ... Those who remembered the grand days before 1939 would be the casualties" (p90).

Empire routes continued to be opened by Imperial up to 1939, often working with associated airlines such as Indian National, Qantas, South African Airways and Wearne's Air Services. There were projected routes to Canada, the USA and New Zealand, but these were delayed by the war.

Imperial Airways was not the only passenger plane operation in 1930s Britain. One such was started by Edward Hillman. He started driving in taxis after serving in the World War I, started a car-hire business and then bought his first coach in 1928. Within three years he owned over two hundred. In 1931, the government reorganised passenger coach services, setting up the London Passenger Transport Board. Hillman's fleet was taken over, with a sizable compensation paid, setting him on a new course buying four small aircraft for a service from Romford to Clacton-on-Sea, 44 miles away. It was labelled Hillman's Airways. He kept costs down and made money. Next, he persuaded De Havilland to design and build him a six-to-eight-seater biplane, the De Havilland Dragon Moth. It started his twice-daily service from Romford to Paris at the comparatively low price of £5 10s (≈£278) return – about what Imperial and Air France charged for a one-way ticket [Davies, 2005]. Hillman's travel-to-tourism progress was an early example of the kind of enterprise shown by Freddie Laker with Channel Air Bridge and Laker Airways' *Skytrain*, and Herb Kelleher's Southwest Airlines in the 1960s and '70s with their 'no frills' approach..

There were others: Spartan, Highland, Midland & Scottish, Olley Air Services, Railway Air Services and more. It might have been free enterprise at its best, but Stanley Baldwin's National Government in 1936 saw problems. The competition between them was cut-throat, some of them were moving into Europe and causing problems for Imperial at a time of economic crisis, and it felt Britain had lost prestige with signs of a threat from Nazi Germany [Higham, 1960]. The Under-Secretary of State for Air, Harold Balfour, moved to set up a 'second instrument' to bring about more British involvement in air travel. A series of mergers, subsidies, special mail contracts and careful encouragements led to the formation of British Airways Ltd in 1935 from a group of smaller airlines.

The Polytechnic Tourist Association, one of the great pioneers of package touring, advertised a kind of Grand Tour in 1934, "the first escorted air cruise of the capitals of Europe". Fourteen days, 2,829 miles and seven countries were to be taken up at a cost of £78.15s (≈£3,952). It was publicised widely but failed to attract enough people and was dropped [Pudney, 1959:180]. The British economic crisis of 1933-37 hit home. The PTA was successful taking people to parts of Europe by ferry and train, mainly using back-to-back bookings in its own hotels in a handful of destinations [see Studd, 1950]. Even in the later days of package travel by air, the multi-destination tour by aeroplane would be a rarity. Even single-destination flights were relatively scarce. There were just 147,000 passenger journeys in total on British airlines in 1938 [O'Connell, 2007].

It was unavoidably a time of trying out ideas, taking opportunities and seeing what worked. This was the case with new airfields. Hounslow Heath had given way to Croydon as London's main airport after World War I as the latter had more space and had grown bigger in the final war years. Shoreham Airport was older than Hounslow Heath, being founded in 1910 as an aerodrome. It claims the title of the oldest purpose-built commercial airport in the world. During the 1930s it acquired a fine Art Deco style terminal building. Shoreham became a Municipal Airport in 1936 and is today known as Brighton City Airport.

Other airfields were tried and, in the long run, abandoned or turned over to other development. For example, Haldon, in Devon, was opened in a private project by W R Parkhouse in 1929. It appeared in schedules by Railway Air Services and Provincial Airways in the mid-1930s. A number of regional flights included Haldon, its position near Exeter being attractive to travellers going to Dawlish and the other English Riviera towns. But it was situated on high ground, suffering from frequent bad weather, and passenger services moved to Exeter Airport in 1937. Some general aviation continued. The 1939-45 war saw its use by the RAF, but it was abandoned soon afterwards (weblist: Haldon).

Manchester, in the North of England, as a busy manufacturing and service centre, needed an airport after the war. A wartime airfield at Alexandra Park could not be used as its landowner refused to sell the ground for a permanent airport. A temporary arrangement was made by Manchester Corporation in Wythenshawe with a barn converted to hold one light aircraft, plus fuel pumps and an administration building. At the same time, a more permanent aerodrome was being prepared at Barton, near Eccles, with a hangar and grass runways. Such a relatively simple structure could be ready in a short time and just over a year later it was in use for a passenger charter flight. Imperial Airways began an experimental three-times a week service to Croydon with a stop in Birmingham on the way. By arriving in the capital in the morning and returning in the evening, it made a useful feeder for ongoing flights into Europe and back. All three airports were owned by the cities on the UK route, a mark of the belief in investment in economic activity by municipal authorities. Flights from and to Liverpool were incorporated. After three months however, only just over two hundred passengers had been carried, too few to keep the inter-city service going (weblist: Barton).

221

The contrast in lead-times before airports like Barton could be up and running, and the present day longer process, is obvious. The airline business all round was both simple and small in those days. Yet Barton started services without a control tower, with manual signalling by ground handling staff being used entirely. Its first tower was opened in early 1933, with a radio station, able to communicate with suitably equipped planes, alongside the first hangar built in that same year. The hangar was England's earliest civil aviation hangar. The control tower is still in use for what is now Manchester's City Airport and is believed to be Europe's oldest still used as such. On entering the airfield, the redbrick building on the left (once part of Foxhill Farm) was the original terminal.

Barton grew but by 1938 all the scheduled flights went to yet another Manchester airport, Ringway, south of the city. Services by small operators continued at Barton and the RAF began to use it for training. Barton had got a problem identified by a test flight pilot from KLM who was considering its use by his airline. Radio masts, pylons and tall chimneys presented hazards (weblist: Barton). Ringway was chosen by the city as being in more open country. It is still the city's main airport, vastly bigger and now the third biggest in Britain. Barton, with its grass runways, tower, original hangar and the terminal building, still operates, with new heliport facilities that are also used by both private and public services. Both Ringway (known now as Manchester Airport) and City Airport are tourist attractions with flight viewing areas open to the public daily, with the larger airport having historic aircraft on show and visitor centre displays. Wythenshawe was turned over to housing after it closed as an aerodrome and the site is no more than a location on a street map.

United States of America

Despite having had the Wright brothers as pioneers in flying, the United States was slow in turning innovation into industry. That might have been because the brothers were reticent about publicity, anxious to obtain patent protections and commercial orders before they gave demonstrations or even further test flights. Between October 1905 and May 1908, they did not fly at all. Instead, they tried to interest the US Army in their aircraft, with little success because the Army had put $50,000 into an embarrassing failure of a project by Samuel Langley a few years earlier (Crouch, 2003). The aeroplane concerned was unsound, crashing on its two flights, the second before even leaving its launch catapult. The Army was not shown by demonstrations or photographs that the Wrights' plane could perform well. Europe took the lead, knowing at least that the aeroplane was likely to have a role in warfare, an activity that it had engaged in often and was threatening again. The USA had not, beyond its Civil War and short affairs like the US-Spanish War of 1898. For nearly two decades after the Wright successes, passenger aircraft were almost non-existent anywhere (see Chant, 1980), the St Petersburg-Tampa flights being a small exception.

Robert Serling (1985) notes that US industry made no contribution to fighting in the air during World War I. US fighter pilots flew French Spads and Nieuports and observation crews used British DH-4s. Deutsche Luft-Reederei (DLR) had been operating in Germany as a passenger airline since 1919. In that year it had ten destinations established from its Berlin base, including an overseas route to Copenhagen. Its AEG J II and LVG CV biplanes carried two passengers each. In six months, they flew 1,574 customers. Its flight and ground crew looked like typical naval personnel (see Lovegrove, 2000) because of the choice of uniforms for these airborne craft. DLR was the earliest of the airlines that grew into what is today known as Lufthansa. Within a few years, German airlines were flying to the Baltic States, Leningrad, Moscow and Smolensk, and within just a few more years were reaching out to other continents (Davies 1991, Crouch 2003).

The first US post-war civilian airline started services in November 1919 flying between Key West and Cuba. This was the flying-boat operation of Aeromarine West Indies Airways. It carried passengers at $50 each, twice the price of a ship voyage, and relied heavily on postal subsidies from both the USA and Cuba (Crouch, 2003). The US Mail was the backbone of early American civil aviation through the contracts it awarded to airlines. It tried using Standard JR-1B biplanes for internal services. They had been converted from wartime use as training aircraft but were soon discarded in favour of 250 war surplus British DH-4s and a number of Junkers F13s. The US Mail had in effect created a government-run airline. Republicans objected to the situation. They pointed out in the mid-1920s that nothing had been done to foster competitive civil aviation. The Kelly, or Contract Air Mail, Act of 1925 closed down the US Mail operation, turning it over to a system of contracts awarded to business operators. Four-fifths of the revenue from mail carried by them would be paid to those operators (Crouch, 2003). In this way, United States' airlines were brought to economic maturity by public money.

It was a key moment in the development of air transport tourism. Plane operators began to make money from carrying the mail and some began to think in terms of attracting paying passengers. Daniel Rust (2009) tells of two newlyweds who paid $2,000 to make a flight of five hundred miles sitting on a pile of mailbags. Western Air Express won the contract to fly mail between Salt Lake City and Los Angeles. Their first passenger was Ben Redman, who paid $90 to fly from LA to Salt Lake City, an eight-hour trip in an open cockpit. Most passengers were men, but a woman named Maude Campbell paid the $180 for a round trip to Los Angeles and back. Western Air Express turned her trip into a publicity run. She was given a flying suit to wear and a parachute, with a briefing on how it would be used if required. The airline president met her in LA with a bouquet while press photographers recorded the scene.

A Lincoln-Page Aircraft Co Standard LS5, in 1926
Reproduced, with permission, from Aero Digest Magazine Vol 8 No 3 March 1926

A new air mail Act of 1930 tried to encourage airlines to carry more passengers as well as contracted air mail, while tightening the rules about carrying bulk junk mail to increase profits. Contracts were renewed giving financial advantages to bigger operators over smaller operators. This was without them necessarily charging the Postal Department the low rate that airlines had used to win the contract. The 1930 meeting about the new contracts, between the Postmaster General, Walter Folger Brown, and the senior staff of the big airlines, saw the latter divide up the contracts between themselves. It was not until 1934 that the carve-up became public knowledge, immediately labelling the 1930 meeting as the Spoils Conference. President Roosevelt cancelled the contracts, ordering the Army Air Corps to take over deliveries.

The Corps found the new winter, night-time job, challenging. There were many crashes, and thirteen airmen were killed. By June, the airlines had new contracts and legal proceedings took place against Spoils Conference participants. The airline industry was then restructured, and passenger services emphasised. From then onwards it became important to market for business and leisure travellers by air. It was a position reached by indirect political, legal and economic actions. Air tourism in the United States did not come about by merely building planes and infrastructure and then selling seats to the public, as had happened in Europe. It involved Federal Government actions and the courts of justice.

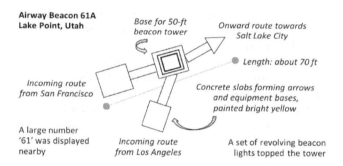

United States Airways Beacon 61A:
Between 1923 and 1933 1,500 Beacons were erected along US airways
to aid daytime and night-time navigation, numbered to aid location. Later beacons
were 3 to 5 miles apart, and every 25 miles there was an emergency landing
field marked by electric lights powerful enough to be seen 75 miles away

Pilots navigated where possible by following familiar rivers and railways or by referencing prominent landmarks, as in Europe. Flight altitudes were low and pilots able to vary them and their flight lines. It was a risky practice, the more so in bad weather. Journeys could be delayed, sometimes heavily. Accidental collisions in fog or low cloud were frequent. Crossing deserts and mountain ranges where there were few rivers and no railroads presented serious problems. The airway beacons of the kind described in the graphic above were an early solution, with later radio systems replacing them [see Lehrer, 2014].

Government money to carry the mail was the first shot in the arm of the American air transport industry. The second was Charles Lindbergh. He had been an airmail pilot, but he wanted more excitement than that [see Bergh, 2013]. Lindbergh thought about expeditions that might need a pilot. Then he thought of a $25,000 prize offered in 1919 for the first non-stop flight New York to Paris (or its reverse) that had not been claimed. He did know it had cost several lives and injuries and it would continue to do so. Lindbergh was 25 when he made his attempt. He was young, fit, a skilled pilot, brave and possessed of insightful ideas about which plane might be successful [Berg, 2013]. Rather than a big tri-motor aircraft with two pilots, he reasoned that a single-seater, single engined plane would do the job.

Alcock and Brown had crossed from St Johns in Newfoundland to Clifden in Ireland, finishing in a not-quite-perfect landing (well, they crashed into a bog). It was a flight of 3,040 kms (1,890 miles) that had taken 15 hours and 57 minutes. Lindbergh had to go much further – 5,800 kms (3,600 miles). His specially built Ryan monoplane had to be stripped of all excess weight (he even trimmed the margins from the maps he used to reduce the load) but filled with as much fuel as could be packed on board. It even had a fuel tank in front of the cockpit, improving the balance of the fuselage. A periscope was fitted to get a forward view, though he probably made the plane yaw from side to side, looking through side windows, to work out what was ahead.

Lindbergh had not slept for several hours before a chance to beat a rival effort presented itself. He took off, at short notice but successfully, from Roosevelt Field on Long Island. His plane, *The Spirit of St Louis*, carried him on an epic 33.5-hour flight to Le Bourget in France. The epic was the mix of accurate navigation, total lack of sleep and the reliability of the plane [see Bergh, 2013]. His home country had begun to see him as a hero just as he took off from Roosevelt Field: it was reported that a French attempt by Nungessor and Coli had failed, and the two men were missing. News reporters on the spot turned their attention to the man they began to call Lindy, making him into the kind of all-American hero who sold newspapers and held the attention of radio audiences [Crouch, 2003]. The kind of adulation that greeted him on his return saw not only his name in the headlines, but popular attention now focused on flying. The pioneering aviator Elinor Smith Sullivan said: "We'd been standing on our heads trying to get them to notice us but after Lindbergh, suddenly everyone

wanted to fly, and there weren't enough planes to carry them" (in Jennings and
Brewster 1998:420).

Lindbergh and air mail laid the foundations for evermore successful American
airline businesses. Tourism by air would still take time to grow. Railroads and
automobiles had a firm hold on the traveller market. The motor car offered
what neither the train nor the aeroplane could give – the freedom for a family
to go where they wanted, when they wanted, deciding their own route,
stopovers, meals and entertainment. Railroads offered relaxed, comfortable,
long distance travel at low cost – no capital investment by travellers required
– with interesting scenery on the way.

Aircraft offered little of these attractions, unless the potential traveller was
wealthy and the weather for the flight was good. But it did supply the
excitement of a new mode of travelling. For those who could afford it, new
international touring with cultural excitement would be on hand. Touring to
Europe needed time and money which were in short supply for Americans of
the inter-war years. Central and South America needed similarly expensive
sea travel or the challenges of road or rail journeys in unfamiliar territory.
Besides, for several decades, guidebooks, resorts and the new National and
State Parks had been trying to boost tourism within the nation. 'See America
First' was pushing back against the lure of European heritage. Using road and
rail access to visit places in the national treasure trove was becoming *the* 20th
century travel occupation for most United States' citizens.

Lindbergh might fly thousands of kilometres non-stop. Passenger service
planes in America could not possibly do so. They could not match the fuel
needs, nor the human endurance required by pilot and passengers. The
solution adopted was to use a transport mix, a sequence of plane-and-coach
hops across country, as described in Chapter 7, *On the Road*. The Californian
bus operator, Pickwick, designed its 'Nite Coach' for long journeys with
sleeping passengers. The company took people to Phoenix, Arizona, overnight
using the coach. A Pickwick aircraft used daytime stages to get passengers to
St Louis, where a Nite Coach continued their journey to Chicago. The
travellers for New York were booked onto other operators' flights to complete
their journey. It was advertised as a two-day journey, but this seems to have
been optimistic. The Universal Aviation Company had a similar rail/air
service taking 67 hours.

On the Move

Trans World Airways

The origins of Trans World Airways lay in a similar multi-mode arrangement. A group of leading businessmen met to discuss a new service. They agreed an airline route from New York to San Francisco. The first stage would be by train to Columbus, Ohio, continuing to Waynoka, Oklahoma in stages by plane, then Clovis, New Mexico via train and finally by air once more in hops to San Francisco (Serling, 2018). The Atchison, Topeka and Santa Fe Railroad and the Pennsylvania Railroad formed a partnership. Neither were fearful of the coming of competition in the air. W W Atterbury, president of the Pennsylvania line, said "the railroads will remain, of course, the backbone of the nation's transportation system" (Rust, 2009:44). Someone from the Santa Fe thought the only users of the rail/air service would be those who were in the greatest hurry. Coast to coast, the rail/air schedule clocked in at 48 hours. The fastest train took twice as long. But the new TAT company air ticket would cost $338, equivalent to $4,500 today and about twice the 1929 cost of a coast-to-coast rail ticket.

This new company was formed as Transcontinental Air Transport (TAT). Charles Lindbergh was its technical adviser, wielding a powerful influence. He insisted on Ford 5-AT-B Trimotor aircraft for the relevant stages. They were noisy and slow but reliable. Ten were purchased, with spares to deal with early breakdowns. Lindbergh ordered that they have two-way radios, something very new in the airline business.

Robert Serling (2018:19) has described the detailed preparations. Lindbergh knew that east of Wichita they could use existing airport facilities. West of the city required new construction of fields, passenger buildings and hangars. He spent months inspecting and checking the route and determining the groundworks needed for each runway. Several Curtiss Aero Cars - closed-in trailers developed from 'fifth-wheel' caravan vehicles - towed by Studebaker Roadsters, were bought to move passengers between cities and airfields. Thirty-eight experienced pilots were recruited and given specific training, and seventy-two weather observers were assembled to report on conditions along the route. Many of these were taken on by the railroads who were TAT operating partners, and even a handful by the US Weather Bureau. A private teletype service along the whole route shared the forecast details and general operations information.

TAT was pipped to the post in June 1929 by another rail/air service. Universal Aviation Corporation took passengers from New York to Cleveland, Ohio by railroad Then they were flown to Garden City, Kansas via Chicago, St Louis and Kansas City before the Santa Fe Railroad completed the journey to Los Angeles. TAT launched on 7 July with the Pennsylvania Railroad's newly named *Airway Limited* leaving Penn station. Each aeroplane stage used two Ford Trimotors to carry the travellers west. The Ford planes were fitted with ten seats each rather than the design quota of 15.

TAT had decided more space allowed more comfort, but fitting radio gear and space for a cabin attendant had to be arranged (Rust, 2009). TAT attendants were called couriers, a title used by the partner Santa Fe Railroad for men looking after tourists on automobile side trips. They were initially male and recruited from wealthy TAT investors. Duties included escorting passengers from city collection points to airports, delivering meals from caterers for the Fred Harvey in-flight services, weighing luggage and stowing it in retractable bins on the aircraft.

The age of mass aeroplane travel was still a long way off. But it was a start. Lindbergh flew one of the two planes on the first leg of the eastbound service with his new wife, Anne Morrow Lindbergh, on board as a passenger. The movie stars Mary Pickford and Douglas Fairbanks saw them off from LA. Good publicity was always needed but could be wiped out by bad within a moment. Within two months of the inaugural, a TAT plane crashed into a mountain in New Mexico, killing all eight people on board, then a Western Air Express F10 hit the same mountain killing its five occupants. Bookings dried up immediately.

Great efforts were spent trying to rebuild bookings, emphasising the Fred Harvey catering, giving away gold fountain pens and advertising "the first aerial motion pictures in the history of aviation". These were a newsreel and some cartoon films on a flight of 8 October 1929. Unfortunately for TAT history, as Robert Serling (2018) points out, Imperial Airways had shown the whole of Conan Doyle's *The Lost World* in April 1925, as noted earlier in this chapter. Ticket prices were slashed to $267, to no avail. In January 1930 they dropped to $160. Bookings increased, but the airline's cut of the ticket price (as opposed to the railroads') was too small. TAT managed a merger with Maddux Airlines operating fifteen Trimotors and a route from Los Angeles to San Francisco. A plan to merge with Western Air Express got nowhere. It was the Great Depression. At the same time in 1930 the reorganisation of airmail contracts through what became known as the Spoils Conference, was under way by the Federal Government.

As part of his reorganisation, the Postmaster General, Walter Folger Brown, forced the merger of TAT and Western Air Express that TAT itself had failed to progress. The new company was known as Transcontinental and Western Air. They dropped the rail/air route across America and began a coast-to-coast service using Ford Trimotors alone on 25 October 1930. It was the beginning of TWA, though it would only become Trans World Airline in 1950 when international routes were being established.

Things went well until a Fokker F-10 from the Western Air fleet crashed near Wichita in wet weather. Everyone aboard was killed, including the famed Notre Dame football coach, Knut Rockne. The US Commerce Department's Aeronautics Branch found the cause of the accident to have been water getting into the plywood-skimmed wing, weakening the glue that bonded the structure together [Serling, 2018]. The starboard wing had sheared off. T&WA sold a few remaining Fokkers, salvaged the engines from the rest and burnt them. It kept going with the Trimotors carrying air mail, the Depression and the accident having reduced passenger demand to low levels. At least the mail contracts allowed the business to buy new planes just to carry the air mail. A dozen Northrop Alphas were purchased, strong planes but difficult to fly. They approached Boeing about buying sixty Boeing 247s, but the manufacturer had a two-year production schedule for the rival United Aircraft and Transport, who at that stage owned Boeing. They wrote to the presidents of five aircraft manufacturers in 1932 with a request. First to reply was Donald Wills Douglas of the Douglas Aircraft Company.

T&WA wanted a metal, three-engined plane capable of flying on one engine in an emergency, carrying twelve passengers, at a cruising speed of 150mph (241kph). The Douglas design team were anxious to make their mark [Crouch 2003, Serling 2018]. They proposed an aircraft using two, not three, engines, but still capable of flying on just one. T&WA agreed to buy one aircraft with a promise of ordering sixty if the prototype succeeded. The new plane was the DC-1, or Douglas Commercial-1. It was first flown in just under a year after T&WA requested designs. T&WA confirmed the main order for sixty planes. Douglas Aircraft made some improvements to the original design and called it the DC-2. Seven months after the first flight, the DC-2 was flown from Santa Monica, California to Newark, New Jersey in thirteen hours and two minutes.

The plane that followed, the DC-3, became one of the most influential in aviation history both in peacetime and war. It resulted from Cyrus R Smith of American Airlines persuading Donald Douglas that his DC-2 could be better. Smith suggested making it a couple of feet longer and a couple of feet wider (61cms each). It would be made in two versions, one for fourteen passengers in seats capable of folding into sleeping berths and a second equipped with twenty-one ordinary seats. American Airlines would buy ten of each. Douglas Aircraft would be free to sell across the market. Smith assured Douglas a federal loan would be obtained to cover research, design and initial production (Crouch, 1983). Donald Douglas was persuaded. The first DC-3 flew on 17 December 1935, thirty-two years to the day after the Wright brothers' Kitty Hawk success. Smith would boast that the plane he helped create was the first that could be flown profitably without a government subsidy (Crouch, 1983).

This was a time when the fall-out from the Spoils Conference scandal was being deposited across the airline business. When the Roosevelt government closed air mail contracts and had the Air Corps fly the mail bags, the T&WA business struggled. Donald Douglas helped by taking on personnel who were surplus to T&WA's needs – and their budgets. When the Roosevelt administration realised the Air Corps could not cope, it passed new legislation returning new contracts to the airline companies. There was a period of making changes to the companies, breaking up some major combines and satisfying the rule that airlines who had taken part in the Spoils Conference could not bid on new routes. Had that been a matter of blocking the big airlines entirely from the bidding process, the smaller ones who had not been involved could not have coped wth the transport requirements (Serling, 2018).

The new Postmaster General, James Farley, let the airline bosses know privately that a change of name would allow them to bid. American Airways became American Airlines, Eastern Air Transport became Eastern Airlines and so on. Transcontinental and Western Air sold its Trimotors to a new company, T&WA Inc which won its old coast to coast route contract to handle the mail. Transcontinental and Western Air kept its DC-2s and carried only passengers. It was probably inevitable that the Post Office Department should eventually suggest the two companies ought to merge. So, they did. The famous tourist airline was taking shape.

On the Move

Pan American Airways

While T&WA was metamorphosing, another airline was getting ready to fledge. It would be a wing-spreading eagle of a flyer: Pan American. Trying to apply simplistic marketing principles to understand how it came about would get a historian nowhere. To apply an appropriate metaphor, Pan Am grew by flying by the seat of his pants by the man who led it – Juan Trippe. Few tourist innovations over the decades, even the centuries, can be analysed properly by marketing principles alone. The elements of chance opportunities and human responses were always too strong. Variables of one kind or another abounded.

Politics, culture, resource availability, technical skills and even the weather and religion could easily override sketchy ideas of market research and planning. To take a famous case, Thomas Cook's personal intuition and beliefs, not market research, started him off as a tourism operator. So many tourism innovations have owed their origins to an individual's bright idea, based on personal belief, experience and sheer determination.

We can take examples from a range of historic periods. It would seem ludicrous to suggest otherwise: the great medieval pilgrim-attracting churches and cathedrals did not come about through marketing research. Neither did the great houses that were designed under the influence of the Grand Tour. Changing the Louvre Palace into a museum that anyone could visit was a political act. Creating the open-air museum of Skansen in Stockholm was a matter of folk observation and educational vision. Preserving and presenting Colonial Williamsburg in the USA stemmed from desires to educate people and regenerate the old community. National Parks in the USA grew out of the desire to conserve areas of wilderness, often with spectacular scenery.

Of course – and especially in the business-minded United States – commercial opportunities were taken up in all kinds of places attracting visitors. Transport services were often begun with a nebulous recognition of potential demand. Britain's pioneering railways, America's transcontinental railroads, shipping companies across Europe and North America and certainly airlines, were responding to perceptive, not statistical, measures of demand. It is far more difficult to predict a demand level that is going to be created from scratch. Those speculative measures were quite different from our modern ideas of market research with its questionnaires and focal group studies. Those things have been more the tools of established, big companies and public service

232

organisations with more to lose if their chosen strategies proved faulty. Change and progress are the offspring of many worldly parents.

Chance caused change when the Western Air fleet's Fokker aircraft crashed in bad weather in 1931, contributing to the Douglas Commercial series of aircraft. Chance events are not divine determinants unless you happen to believe in a prescriptive divinity. Thomas Cook, of course, believed in the Will of the Lord, though it fell to Cook to bring about what he thought God wanted.

International conflicts boosted technical developments, notably in military vehicles that in subsequent years could be used for peaceful purposes. Bombers became airliners, staff cars turned into taxis, torpedo boats into pleasure craft.

The origins of Pan American again lay in the whirlpool of American business between the two World Wars. Entering World War I in 1917 took the country into new relationships around the globe. Transport had to be the key to taking part. Opportunities were opening fast in the mass media, sharing ideas while offering places to promote pet projects. European traditions meant state ownership, coordination or encouragement in the air passenger business. Such influences were made all the more essential by nationalist pride and economic post-war stress. After initial periods of smaller-scale enterprises, the policy was for mergers into flag carriers (such as KLM 1919, Imperial Airways 1924, Lufthansa 1926, Air France 1933) or, in the case of the Soviet Union, state run departments (Aeroflot, 1932).

The traditions in the USA were for independence from government in line with the founders' philosophy of freedom in everything. It meant freedom to form businesses making profits. It also meant freedom from any federal efforts to impose the kind of flag-waving carriers seen in Europe. The airmail situations of those years showed wavering policies and limitations to the philosophies. Successful airlines depended in large part on federal contracts. The businesses might be formed by free association, but they struggled to survive without the subsidies the contracts provided. Roosevelt's years saw numerous initiatives by federal agencies such as the WPA Guides programme, the Blue Ridge Parkway (and others) and the Boulder/Hoover dam project. Taking over the airmail deliveries with Air Corps operations fitted this strategy, but failed, and the work returned to the private sector. Even so, the contracts themselves were set out by the Postmasters General and remained federal initiatives.

The story of TWA showed how commercial and federal interplay shaped the new passenger airlines and therefore the nascent air tourism services. That of Pan American Airways Corporation was similar. A difference however was that TWA was built first on internal routes and Pan American was almost from the start internationalist. The airline was also driven by an American hero-figure, Juan Terry Trippe (1899-1981) who learned to fly in the US Navy. Robert Daley's account of *Trippe and his Pan Am Empire* [(1980)] calls him, when young, "both a dreamer and a daredevil, a youth with mind and heart literally in the clouds". He was "well-bred, a gentleman ... He was affable, polite and shy with girls". Though he had played football and rowed, an accident at Yale damaged his spine so golf was his sport thereafter. Daley picks out a particular strength that would serve him in later business days: "He would argue patiently until no-one had any energy left to argue back". And after graduation, rather than follow his father into banking, "He was determined to make a business out of aviation" [(Daley, 1980)] after learning to fly and winning an intercollegiate air race between college clubs.

Trippe's first foray into flying came through his start-up of Long Island Airways in 1923, a rich man's charter service [(Davies, 1987)] using seven ex-Navy aircraft. Small companies were added in partnership with others and then either left behind or merged into his Aviation Corporation of America (1927). Pan American Airways was not formed by Trippe but was one of seven companies, three of which were his by midsummer of that year. However, the seven merged into the Aviation Corporation of America, which from June 1928 operated as Pan American Airways.

An airmail contract was won that year running between Key West and Havana. A new airport was opened at Miami in 1928. Services were transferred there. Pan Am was able to open up passenger services to the Cuban capital, a lucrative destination for the airline as it offered exotic nightlife in a place contrasting with the USA. For those who could afford it, Pan Am took people abroad on short flights at costs lower than any going to Europe by sea or air. Over two years the airline opened flights to many destinations around the Gulf of Mexico and the Caribbean and then down the Pacific coast of South America before reaching Santiago and crossing the continent to Buenos Aires and Montevideo [(see Hudson & Pettifer, 1979)]. 1930 saw Trippe's company capture the New York, Rio and Buenos Aires Line (NYRBA) in what Davies has called Trippe's "greatest coup, and his most ruthless" in a predatory takeover bid for NYRBA [(Davies, 1987:20)]. "Those fellows were just damn dumb" Trippe said privately about the NYRBA board of directors, after his manoeuvrings had led to victory [Daley, 1980].

Trippe had a new flying boat station opened on Dinner Key, Miami (named as a popular place for boat owners to take a midday break). Alastair Gordon says it was

> "the most advanced American airport of its day. It was certainly the most elegant. Tall, swaying palm trees lined the processional drive that led to the main terminal ... The colour scheme was meant to suggest the 'brilliance of sky, sand and sea'" [Gordon, 2004:94].

It had an Art Deco terminal building in keeping with Miami's seafront style. It had a limited life with Pan Am, as the Navy requisitioned it in 1943, Pan Am transferring operations then to Miami International using land planes. The old terminal survives as Miami City Hall.

Central and South American development continued during the 1930s, some of it by flying boats, soon to be a major development aimed at the top end of the market of the travelling US public. The Sikorsky S-40, carrying up to 38 passengers at 115 mph (185 kph) led the way in the Gulf and Caribbean. Another Sikorsky, an S-42, was stripped of passenger accommodation and given extra fuel tanks. In 1935, it carried out a series of survey flights to Honolulu, Midway, Wake and Guam. The crossing of the Pacific by regular services was becoming possible.

Flying boats were thought safer in an emergency as they could land on water and radio for help. They were big, making them suitable for combinations of cabins and service areas with some space for passengers to move around at leisure. Pan Am bought Martin M-130s, slower than the Sikorsky S-42 but with greater fuel capacity and 41 passenger seats. A new service began in late November 1935 to Manila, the *China Clipper*. Two thousand special guests awaited the plane's arrival after the inaugural flight. Military fighter planes escorted it to the harbour. The pilot, Ed Musick, carried a letter from President Roosevelt to his counterpart in the Philippines, President Quezon. In the excitement of the day it was handed over, but the ceremony had to be restaged later for the newsreel cameramen.

The one-way fare to Manila was $799, equivalent to $10,000 in the 1980s when Ron Davies wrote about it [Davies, 1987:38]. For a few years, *Clipper*-styled services were a powerful luxury brand. Pan Am wanted to fly Atlantic routes as well, but it either had to fly via Newfoundland, Greenland and Iceland, or island-hop across via Bermuda and the Azores. Getting relevant permissions was not easy. Britain's influence over Canada put Newfoundland out of the question for some time, for example. The British had wanted its Short S.23 *Empire* flying boats, of Imperial Airways, protected. Then in 1939 Britain decided its S.23 could withstand competition. Permissions were granted for Pan Am to use Botwood (later known as Gander) in Newfoundland. The American airline introduced its B.134 flying boat from Boeing, with 74 seats, a cruising speed of 180 mph (290 kph) and a range of 3,500 miles. It could reach the new airport at Foynes, in the west of the Republic of Ireland, from Canada. From there it continued to Southampton in a service begun in June 1939. The previous month had seen Boeing 314 *Yankee Clipper* reach Marseilles via the Azores and Lisbon.

It seemed flying boats were well established in the skies. But they were not. A Focke-Wulf Fw 200 Condor belonging to Deutsche Lufthansa made a non-stop flight from Berlin to Floyd Bennet Field, New York, in the summer of 1938 (Davies, 1987). Land-based aircraft were not at the mercies of bad weather, which could make sea landings impossible. The Second World War would supply many new airports with paved runways for the following years of peace. The end of the war would again make available thousands of military aircraft at low cost for later conversion to passenger planes.

Part of the tourist experience was the flight itself; another part was the onboard entertainment. Simple refreshments or more sophisticated meals with alcohol and hot drinks pleased the customers and helped while away the time aloft. Showing movies had been tried by Imperial Airways and TAT in the late 1920s, but aircraft noise and the projector's instability defeated the idea. In 1939 there were experiments by TWA, providing on request a small loudspeaker for each passenger relaying radio station entertainment. Stewardesses had to guess which station would be popular on each flight and choose the wavelength on the aircraft receiver. Long distance flights required retuning of receivers as the plane passed beyond each reception area (Pettifer & Hudson, 1979).

Gazing out of the cabin window fulfilled one of the main promises of flying – a view of a world that was impossible to get at ground level. The TWA loudspeakers could be used by the captain to tell passengers about notable sights coming into view. Stewardesses could do the same for individual travellers while they served refreshments or answered queries. What they

236

knew about places in view varied. They were not trained as tour guides, whereas the captain's job required him to know exactly where he was – even if it did not always work out accurately. Unlike railroads, airlines could not easily supply guidebooks with out-of-the-window descriptions – the actual route taken might depend on the weather or another variable. Bad weather or clouds might prevent people from seeing anything.

KLM did give customers on its prestige Amsterdam to Batavia service a hardback guide in Dutch or English editions, *Wings Across Continents* (Rusman, 1935). It included strip maps of each stage, though the scale was too small to show much detail. Information about the aircraft, stopping points and activities affecting the planes was interspersed with short chapters about the countries and cities along the way. Photographs and drawings illustrated each of them. Passengers who used the guides were entertained and gained some familiarity with their journey, courtesy of KLM.

A very unusual guidebook was published by the Geographical Press of Columbia University in 1933. It marked the occasion of the sixteenth Geological Congress held in Washington. The title was *Airways of America*, subtitled *Guidebook No 1: The United Air Lines* (Lobeck, 1933). Whether others were produced, I have not been able to discover, but it looks too specialist to be an ongoing proposition. My own copy used to belong to a university library where its wealth of information must have made it an excellent textbook.

Airways of America was based on a transect of the United States from New York to San Francisco, along the route followed by United. The airliner principally used was the Boeing 247, new and exhibited in pride of place at the 1933 Chicago World's Fair (and the one not available to TWA at the time, leading to TWA's adoption of Douglas Commercial aircraft). The 247 carried ten passengers. The guidebook had a revealing chapter on Airways and Navigation, detailing many aspects of the personnel, equipment and operations assembled to carry out the airline service. Ground beacon 'lighthouses', radio communications and 14 radio beam guidance aerials are shown, together with weather stations and forecasting services for pilots.

Aircraft heading west for San Francisco flew at altitudes of 1,000-2,000 feet to avoid strong headwinds from the west. Those flying east would benefit from the same, tail, winds around 10,000 feet or so. The result was that travellers had a better chance of detailed views of the ground when going west, though at the higher east-bound levels the view was more panoramic. But there was a problem with the Boeing 247. There were six windows on each side for the passengers. Unfortunately, they all looked out onto the wings. Perhaps there was still a distant view possible. The rearmost window gave a better chance if the passengers could crane their necks to look back as far as possible.

All in all, the guidebook would have its best use in the home or the office. Good photos and bird's eye view sketches abounded. Both the geologist and the geographer, from school to professional in the field, would have found it a delight, great for the one transect it covered - the aeroplane route across the mid-latitude USA. In flight, chatting, eating, drinking and sleeping might leave little time for matching the window view with the detail on each page.

Cabin crew

European airlines had put young men on aircraft to look after passengers from immediately after the 1914-18 war. The United States companies were at first slower to add cabin staff since it was airmail business that counted most until after Lindbergh's adventure stimulated passenger flying. The first was Stout Air Services between Detroit and Grand Rapids in 1926 [Rust, 2009]. Then Western Air Express put them onto its San Francisco to Los Angeles route.

As described earlier, TAT employed male 'couriers' to look after passengers. Daniel Rust quotes a female passenger on a TAT flight who wrote that the courier was "a college boy, tall, clean cut, intelligent ... very eager to make each passenger as comfortable and happy as possible" [Rust, 2009:53]. Couriers were given a uniform modelled on those of the stewards on passenger ships [see Lovegrove, 2000]. It suggested both discipline and service. TAT's successor, TWA, began to have copilots serve coffee on flights, something noted by Serling as a hated duty for a pilot to do. Jack Frye of TWA had believed survey data suggesting passengers preferred being looked after by copilots. But then he found his passengers "were going over to United and American because they had attractive girls" [Serling, 2018:83]. United had taken on stewardesses in 1930 and American in 1933. Frye followed suit but insisted on calling the women 'hostesses' who served the airline's 'guests' on board.

The US industry as a whole adopted the practice of recruiting registered nurses for the job. It was ostensibly because the number one problem on a flight was air sickness. Again, it was partly copying from railroads that had taken on nurses as attendants on its long-distance services. It was a way of reassuring the public who might be wary of travel adventuring – by rail or air – that they would be looked after. Perhaps it was also the maternal image and partly the implication that military-looking males were not necessary, and females could be quite at home on aeroplanes. Travelling by air demanded careful marketing. Railways were well past the days when people were afraid to travel faster than speeding horses. Dark tunnels no longer needed ladies to ward off male advances. There was much to explain to nervous travellers about the sights, sounds and careering motions experienced in flight. 'Welcome on Board' booklets would become standard as flying increased in popularity after 1945. Competition would cause airlines to use female attractiveness in barely disguised ways. They would appear as servants to be summoned by pressing a button, ready to look after every need. Back in the 1930s, was there even the hint of the school matron? There certainly would be post World War II.

In the late autumn of 1939, Imperial Airways was merged with British Airways Ltd that had been formed itself from merging smaller companies in 1935. The new organisation was state owned and called the British Overseas Airways Corporation. It would operate throughout the Second World War and become in due course, and after other changes, British Airways, in 1974. Daniel Rust reproduces an image from the TWA archives of the 1970s (Rust, 2009:11). Listed against an outline map of the USA is a summary of coast-to-coast flying times from 1929 to 1976. The rail/air journey of 1929 took two days. A Ford Trimotor of 1930 flew the whole way in a day and a half. Travelling by both day and night in 1932 cut the time to 24 hours. Post-World War II aircraft took the time down rapidly to where in 1976 it was scheduled as eight minutes under five hours.

The Second World War was even more destructive of life and places than the first. Both wars reshaped political maps, national attitudes, economic and social conditions in radical ways. There were three deep-seated changes to travel and tourism. The first, quite obvious, was the redrawing of political boundaries and policies. They were numerous. Europe had suffered, the United States became more dominant; Eastern Europe soon became a communist bloc behind a so-called 'iron curtain'. The old Indian Empire sought independence from Britain. Japan underwent painful transformation from a once-closed society, hit by atomic bombs and international defeat in 1945, towards a recovering, more open and vibrant nation. Victorious imperial countries tried to recover and continue with their lives while many of their colonies were becoming ever more ready to press for their own independence.

On the Move

The second change was brought about, as in 1919, by the releasing of military transport and equipment now surplus to requirements. Tents and camping gear were prominent in new army and navy surplus stores. They were just what people within new years of austerity needed. Tents, folding beds, tables and the like would help create new holiday camps abroad with surplus DC-3 and other troop transport aircraft converted to tourist carriers.

The third change was similar to what happened after earlier wars. Military veterans, their interested families and casual adventurers began to travel to previous war zones. European Town Twinning schemes led to peace-time reconstruction work and reconciliation visits. The war had opened the eyes of combatants, while showing them that foreign travel was not so difficult. Many found themselves welcomed back as previous liberators. It was not the same with countries like Germany, which would be occupied by Allied forces for years. Yet even that gradually meant that the occupiers became peacetime explorers who knew more about the world from their experiences than any previous generation.

All of this was for the future. The end of the 1930s brought tourism to a sudden stop. The progress made with land, sea and air transport had to service a wide-ranging conflict moving at an ever-greater pace. Tourism closed down. Travel was now a function of war. Few people could ever be on the move unless they could answer the question: "Is your journey really necessary?".

Bleriot's Landing Site Near Dover Castle:

marked out by the shape of his aircraft.
An interpretive panel tells the story

.

Bibliography

Works marked with [a] were consulted online by using, eg the free library at www.archive.org, Google books and other web pages.

Books, Journal Papers, Articles
Recently reprinted older books are shown with both relevant dates and publishers.

AA & MU (1914) *The Automobile Association and Motorists' Union Handbook 1914-15,* London, AA & MU.

Akerman, James R (2006) *Twentieth-Century American Road Maps and the Making of a National Motorized Space,* in Akerman (ed)(2006) <u>Cartographies of Travel and Imagination</u>, Chicago, Chicago University Press

American Automobile Association (1938) *Motoring Abroad,* New York, AAA

Anderson R C A & Frankis, G (1970) *History of Royal Blue Express Services,* Newton Abbott, David & Charles

Appleton & Co (1857) *Appletons' Illustrated Hand-Book of American Travel,* New York, D Appleton & Co

Arkell, Reginald (1933) *Richard Jefferies and his Countryside,* London, Herbert Jenkins

Army & Navy Stores (1883) *General Catalogue,* London, Army & Navy Co-operative Society Ltd [a]

Ash, Russell (1974) *The Wright Brothers,* London, Wayland

Automobile Association (1914) *The Automobile Association and Motor Union Handbook 1914-15,* London, The AA

Automobile Association (1931) *The Automobile Association and Motor Union Handbook 1931-32,* London, The AA

Barr, Robert (1945) *I Travel the Road,* London, Quality Press Ltd

Bassett, Philippa (1980) *A Brief History of the Caravan Club of Great Britain and Northern Ireland*, Birmingham, University of Birmingham, *available online* at discovery.nationalarchives.go.uk

Berg, A Scott (2013) *Lindbergh*, London, Simon & Schuster UK

Botting, Douglas (2001) *Dr Eckener's Dream Machine,* London, Harper Collins

Boyle, Andrew (1994) *Pictorial History of Arran,* Darvel, Alloway Publishing

Boy Scouts of America (1911) *Boy Scouts Handbook,* Garden City NY, Doubleday, Page & Co

Bradley, Simon (2015) *The Railways: Nation, Network and People,* London, Profile Books

Bradshaw, George (ed)(1863/2012) *Bradshaw's Descriptive Railway Hand-Book of Great Britain and Ireland,* reprinted, Oxford, Old House Books

Bradshaw Editors (1934/2013) *Bradshaw's International Air Guide,* London, Henry Blacklock & Co Ltd, reprinted, Oxford, Old House Books

Brendon, Piers (1997) *The Motoring Century: The Story of the Royal Automobile Club,* London, Bloomsbury Publishing

Briggs, Asa (1961) *The History of Broadcasting in the United Kingdom: 1, The Birth of Broadcasting,* Oxford, OUP

Browne, John Paddy (1991) *Map Cover Art: A Pictorial History of Ordnance Survey Cover Illustrations,* Southampton, Ordnance Survey

Bull, Bartle (1992) *Safari: A Chronicle of Adventure,* Harmondsworth, Penguin Books

Burdett Wilson, Roger (1970) *Go Great Western: A History of GWR Publicity,* Newton Abbot, David & Charles

Burrow, Ed (ed)(?1922) *On the Road: The Dunlop Pictorial Road Plan: VI - The Great North Road,* London, Ed J Burrow Ltd

Butko, Brian (2013) *Greetings from the Lincoln Highway: A Road Trip Celebration of America's First Coast-to-Coast Highway,* Mechanicsburg PA, Stackpole Books

Chadwick, F E et al (1891) *Ocean Steamships: A Popular Account of their Construction, Development, Management and Appliances,* New York, Charles Scribner's Sons [a]

Chant, Chris (1980) *Early Airliners,* London, Phoebus Publishing

Chase, Stuart (1940) *Idle Money, Idle Men,* New York, Harcourt, Brace & Co [a]

Chicago & North Western Railway (1937) *Every Kind of Vacation,* Chicago, CNWR [a]

Childers, J W et al (1868/1993) *Lord Orford's Voyage Around the Fens in 1774,* reprint 2nd ed, Cambridge, Cambridge Libraries [corrected author reference]

Class Journal Company (1907) *The Automobile Blue Book 1907,* New York, Class Journal Co

Clawson, Marion & Knetsch, Jack L (1966) *Economics of Outdoor Recreation,* Baltimore, Johns Hopkins Press:

Cluett, Douglas et al (1980) *Croydon Airport, 1928-39: The Great Days,* Sutton, London; Sutton Libraries and Arts Services

Cole, Beverley (2006) *It's Quicker by Rail,* Harrow, Capital Transport/NRM

Cole, Beverley & Durack, Richard (1992) *Railway Posters 1923-1947,* London, Laurence King

Constance, Hazel (2001) *First in the Field: A Century of the Camping and Caravan Club,* Coventry, The Camping and Caravan Club

Cook & Son, Thomas (1930) *Around-the-World Cruise RMS 'Franconia' 1930: North China Arrangements* booklet, Pekin, Cook & Son Office

Cudahy, Brian J (2003) *A Century of Subways,* New York, Fordham University Press

Cullen, Gordon (1962) *Townscape,* London, The Architectural Press

Cynk, J B (09.05.1963) *Letter* in <u>Flight International</u>, p695 [a]

Daley, Robert (1980) *Juan Trippe and his Pan Am Empire,* New York, Random House

Davies, G Christopher (1882) *The Handbook to the Rivers and Broads of Norfolk and Suffolk,* London, Jarrold & Sons

Davies, Roger & Barber, Stephen (2007) *Glory Days: Wallace Arnold,* Shepperton, Ian Allan Ltd

Davies, Ron E G (1987) *Pan Am: An Airline and its Aircraft,* Twickenham UK, Hamlyn Publishing Group

Davies, Ron E G (1991) *Lufthansa: An Airline and its Aircraft,* McLean VA, Paladwr Press

Davies, Ron E G (2005) *British Airways: An Airline and its Aircraft, Vol 1 1919-1939,* McLean VA,

Delgado, Alan (1977) *The Annual Outing and Other Excursions,* London, George Allen and Unwin

Dye, Victoria E (2007) *All Aboard for Santa Fe: Railway Promotion of the Southwest, 1890s to 1930s,* Albuquerque NM, University of New Mexico Press

Ellesmere, Roger (2012) *British Caravans: Makes Founded Before World War II,* Shebbear, Devon; Herridge & Sons

Ellis, Christine (2006) *The History of the Caravan Club,* East Grinstead, The Caravan Club

Everitt, Nicholas (1902) *Broadland Sports,* London, R E Everett & Co [a]

Flitton, David (2004) *50 Years of South Midland: 1921-1970,* Wokingham, Paul Lacey

Flower, Raymond & Wynn Jones, Michael (1981) *100 Years of the Motor Car: An RAC Social History of the Car,* Maidenhead, McGraw-Hill/RAC

Foote Wood, Chris (2008) *Walking Over the Waves: Quintessential British Seaside Piers,* Dunbeath, Whittles Publishing

Forbes, A S C (1925) *California Missions and Landmarks: El Camino Real,* Los Angeles, privately published [a]

Fox, Stephen (2004) *The Ocean Railway: Isambard Kingdom Brunel, Samuel Cunard, and the Revolutionary World of the Great Atlantic Steamships,* London, Harper Perennial

Fried, Stephen (2011) *Appetite for America: Fred Harvey and the Business of Civilising the Wild West – One Meal at a Time,* New York, Bantam Books

Garland, Ken (1994) *Mr Beck's Underground Map*, Harrow Weald, Capital Transport Publishing

General Motors (1939) *Futurama*, Detroit, General Motors Company

Gladwell, Andrew (2013) *Pleasure Steamers*, Oxford, Shire Publications

Gordon, Alastair (2004) *Naked Airport: A Cultural History of the World's Most Revolutionary Structure*, New York, Metropolitan Books

Green, Oliver (1990) *Underground Art*, 2nd edition, London, Laurence King

Green, Oliver (2004) Introduction to facsimile of *Metro-land* 1924 edition, Harpenden, Southbank Publishing [a]

Green, Oliver (2016) *Rails in the Road: A History of Tramways in Britain and Ireland*, Barnsley, Pen and Sword Transport

GWR (1924/2008) *Through the Window: The Great Western Railway from Paddington to Penzance, 1924*, reprint edition, Moretonhampstead, Old House Books

Harp, Stephen L (2002) *Marketing Michelin: Advertising and Cultural Identity in Twentieth Century France*, Baltimore, Johns Hopkins University Press

Harper, Charles G (ed)(c1931) *The Travelogue of Knowtoring: Raising the Curtain*, Exeter, ? Western National Omnibus Company

Harrison, James P (1996) *Mastering the Sky: A History of Aviation from Ancient Times to the Present*, New York, Sarpedon

Harveycar Courier Corps (1930) *Indian-Detours: Most Distinctive Motor Cruise Service in the World*, Santa Fe NM, Harveycars

Heald, Bruce D (2011) *The Mount Washington Mountain Railway: Climbing the White Mountains of New Hampshire*, Charleston SC, The History Press

Hewison, Robert (1987) *The Heritage Industry: Britain in a Climate of Decline*, London, Methuen

Hewitt, Rachel (2010) *Map of a Nation: A Biography of the Ordnance Survey*, London, Granta Publications

Hibbs, John (1989) *The History of British Bus Services*, Newton Abbott, David & Charles

Higham, Robin (1960) *Britain's Imperial Air Routes, 1918-1939: The Story of Britain's Overseas Airlines*, revised edition 2016, Stroud, Fonthill Media

Holland, Clive (1922) *Caravanning for a Holiday: Its Attractions, Experiences and Expenses* in The Windsor Magazine, Vol 34 1922 pp240-249 [a]

Homberger, Eric (1994) *The Historical Atlas of New York City: A Visual Celebration of Nearly 400 Years of New York City's History*, New York, Henry Holt & Co

Hopkinson, Tom (1970) *Picture Post 1938-50*, Harmondsworth, Penguin Books

Howard, Fred (1988) *Wilbur And Orville: A Biography of the Wright Brothers*, New York, Ballantine Books

Hudson, Kenneth (1972) *Air Travel: A Social History*, Bath, Adams & Dart

Hudson, Kenneth & Pettifer, Julian (1979) *Diamonds in the Sky: A Social History of Air Travel*, London, BBC/Bodley Head

Huntley, John (1969) *Railways in the Cinema*, Shepperton, Ian Allen Publishing Ltd

Hurley, Edward N (1927) *The Bridge to France*, Philadelphia, J B Lippincott Company [a]

Huxley, Aldous (1925) *Along the Road: Notes and Essays of a Tourist*, London, Chatto & Windus

Jacob, John P (ed) (2012) *Kodak Girl: From the Martha Cooper Collection*, Göttingen, Steidl Verlag

Jenkinson, Andrew (1998) *Caravans: The Illustrated History 1919-1959*, Dorchester, Veloce Publishing

Jenkinson, Andrew (2003) *Motorhomes: The Illustrated History*, Dorchester, Veloce Publishing

Jerome, Jerome K (1989) *Three Men in a Boat*, London, J W Arrowsmith [a]

John, Richard R (2000) *Recasting the Information Infrastructure for the Industrial Age* in Chandler, Alfred D & Cortada,

James W (ed)(2000) <u>A Nation Transformed by Information: How Information Has Shaped the United States from Colonial Times to the Present</u>, New York, OUP USA

Johnson, Lynn & O'Leary, Michael (1999) *All Aboard! Images from the Golden Age of Rail Travel,* San Francisco, Chronicle Books

Johnson, Peter (2010) *An Illustrated History of the Snowdon Mountain Railway,* Oxford Publishing Company

Jordan, Arthur & Jordan, Elizabeth (1991) *Away for The Day,* Kettering, Silver Link

Kaye, David (1970) *Buses and Trolleybuses 1919 to 1945,* London, Blandford Press

Kaye, David (1972) *Buses and Trolleybuses before 1919,* London, Blandford Press

Kaye, David (1981) *The British Bus Scene in the 1930s,* Shepperton, Ian Allan Ltd

Keir, David (1955) *The Early Story,* in Keir, David & Morgan, Bryan (1955) <u>Golden Milestone: Fifty Years of the AA</u>, London, The Automobile Association

Klapper, Charles (1974) *The Golden Age of Tramways,* Newton Abbot, David & Charles

Law, Michael John (2017) *1938: Modern Britain – Social Change and Visions of the Future,* London, Bloomsbury

Learmonth, Bob et al (1977) *The First Croydon Airport, 1915-28,* Sutton, London; Sutton Libraries & Arts Services

Lehrer, Henry R (2014) *Flying the Beam: Navigating the Early US Airmail Airways, 1917-1941,* West Lafayette IN, Purdue University Press

Levey, Michael F (1976) *London Transport Posters,* Oxford, Phaidon Press

Lewis, Sinclair (1919) *Free Air,* New York, Harcourt, Brace and Howe

Leyland, John (1897) *The Thames, Illustrated: A Picturesque Journeying from Richmond to Oxford,* London, George Newnes

Lobeck, Armin K (1933) *Airways of America: 1 The United Airlines,* New York, Columbia University

Lockwood, Stan (1980) *Kaleidoscope of Chara-Bancs and Coaches,* London, Marshall Harris & Baldwin

London & North Western Railway Co (1914)(reprint 2010) *Programme of Excursion Bookings for the Summer Holidays,* Rothbury, L&NWR Society

London Underground (?1920s) Map of London's Underground Railways

Lord, Walter (2012/1955) *A Night to Remember,* Harmondsworth, Penguin Books

Lovegrove, Keith (2000) *Airline: Identity, Design and Culture,* London, Laurence King

Lovegrove, Keith (2004) *Railway: Identity, Design and Culture,* London, Laurence King

Low E H (1895) *The Passenger,* New York, Low's Exchange

Lydecker, Ryck & Podlich, Margaret (1999) *A Profile of Recreational Boating in the United States* in Cicin-Sain, Biliana; Knecht, Robert W & Foster, Nancy (eds)(1993) <u>Trends and Future Challenges for U.S. National Ocean and Coastal Policy: Workshop Proceedings</u>, Silver Springs MD, National Ocean Service [a]

Machin, Alan (2016) *Making Sense of Tourism: 1 The Beckoning Horizon,* Halifax UK, Westwood Start [obtainable via amazon.com or amazon.co.uk]

Mansfield, Robert E (1853) *The Water Lily on the Danube,* London, John W Parker & Son

Marchand, Roland (1992) *The Designers Go to the Fair II: Norman Bel Geddes, the General Motors "Futurama" and the Visit to the Factory Transformed,* in <u>Design Issues</u> pp22-40, Vol 8 No 2, the MIT Press [a]

Martin, Albro (1992) *Railroads Triumphant: The Growth, Rejection and Rebirth of a Vital American Force,* New York, Oxford University Press

Martin, Andrew (2012) *Underground Overground: A Passenger's History of the Tube,* London, Profile Books

McCullough, David (2015) *The Wright Brothers: The Dramatic Story-Behind-the-Story,* New York, Simon & Schuster

McKay, John P (1976) *Tramways and Trolleys: The Rise of Urban Mass Transport in Europe,* Princeton NJ, Princeton University Press

Megoran, John (2016) *British Paddle Steamers: The Heyday of Excursions and Day Trips,* Stroud, Amberley Publishing

Meier, Albert E & Hoschek. John P (1975) *Over the Road: A History of Intercity Bus Transportation in the United States,* Upper Montclair NJ, Motor Bus Society Inc

Metcalfe-Shaw, Gertrude E (1926) *English Caravanners in the Wild West: The Old Pioneers Trail,* London, William Blackwood & Sons

Michelin (1900) *Guide Michelin, Offert Gracieusement aux Chauffeurs,* reprinted, no date, Paris, Michelin Tyre Co

Milward, Alan (1999) *The Routledge Historical Atlas of the American Railroads,* New York, Routledge

Monmonier, Mark (2017) *Patents and Cartographic Inventions: A New Perspective for Map History,* Basingstoke, Palgrave Macmillan [a]

Monmonier, Mark et al (2018) *A Directory of Cartographic Inventors: Clever People Awarded a US Patent for a Map-Related Device or Method,* Syracuse NY, Bar Scale Press [a]

Moran, Joe (2010) *On Roads: A Hidden History,* London, Profile Books

Murphy, Thomas D (1908) *British Highways and Byways from a Motor Car,* Boston USA, L C Page & Co

Nelson, N (1960) *The Shepheard's Hotel* in Pirie, G (2009) Incidental Tourism: British Imperial Travel in the 1930s, Journal of Tourism History Vol 1:1 49-66 [a]

Nilsson, Jeff (2012) *The First GPS: Hi-Tech Navigation in 1909,* in The Saturday Evening Post 4 February 2012 [a]

North, Arthur E (1952) *The Book of the Trailer Caravan,* London, Sir Isaac Pitman & Sons

North, Rex (1962) *The Butlin Story,* London, Jarrolds

Nugent-Bankes, George (1892) *Across France in a Caravan: Being Some Account of a Journey from Bordeaux to Genoa in the 'Escargot',* London, William Blackwood & Sons

O'Connell, Sean (1998) *The Car and British Society: Class, Gender and Motoring, 1896-1939,* Manchester, Manchester University Press

O'Connell, Sean (2007) *Motoring and Modernity* in Carnevali, Francesca & Strange, Julie-Marie (eds) Twentieth Century Britain: Economic, Cultural and Social Change, Abingdon, Routledge

O'Dwyer, William J & Randolph, Stella (1978) *History by Contract,* Leuterhausen, Germany, Fritz Majer & Sohn [a]

Opie, Robert (2005) *Remember When: A Nostalgic Trip Through The Consumer Era,* London, Bounty Books

O'Sullivan, John L (1845) *Annexation* in The Democratic Review July-August 1845 [a]

Ovenden, Mark (2003) *Transit Maps of the World,* London, Penguin Books Ltd

Owen, Tim & Pilbeam, Elaine (1992) *Ordnance Survey: Map Makers to Britain Since 1791,* Southampton, Ordnance Survey and London, HMSO

Palin, Michael (2015) *The Golden Age of Railway Posters,* London, Batsford

Parker, Mike (2013) *Mapping the Roads: Building Modern Britain,* Basingstoke, AA Publishing

Parissien, Steven (2013) *The Life of the Automobile: A New History of the Motor Car,* London, Atlantic Books

Paterson, Alan J S (1969) *The Golden Years of the Clyde Steamers: 1889-1914,* Newton Abbot, David & Charles

Payne, Lee (1991) *Lighter than Air: Illustrated History of the Airship,* New York, Orion Books

Petroski, Henry (2016) *The Road Taken: The History and Future of America's Infrastructure,* New York, Bloomsbury

Pike, Stuart N (1947, 2017) *Mile by Mile: An Illustrated Journey on Britain's Railways,* London, Aurum Press

On the Move

Pirie, G (2009) *Incidental Tourism: British Imperial Travel in the 1930s,* Journal of Tourism History Vol 1:1 49-66 [a]

Pittard, Christopher (2013) *Purity and Contamination in Late Victorian Detective Fiction,* Farnham, Ashgate Publishing [a]

Porter, Horace (1888) *Railway Passenger Travel* in <u>Scribner's Magazine,</u> Sept 1888; reprinted 1987, Maynard MA, Chandler Press [a]

Post, Emily (1916) *By Motor to the Golden Gate,* New York, D Appleton Co

Potteiger, Mathew & Purinton, Jamie (2008) *Landscape Narratives: Design Practices for Telling Stories,* New York, John Wiley & Sons

Pudney, John (1959) *Seven Skies: A Study of BOAC and its Forerunners Since 1919,* London, Putnam

Pye, Denis (1995) *Fellowship is Life: The National Clarion Cycling Club 1895-1995,* Bolton, Clarion Publishing

Quartermaine, Peter & Peter, Bruce (2006) *Cruise: Identity, Design and Culture,* London, Laurence King

Ransome, Arthur (1923) *Racundra's First Cruise,* London, George Allen & Unwin

Ransome, Arthur (1930) *Swallows and Amazons,* London, Jonathan Cape

Raymond-Whitcomb (1927) *Log Book: Raymond-Whitcomb Agents' Convention 11-13 September 1927,* Boston, Raymond-Whitcomb Company

Ribeill, Georges (trans: Judith Crews,) (1991) *From Pneumatics to Highway Logistics: André Michelin, Instigator of the 'Automobile Revolution'* (Part II) in Flux No 5 1991, pp5-19 [a]

Robertson, C J A (1983) *The Origins of the Scottish Railway System: 1722-1844,* Edinburgh, John Donald [a]

Roden, Andrew (2010) *The Great Western Railway: A History,* London, Aurum Press

Rojek, Chris & Urry, John (eds)(1997) *Touring Cultures: Transformations of Travel and Theory,* London, Routledge

Rolt, Tom (1944) *Narrow Boat,* London, Eyre & Spottiswoode

Rolt, Tom (1985) *The Aeronauts,* Gloucester, Alan Sutton Publishing

Ross, David (2014) *The Glasgow and South Western Railway: A History,* Catrine, Stenlake Publishing [a]

Rumsey, David & Punt, Edith M (2004) *Cartographica Extraordinaire, The Historical Map Transformed,* Redlands CA, ESRI Press

Rusman, E (1935) *Wings Across Continents: The KLM Amsterdam-Batavia Line,* Amsterdam, Andries Blitz

Rust, Daniel L (2009) *Flying Across America: The Airline Passenger Experience,* Norman OK, University of Oklahoma Press

Sarnoff, David (1968) *Looking Ahead: The Papers of David Sarnoff,* New York, McGraw-Hill

Schisgall, Oscar (1985) *The Greyhound Story: From Hibbing to Everywhere,* Chicago, J G Ferguson Publishing Co

Schivelbusch, Wolfgang (1980) *The Railway Journey: Trains and Travel in the 19th Century,* trans. by Anselm Hollo, Oxford, Basil Blackwell

Scidmore. Eliza R (1893) *Appletons' Guide-Book to Alaska and the Northwest Coast,* New York, D Appleton & Co

Serling, Robert J (1985) *Eagle: The Story of American Airlines,* New York, St Martin's Press

Serling, Robert J (2018) *Howard Hughes' Airline: An Informal History of TWA,* London, Endeavour Media

Seton, Ernest Thompson (1913) *The Book of Woodcraft and Indian Lore,* Garden City NY, Doubleday, Page & Co [a]

Sevareid, Eric (1967) *All England Listened: The Wartime Broadcasts of J B Priestley,* New York, Chilmark Press

Shaffer, Marguerite S (2001) *See America First: Tourism and National Identity 1880-1940,* Washington, Smithsonian Institution Press

Shepherd, Robert (2002) *Commodification, Culture and Tourism,* in <u>Tourist Studies</u> Vol 2(2) 183-201 [a]

Simmons, Jack (ed) (1971) *The Railway Traveller's Handy Book,* (original edition 1862), Bath, Adams and Dart

Sinclair, Upton (1906) *The Jungle,* New York, Doubleday Page & Co

Slater, David (1982) *Yelloway Motor Services of Rochdale,* Buses Extra magazine No 22 pp19-25, Shepperton, Ian Allan Ltd

Slocum, Joshua (1900) *Sailing Alone Around the World,* New York, The Century Co [a]

Stables, William Gordon (1886) *The Cruise of the Land Yacht 'Wanderer' or Thirteen Hundred Miles in My Caravan,* London, Hodder & Stoughton

Steves, Rick (2018) *Rick Steves' Best of England,* Berkeley CA, Avalon Travel

Stilgoe, John (1983) *Metropolitan Corridor: Railroads and the American Scene,* New Haven CT, Yale University Press

Stone, Joel (2015) *Floating Palaces of the Great Lakes: A History of Passenger Steamships on the Inland Seas,* Ann Arbor MI, University of Michigan Press [a]

Stover, John F (1997) *American Railroads,* Chicago, University of Chicago Press

Studd, Ronald G (1950) *The Holiday Story,* London, Percival Marshall

Suffling, Ernest Richard (1887) *The Land of the Broads,* London, L Upcott Gill

Suffling, Ernest Richard (1899) *How to Organise a Cruise on the Broads* 3rd ed, Norwich, Jarrolds

Swenson, Stephen P (2006) *Mapping Poverty in Agar Town: Economic Conditions Prior to the Development of St. Pancras station In 1866,* London, Dept of History, London School of Economics [a]

Swinglehurst, Edmund (1982) *Cook's Tours: The Story of Popular Travel,* Poole, Blandford Press

de Syon, Guillaume (2002) *Zeppelin! Germany and the Airship,* Baltimore MD, Johns Hopkins University Press

Talwin Morris, Alice (1911) *Our Holiday on a Barge,* Glasgow, Blackie & Sons

Taylor, Sheila (ed)(2001) *The Moving Metropolis: A History of London's Transport Since 1800,* London, Laurence King Publishing

Thomas, David St J; Whitehouse, Patrick (2002) *LMS 150: The London Midland & Scottish Railway: A Century and a Half of Progress,* Newton Abbott, David and Charles

Thomas, Joseph (1839) *Railroad Guide from London to Birmingham,* London, J Thomas

Thurley, Simon (2013) *The Building of England: How the History of England has Shaped our Buildings,* London, William Collins

Tilden, Freeman (1957) *Interpreting Our Heritage,* Chapel Hill NC, University of North Carolina Press

Tuan, Yi-Fu (1974) *Topophilia: A Study of Environmental Perception, Attitudes and Values,* New Jersey, Englewood Cliffs

Tuan, Yi-Fu (1977) *Space and Place: The Perspective of Experience,* Minneapolis, University of Minneapolis

Twain, Mark (1884) *Adventures of Huckleberry Finn,* London, Chatto & Windus [a]

USCB (United States Census Bureau), *Report on Transportation Business in the United States at the Eleventh Census 1890,* Washington DC, USCB [a]

USSB (1922) *Going Abroad: A Booklet of Information for Travellers,* Washington DC, United States Shipping Board

Urry, John (1990) *The Tourist Gaze: Leisure and Travel in Contemporary Societies,* London, Sage Publications

Verne, Jules (1873) *Around the World in 80 Days,* Paris, Pierre-Jules Hetzel

Vine, P A L (1983) *Pleasure Boating in the Victorian Era,* Chichester, Phillimore & Co

Watts, Steven (2005) *The People's Tycoon: Henry Ford and the American Century,* New York, Vintage Books

Weigel, Marta & Babcock, Barbara A (1996) *The Great Southwest of the Fred Harvey Company and the Santa Fe Railway,* Phoenix AZ, The Heard Museum

Wenham, Simon 2006) *Salters' of Oxford: A History of a Thames Boating Firm over a*

Century of Evolution, (1858-c1960), in Oxoniensa 2006, Oxfordshire Architectural and Historical Society [a]

West, Nancy Martha (2000) *Kodak and the Lens of Nostalgia,* Charlottesville VA, University of Virginia

Whisnant, Anne Mitchell (2003) *Public and Private Tourism Development in 1930s Appalachia: The Blue Ridge Parkway Meets Little Switzerland,* in Starnes, Richard D (ed) Southern Journeys: Tourism, History and Culture in the Modern South, Tuscaloosa AL, University of Alabama Press [a]

Whisnant, Anne Mitchell (2006) *Super Scenic Motorway: A Blue Ridge Parkway History,* Chapel Hill NC, University of North Carolina Press

Whitfield, Peter (2003) *The Mapmakers: A History of Stanford's,* London, Compendium

Williams, John A (2002) *Appalachia: A History,* Chapel Hill NC, University of North Carolina Press

Williamson, Tom (1997) *The Norfolk Broads: A Landscape History,* Manchester, Manchester University Press

Willrich, John (2013) *Did You Notice the Signs by the Way?* Beaulieu, Beaulieu Enterprises

Withers, Charles W J (2008) *Placing the Enlightenment: Thinking Geographically about the Age of Reason,* Chicago, University of Chicago Press [a]

Wolmar, Christian (2004) *The Subterranean Railway: How the London Underground was Built and how it Changed London Forever,* London, Atlantic Books

Wolmar, Christian (2007) *Fire and Steam: A New History of the Railways in Britain,* London, Atlantic Books

Wolmar, Christian (2009) *Blood, Iron and Gold: How the Railways Transformed the World,* London, Atlantic Books

Wolmar, Christian (2012) *The Great Railway Revolution,* London, Atlantic Books

Wolmar, Christian (2019) *Railways,* London, Apollo Books

Wragg, David (1978) *Flight With Power: the First Ten Years,* London, Barrie & Jenkins

Wynne, Nick (1999) *Tin Can Tourists in Florida, 1900-1970,* Charleston SC, Arcadia Publishing Library

Zega and Gruber (2002) *Travel by Train: The American Railroad Poster,* Indianapolis, Indiana University Press

Web pages:

Albatross 01 – *please read through the additions in the comments page listed*

http://www.old-bus-photos.co.uk/wp-content/themes/Old-Bus-Photos/questions/mystery_sleeper_coach.php *accessed 06.11.2018*

Albatross 02 – *NB accessed again in June 2020: page appears changed.*
http://archive.commercialmotor.com/article/18th-december-1928/4/wheels-of-industry *accessed 06.11.2018*

Anita King

www.lincoln-highway-museum.ord/king/king-index.html *accessed 20.05.2017*

Barton

https://www.mangeogsoc.org.uk/pdfs/manchestergeographies/Manchester_Geographies_5_Brumhead.pdf *accessed 03.04.2019*

Brecon

(Powys in 1891: An attractive, detailed website with much relevant material):

http://a-day-in-the-life.powys.org.uk/eng/trans/et_brecref.php *accessed 04.09.2018*

Broadlands

http://www.broadlandmemories.co.uk/pre1900history.html *accessed 16.06.2018*

Cargo

https://www.indy100.com/article/remote-religion-planes-sky-7382991 *accessed 08.03.2019*

Cold Spring Tavern

https://www.coldspringtavern.com *accessed 27.08.2019*

Cuba

http://alanmachinwork.net/Back-to-Basics-Presentation-given-at-the-Cuba-EduTourism-Conference
accessed 09.07.20

Currency:

http://www.nationalarchives.gov.uk/currency/results.asp#mid *accessed* 30.01.2017

Elliott *see a discussion by Dr David Turner:*

https://davidturnerrailway.wordpress.com/2018/01/05/the-art-of-railway-pr-learning-from-the-past/ *accessed* 25.09.2018

FHWA (Federal Highways Administration)

https://www.fhwa.dot.gov/highwayhistory/dodge/03.cfm *accessed* 13.06.2018

Gould 1

http://www.petergould.co.uk/local_transport_history/generalhistories/general/horsebus.htm *accessed* 27.07.2018

Gould 2

http://www.petergould.co.uk/local_transport_history/generalhistories/general/tramcar.htm *accessed* 01.08.2018

Great Lakes

https://en.wikipedia.org/wiki/Great_Lakes_passenger_steamers *accessed* 19.04.2018

Haldon

https://devonairfields.hampshireairfields.co.uk/hald.htm *accessed* 27.04.2019

Ivernia

https://www.gjenvick.com/Passengers/Cunard/Ivernia-PassengerList-1905-06-20.html *accessed* 24.07.2019

Kitty Hawk Tourism

https://teachinghistory.org/history-content/ask-a-historian/20402 *accessed* 12.04.2019

Langham

https://actonbooks.com/2017/03/28/sanderson-at-the-langham-hotel/

Lehwess

https://gracesguide.co.uk/Edward_Ernest_Lehwess *accessed* 09.02.2019

Lincoln Highway

https://www.fhwa.dot.gov/infrastructure/lincoln.cfm *accessed* 09.06.2018

Manure

https://www.historic-uk.com/HistoryUK/HistoryofBritain/Great-Horse-Manure-Crisis-of-1894/ *accessed* 15.01.2019

Marriott (Paul Daniel)

http://www.historicroads.org/documents/GUIDE.pdf *accessed* 14.06.2018

Michelin

https://archive.is/20130505100337/http://www.viamichelin.co.uk/tpl/mag6/art200903/htm/tour-saga-michelin.htm *accessed* 11.07.2017

Pickwick

http://www.coachbuilt.com/bui/p/pickwick/pickwick.htm *accessed* 01.11.2018

Rand, McNally

https://www.davidrumsey.com/ - search for Rand McNally, scroll down to view Photo-Auto Maps *accessed* 04.12.2018 *This is a major historical map collection freely viewable online*

Raymond-Whitcomb *1892 Programme*

https://babel.hathitrust.org/cgi/pt?id=aeu.ark:/13960/t1zc8fg9k&view=1up&seq=5
accessed 15.02.2020

Rheims

https://www.thosemagnificantmen.co.uk/rhiems *accessed* 18.10.19

Rumsey

https://www.davidrumsey.com/maps499.html *accessed* 27.02.2020

SF Cable cars

https://www.sfcablecar.com/history.html *accessed* 04.08.2018

Slocum 1

http://www.allthingsransome.net/literary/sloc2_0.htm *accessed* 23.04.2018

Slocum 2

https://asa.com/news/2015/07/09/5-greatest-sailors-of-the-modern-era/# *accessed* 23.04.2018

Soyer

http://cabinetmagazine.org/issues/37/va nleeuwen.php *accessed* 20.02.2019

Sternwheelers

http://www.captainjohn.org/History3.ht ml *accessed* 24.04.2018

The Scotsman

http://www.scotsman.com/news-how-the-invention-of-the-caravan-forced-us-into-life-in-the-slow-lane-1-1296411 *accessed* 10.02.2019

Trans-Atlantic Fares

http://eh.net/eha/wp-content/uploads/2013/11/Weissetal.pdf *accessed* 25.04.2018

Turnpikes

http://www.geog.port.ac.uk/webmap/ha ntsmap/hantsmap/turnpike.htm *accessed* 23/01.2019

USGS1

https://en.wikipedia.org/wiki/United_St ates_Geological_Survey *accessed* 22.12.2018

USGS2

https://pubs.usgs.gov/gip/usgsmaps/us gsmaps.html *accessed* 22.12.2018

US transport

https://www.fhwa.dot.gov/ohim/summa ry95/mv200.pdf *accessed* 12.06.2018

Whitehead

http://www.gustave-whitehead.com/history/jane-s-foreword-march-8-2013/ accessed 06.04.2019

Index

260

Goodyear-Zeppelin Corporation, 202
Gordon Bennett International Aviation
  Cup, 210
Gordon, Alastair, 212, 217, 235
Göta Canal, 131
Gould, George, 94
Gould, John H
  influence of Paris Exposition, 48
Gousha, H M, 155
government, 2, 53-54, 56, 71, 90-91, 94, 96,
108, 125, 132, 136-38, 146-147, 151-52, 155-
157, 167, 170, 181,194, 201, 213-14, 218, 220,
223, 225-226, 230-31, 233
Government Disposals Board, 181
Grace's Guide, 135
Graf Zeppelin, 193, 197, 199, 200, 201, 202
Graham, Kenneth, 34
  boating, 26
Grand Canyon, 96
Grand Central station NY, 82, 95
Grand Cruise, 57
Grand National horse race, 79
Grand Pacific Hotel, Chicago, 96
Grand Prix, 170
Grand Prix de la Champagne, 210
Grand Rapids, 238
Grand Tour(s), 1, 21, 27, 46, 56, 220, 232
Grandfather Mountain, 184
Grantham, 81
grass roots, 2
Graves, Clifford, 125
Great Britain, 53, 79, 147, 149, 170, 147
  sail/steamship, 44, 51
Great Britain Times, The, 51
Great Central Railway, 105
Great Cumbrae, 58
Great Depression, 32, 33, 77, 94, 123, 125-
126, 230
Great Exhibition, The, 62, 100-101, 116, 132
generating tourism, 101
Great Lakes, 32-33, 248, 250
Great Marlow, 174
Great North Road, 165
Great Northern Railroad, 125
Great Northern Railway, 100
  onboard restaurant, 68
  Skegness poster, 74
Great Orme, 84

Great Orme Tramway, 84
Great Plains USA, 119
Great Railway Journeys TV series, 64
Great Railway Revolution Wolmar, 69
Great Smoky Mountains National Park,
183
Great Western, SS, 71, 72
  Atlantic crossing, 47
Great Western Railway, 10, 65, 69, 73, 79-
80, 115
  Through the Window, 10, 19, 69
  lavatories, 65
  using motor buses as feeders, 115
Great Yarmouth, 70
  journeys by ship to Wales, 57
Greece, 198
  tramways, 84
Green Line buses, 106
Green, Charles, 190
Green, Oliver, 104
  on Edinburgh trams, 85
Greenfield Village Museum, 209
Greenland, 236
Greenock, 58
Greenwich, UK, 44
Greetings from the Lincoln Highway, 141
Grein whirlpools and rapids, 28
Grenoble, 178
Gresley, Sir Nigel, 81
Greyhound buses, 123-127, 247
Greyhound Corporation, 125
Greyhound Story, The, 124
Grise, C W, 121
Ground beacon 'lighthouses', 237
ground handlers, 52
Grouping, Railway, UK, 71
Guam, 46, 235
guaranteed hotel rooms, 126
guard's compartment, 64
Guatemala, 123
guest houses, 59, 108
guests, airline, 238
guidebooks, 4-5, 10, 11, 16, 18, 27-28, 31, 54,
63, 79, 108, 149, 154, 159-160, 167-68, 227,
237-238
Guimard, Hector, 109
guinea (coin), 45
Guines, 190

multi-course meals on future airlnes, 66
multi-media attraction, 10
multi-storey car park, 143
Mumbles Railway, 113
munitions, supplies of, 53
Murdoch, Jacob M, 141
Murphy, Thomas Dowler, 143
Murrays, 54
Musick,, Ed, 235
Mussolini, 170, 214
mythology, 128
myths, 188

Nadar. *See* Tournachon
Naked Airport, 212
Nansen, Fridtjof, 179
Nantasket Beach, 87
Nantes, 114
narrative, 21-22, 27, 191
Narrow Boat (Tom Rolt), 37
narrow-gauge line, 114
NASA, 203
Nashville train wreck, 52
Nassau balloon, 190
Natchez, 36
  name of several sternwheelers, 36
nation, discovery of the, 3
National Aircraft Factories, 211
National and State Parks, 227
national anthems, 50
National Archives currency converter, 45
national cycling clubs, 167
national events, 57
National Geographic Society, 199, 201
National Parks, 130, 182-183, 232
National Parks Service, USA, 182
national policies, 56
National Road, US, 89, 165
national treasure trove, 227
Native American crafts, 17
Native American lands, 156
Native American peoples, 78, 91, 183-184
  loss of land, 92
Native American way of life
  degradation through settlement, 78
Natural History Museum, 100
Nautical Magazine on comfort, 49
Navarac, 181

navigable rivers, 153
navigation aids, 160
Navy Pier, Chicago, 42
Nazi Party, 171
Nazi programme, 56
Nebraska, 120
Nehlsen, Charlie, 202
Nelson's Victory, 57
Neptune, July 1896 cuises summary, 59
Netherlands, the, 197
network of lines
  railway growth, 29
Neustadt am Rübenberge, 191
Nevada, 141
Nevada Basin, 158
new and clearer view of today, 11
New Brighton, 84, 103
New Deal, 11, 14, 182, 183
New Forest, 177
New Generation of Americans, 178
New Hampshire, 70
New Haven Railway excursion
  programme, 159
New Jersey, 47, 52, 95, 109, 120, 131, 136,
  143, 196, 198, 200, 202, 230, 248
new media, 46
New Orleans, 22, 36, 82
  strenwheeler, 36
new world, of new buildings, 12
New York, 43, 47, 49-50, 54, 82, 95, 109, 119-
  121, 126, 131, 135, 140, 155, 171, 199-200,
  226-229, 237
  opening its hinterland, 89
New York Central Lines, 77
New York City, 158, 196
New York Morning News, 91
New York State, 89, 137
New York State Lackawanna Railroad, 95
New York Times, 171
New York transport needs, 109
New York World's Fair 1939-40, 10, 127
New York, Rio and Buenos Aires Line, 234
New Zealand, 219
Newark, NJ, 230
Newbould, Frank, 74
Newcastle-upon-Tyne, 80
Newfoundland, 196, 236
Newport RI, 35, 136